AFGHAN CARAVAN

edited by

Safia Shah

THE OCTAGON PRESS
LONDON

Copyright © 1990 by The Octagon Press Ltd

ISBN 0 863040 59 4

Published 1991

Photoset, printed and bound in Great Britain by
Redwood Press Limited, Melksham, Wiltshire

CONTENTS

Contents

Contents

Introduction –
LAND OF FOOD AND WAR

A magazine editor once asked me for 'six hundred words on Afghanistan – you know the kind of thing'. I looked up a year's issues of his journal, to get the flavour of what it published, and wrote:

'Beyond the frowning, famed Khyber Pass, where grim-faced, loopholed forts guard the realm of the warrior Pashtun clans, lies the God-Given Kingdom of Afghanistan. The British Lion and the Russian Bear have cast envious eyes upon the keystone of Asia, blessed by Nature with haunting scenery and seventy different varieties of grapes.'

And so on. The Editor rang me up. 'Everyone knows all that stuff of yours about Afghanistan. Let's have something they don't know.'
I started again:

'One of the world's greatest faiths – Zoroastrianism – and some of the world's great scientists in the Middle Ages came from Afghanistan; this strange, multi-ethnic country perched above the world. A way-station on the Silk Road from China to Rome, it is the country of some of the world's great mystics, such as Rumi and Attar. For centuries it was the home of Buddhism, which diffused from here throughout the East.'

And much more.
I got a telex back:

TOO   OBSCURE.   RECONDITE   INFORMATION,

1

SOUNDS NATIONALISTIC LIKE THE WAY RUSSIANS CLAIM POPOV INVENTED RADIO. DO A PIECE ON FOOD AND WAR IN AFLAND.

It was midnight; nobody to take dictation and the typewriter would disturb the household. I got out my cassette-recorder and whispered into it:

'Palao, which the Turks mispronounce *Pilaf*, was invented, or discovered – so legend says – in Afghanistan. When Genghiz Khan's men, descending in their hordes on the fertile plains, were once cooking meat, some gravy dripped into a pile of rice which had leaked from a sack. The Mongols had never seen rice before, but they tasted it, flavoured by the herbs which grow abundantly in Afghanistan – and palao had come into being.'

Food, war, history, local colour, all in one sentence. Now for war. I continued:

'Afghan food is ideal as war rations. Again and again, the men of the all-conquering armies of the Moguls taking India, or the Sultan of Ghazni's men carved-out empires, fed on fresh lamb, yoghurt, dried white sultanas and sun-dried bread. Food and war are the recurring themes of High Asia: where one warrior was awarded the city of Kandahar for devising, as military supplies, what the British believe to be the invention of Lord Sandwich.'

And more. In the end the Editor made a pastiche of all my pastiches. Afghanistan has that kind of effect on you: after all, where do you begin, or end? With the Land of High Banners, with Kabul, reputedly the City of Cain, with Alexander of Macedon, with the quarries of Lapis Lazuli or the rubies of Badakhshan?

Let's begin anyway. Get on your stunning Arab-Mongol mare and join me, in an Afghan caravan.

Idries Shah

PART ONE

LOOKING AT EACH OTHER...

I MARRIED AN AFGHAN

Morag Murray was not the first Scottish woman among the Afghans: King Abdur-Rahman's Court Physician in the 1890s was a Scotswoman. But Morag, a teenage student in Edinburgh in the early 1920s, married the son of an Afghan chief and ultimately became mistress of a string of castles in the trans-border territory still known as No Man's Land . . .

The war raged on. It was 1916. Trainloads of troops kept leaving. The streets of Edinburgh were full of wounded men. Everybody was doing something, some war work. Up till then I had spent my time painting, but I felt anxious to get away from this solitary occupation and mix with people who might help me to forget the shock of my brother's death in France. A friend suggested I might do voluntary work at the bandage and sphagnum moss depot, or at the flag depot. I chose the latter, and worked hard getting boxes and flags ready for hundreds of sellers, and then sold flags myself from 5.30 a.m. until after 6 at night.

It was during one of these flag days that a lady in charge of a depot invited me to a reception at the University. All the voluntary flag-sellers were to go. My father gave his views on the affair and was not flattering in his remarks about the 'wild students' I should meet there. In the end he agreed to my going provided I reached home no later than ten o'clock. This meant I should have only two hours there, but, having been to so few entertainments of the kind, I was tremendously excited.

At last the day came. I had spent all my available spare time choosing a frock of pink taffeta, pink shoes and stockings, and a double row of pink moss-roses for my hair. On my arrival the Professors were receiving. I felt lost among so many students and wished I had never come. The lady who had invited me introduced me to a girl student, then left us together. There were all nationalities – I watched them all arriving. It amused me to see how nervous some of them seemed, and so I was somehow a little more at ease. The big room was becoming full and the guests ranged themselves nearer to the walls.

Suddenly an Eastern student appeared at the entrance. He looked different from the others. I could not think what his nationality might be and asked my companion.

'Oh, that is Syed Abdullah. I believe he's the son of an Indian Frontier chieftain. He's terribly clever. Would you like to meet him? I know him well.'

Seeing and meeting seemed a different thing, however, and I said nervously, 'Not just now.' Nevertheless I followed the chieftain's son with my eyes as he crossed the room.

He walked so erectly and looked like the popular idea of a handsome sheikh. He was tall, with finely chiselled features and a swashbuckling air, yet there was no 'side' about him. I could tell that his bearing was natural. He seemed defiant and yet devil-may-care, and I could look at no one else. To me he was the principal actor on the stage. How delightfully he bowed, I thought, to the women there. Why had it not been my luck to be one of them and to be in that particular corner? Yet, on the other hand, I felt glad to be half-hidden where I could see him. He glanced round the room as a conqueror might have surveyed captured legions, but there was nothing insolent in the gaze. It was not for anyone in particular.

He was coming our way now!

'There he is!' I said excitedly to my student companion, while my confusion was almost overpowering. Too late I whispered to her, 'Don't ask him to come'; she was already speaking to him, while he bowed again in that inimitable way of his. They were now beside me, but I continued to hide behind some guests and the girl had to pull me out.

'Meet my fellow-student, Syed Abdullah. This is Morag Murray.' He was now bowing to me, while I, faced with the only person I wanted to meet felt suddenly too shy to look at him and heartily wished the ground would swallow me up. The girl left us together, and my new companion asked whether he might bring me some tea.

I felt it must all be a dream – the likelihood of my being allowed to attend a reception at the University, and now to be waited upon by such a cavalier! Syed Abdullah returned with a cup of tea and some chocolate cake. I found my tongue and thanked him, asking why he had not brought any for himself.

'We men of the hills we drink only green tea and do not like this black tea. Moreover, we are men of the sword and do not care for sugar cakes.'

How marvellously he spoke! 'Men of the hills,' he had said. Then I would talk to him of the hills I loved too; he would understand. So we talked of my hills and of his, until suddenly, like Cinderella, I discovered it was 10.30 p m. I had promised my father to be home at ten, and on this, really my first outing, I had broken my promise!

Fear seized me. 'Oh!' I gasped. 'I ought to have been home by now. My father will be angry. What shall I do? I'm half an hour late, and I have some distance to go.'

'Where do you live?'

I told him, already almost weeping.

'Perhaps I may take you home in my car with your chaperon?'

I could not find my chaperon anywhere, and perhaps was not too anxious to. In any case, within the next few minutes Syed Abdullah and I were sitting in the little car speeding towards our house. My thoughts meanwhile were torn between the bliss of being alone with such a wonderful companion and the fear of my father seeing me arrive back with an unknown young man – and at that late hour.

I got out quickly and my companion stood beside me. Fearful lest I might be seen by my father, I hurriedly said, 'Good night and thank you!'

'Good night. I hope to have the pleasure of meeting you again,' replied Syed Abdullah as he kissed my hand. I am afraid even the street lamps showed only too plainly that we were unwilling to part.

'My father would not allow us to meet again,' I said disappointedly and ran up the few steps to the door. As I opened it I looked once again at my escort, who was still standing on the pavement. I quickly closed the door and thought about nothing but the way Syed Abdullah had looked at me, spoken to me, and attended to me, until I went to sleep.

Next morning I awoke late to find a letter awaiting me. It ran:

Please, Morag, do me the kindness of having tea with me this afternoon at Mackie's at 4 o'clock.

SYED ABDULLAH

I was so delighted at the prospect of seeing him so soon that the day seemed never to pass. Telling my parents I was going to tea with a friend of the family I left an hour before the time, so afraid was I of being late, although it was only a few minutes' walk to reach the cafe.

By 3.30 Syed Abdullah had arrived, and I suddenly became silent. We sat at a window-table looking over Princes Street gardens. By and by I told him of the old home we had left the year before, of my pets in the country – and about my brother.

'I am so sorry for you, poor child,' he said so comfortingly that the sympathy made me cry. He changed the subject and told me about his home, a fort in the 'no man's land' of the Khyber Pass, and I became so interested in hearing about his clansmen that my sorrow was forgotten.

When he told me of the fighting men at home his eyes became almost gripping in their intensity; next moment, with eyes as soft as a woman's, he was telling me of his mother and sisters.

The time passed so quickly, like all happy times, that it was late before we realized it.

'Is it really five o'clock?' said my companion, and I felt glad he had not thought the time long.

We met nearly every day after that – went to the Braid Hills to golf, had tea at the hotel there, and were ridiculously happy. Yet this man, although always anxious to see me and seemingly happy when we were together, never kissed me and spoke only of everyday things. When we parted he raised my hand to his lips. He did not now seem like the Eastern sheiks at the cinema! He said none of the things the picture heroes had said, and did not tell me whether he even liked me, although his attitude was always so kind and protective that I felt he must, or why should he want to see me so often?

8

About this time, a few months after we first met, my father told me he wanted to speak to me.

The son of a boyhood friend of his, he said, was coming home from France, and the two fathers thought that as we got on so well together we might become engaged and be married when the War was over.

I replied that I did not want to become engaged to Roy and that I did not want to marry him.

Whether my father had any knowledge of Syed Abdullah and wanted to be diplomatic about it I do not know; if so, he hid it very well. I told him about my student friend. He listened until the whole story was out, then very determinedly said: 'Morag, this friendship must cease. I forbid you to see this Eastern student again, and I shall certainly communicate with the University authorities if I find any disobedience on your part. Sit down now and write a letter I shall dictate to you.'

I sat down and wrote the following as instructed by my father as he paced up and down the room:

SYED ABDULLAH

I shall not be able to see you again and hope you will not make any effort to see me. I am about to become engaged to be married and in these circumstance you will understand our meetings must cease.

MORAG MURRAY

My father went to post the letter himself. I was too stunned to cry. All the old misery came back. Yesterday I was happy, today in the depths of despair.

That night I begged my father to ask Syed Abdullah to come to talk to him.

His 'word', he said, was final, and in view of the recent sorrow we had sustained he hoped I would not distress him and my mother by any disobedience.

The following day Roy arrived in Edinburgh. He had been in hospital and was given ten days home leave. Naturally I was glad to welcome a War hero, but I could think of no one but Syed Abdullah. What would he think of me? How mean I must appear!

I could not bear the suspense and parting, and wrote telling him

9

the letter had been written under my father's direction, and that I did want to see him soon.

A reply came by special messenger the same evening to say he was waiting to see me in the Caledonian Station. Not a very romantic setting!

Hurriedly putting on my coat and hat I ran all the way and arrived to find him waiting. I wanted to throw my arms round his neck, so relieved was I to see him, but he looked so sadly at me that I felt something terrible must have happened since we parted.

'Morag,' he said, 'I thought you were not coming. I have missed seeing you.'

'And I have missed you,' I said.

'My car is outside. Let us go to the Braid Hills and talk.'

We did not speak until we were actually on the hills. Syed Abdullah was deep in thought.

'Your letter,' he began, 'was a great surprise to me. If you had told me before I should not have been so distressed.'

'I had to write it, my father was so angry,' I protested.

'I want you to understand that we – that is, my clan – look upon our women with the greatest respect. The care we lavish on them and our anxiety to protect them from any harm has gained for us the reputation of making slaves of them. That is not the case. We revere them, and the worst crime in my hills is abduction. I have no wish to claim another man's bride. Such a thing, at home, would cause clan warfare which would not stop until every male member of the offending one's clan had been wiped out.'

'But there's no reason for you to think like this. I'm not engaged to anyone – my father and a friend have set their minds upon this marriage, that is all. I shall not marry Roy Graham. I don't like him well enough.'

'Morag, is there any man, any one of your fellow-countrymen you would marry?'

'No,' I replied.

'Then you will not have to obey your father and marry someone of his choice?'

'No.'

'Then as you are free I want to tell you I love you – ever since I saw you at the reception – and I always shall love you. If I get my father's permission, and your father's, will you marry me?'

'Yes,' I said.

We stood for long that afternoon, too deliciously happy to part.

Next day we met and discussed Syed Abdullah's visit to my father. Roy was going back to France next day, and we arranged for the visit to be on the day following. My mother was quite pleased when I asked whether my friend might come to tea; as she had agreed, I left it to her to break it to Father. The day came, and teatime brought Syed Abdullah. My mother was delighted with him, but my father, in their talk after tea, told him that I was too young to marry and looked older than I was, and he would not give his consent.

Syed Abdullah cabled to his own father. The reply was short: 'Positively not.'

Syed and I were distracted between the two fathers. Another cable came to say, 'Important letter follows'. This arrived weeks later. In it the Chieftain said he was then thinking of negotiating a marriage between Syed Abdullah and the daughter of a powerful rival chieftain and that once it was arranged it was irrevocable – for in the Pashtun country an engagement must never on any account be broken. He also pointed out that I was not of the Muslim faith, and he asked whether I came of a Highland clan of warriors and whether I would able to hold the fort if called upon.

Syed cabled back that I belonged to a Highland clan and was willing to become Muslim, and he took it upon himself to vouch for my ability to guard any fort!

The reply said: 'If you two are sure of your ability to remain faithful for life to each other, marry by both Eastern and Western law, and afterwards marry here in the ancient stronghold of your ancestors. Blessings upon you both! May Allah keep you! This is my permission.'

TO 'NO MAN'S LAND'

The cable with the Chieftain's consent set our minds at ease, but my father refused to consider our engagement, and all day and until late at night my life was one long-drawn-out repetition of stories about girls who had married Orientals only to find on the first visit to their husband's country that he was already married, perhaps more than once, and that the new bride was obliged to wait hand and foot on her new relations and finally, having been

11

starved or deserted, was obliged to throw herself on a missionary's mercy.

There were wild tales of British girls having been killed mysteriously and never heard of again. I was told that all Orientals were married in their cradles and that it was a ninety-nine-per-cent possibility that Syed Abdullah was married and that once in his country he would return to the degenerate ways of his clan and I would either be given ground glass in my food or be made a slave to his relations, whose womenfolk would be madly jealous of me. I would also be beaten regularly.

I felt ashamed to tell Syed these things at first, but determined to give him the chance of contradicting them. He was quite aware of what the Western opinion was and told me that most of the tales were carried by women who had married Orientals thinking them to be princes and looking forward to a life of luxury in some Aladdin-like palace of their own imagination, and, when they found out that there were neither princes nor palaces in their new lives, 'went wild' with the probably rather sketchy local European population who could be persuaded to act like that, and finally – if lucky and still unashamed – they had found their disillusioned way home. Most people assured me that Orientals lived in mud huts, were half clad, heathen, and no better than wild savages.

Syed, on his side, was told by his compatriots of the mistake of taking a Western wife. They said all Western women were the same – waited until they got out East and then danced and drank with their own people; flirted with other women's husbands and generally became impossible to live with; and then, returning home, wrote lurid stories that editors were only too glad to print.

Syed stressed the point that the Khyber men were not Indians, and after learning about his home life I was quite willing to share it.

My aunt alleged she had had two weak turns and several fainting fits since hearing the news, and descended upon me escorted by her Scrooge-like lawyer, who showed me her Will in which everything she possessed in this world, and all the prayers she would have power to offer for me in the next, were mine if I would marry the man my father had chosen for me. She did not want a reply, but thought the longing to possess her considerable wealth would outweigh a very uncertain future in foreign hills where every man had at least four wives!

Every day for a week she and the lawyer came to see me. I

refused to listen to her persuasions, whereupon she finally drew up a new Will to which my father and mother were witnesses. In this Will she left everything to a home for strayed cats.

When my father saw I was not to be influenced, he grudgingly allowed Syed Abdullah to come to our house. They became good friends and within three months of our meeting we were married. Three prominent Muslims who were then in Edinburgh came to my home, and the ceremony – a very simple one – took place in our drawing-room. One acted as priest, the other two as witnesses. I was asked thrice the same question:

'Do you take this man Syed Abdullah, son of Chieftain Secunder Khan, as your husband, and do you accept a thousand pounds as your dowry?'

Then it was Syed's turn:

'Do you take this woman, Morag Murray, the daughter of James Murray, as your wife, and do you agree to pay one thousand pounds as dowry to her at any time she may demand it during your lifetime, or, should she not demand it, do you agree that it be the first claim paid from your estate after your death?'

Three times the question was put and three times answered in the affirmative.

The two witnesses were now asked whether they had heard the parties agree to the contract, and whether they were willing to witness. The reading of a chapter of the Koran in which the contracting parties are enjoined to respect the marriage agreement, and to live with respect and devotion towards each other, was followed by the drawing up of terms of agreement. My husband, myself, the cleric, and both witnesses, appended their signatures. The ceremony was over. It had been solemnized strictly in accordance with Muslim laws, since I had previously embraced the Muslim faith with its simple belief in the unity of God and the prophethood of Mohammed.

The following year a daughter was born to us. The event occurred during the awful influenza epidemic, when my husband was in a nursing-home just recovering from the disease. Thinking to cheer him up, my father sent the good news to him. That night at 12 o'clock my nurse thought she heard someone outside the front door. Opening it she found a man huddled up on the doorstep, soaked through and wearing nothing but pyjamas and a dressing-gown. It was Syed, who had run away when told he was not well

13

enough to leave! The exertion of the four-mile walk had been too much for his strength. He remained unconscious for several hours, and had a relapse from which he almost died.

Shortly after this the Armistice came. The bells and sirens did not bring to some of us the joy that others felt, but it was certainly a relief, and in the first rush of new freedom we vowed to be better than we had ever been before!

Some well-meaning friends had told me that my 'in-laws' would not care for the child and that it would be better not to inform them of her birth; they assured me that only boys were welcome 'anywhere in the East'.

Judging his family's reaction by my husband's, however, I cabled the news, and to my infinite relief received this answer: 'The Chief of the Clan and all the members thereof send their blessings on the arrival of the little one. May the blessing of Allah be with you too! We desire to celebrate the occasion in these hills and are preparing for your coming. Peace be with you!'

A letter came next asking us to leave as soon as possible. But to undertake the long, fatiguing journey with so young a child was too great a problem for us, and our war-shattered nerves and half-starved bodies made a rest imperative. It was not till two and a half years later that we left for the Khyber.

My Scottish nurse left us at Karachi and I engaged instead an Indian hill-woman who had good references from a former employer.

The journey took two days, but luckily the weather was cool. After we crossed the Indus the country changed and we began to see a different type of men – tall, fairer-complexioned, dressed in baggy trousers and embroidered waistcoats, with loose shirts hanging outside the trousers, and turbans.

Near Peshawar men were ploughing with rifles slung over their shoulders. As the train entered the barbed-wire encircled station hall, Pashtun Guards (Military Police) boarded it to see our papers. It was as though we had entered a war area and were suspects – as indeed every one was in those parts until he had proved his innocent identity.

Having satisfied the Military Police that we had not arrived to lay siege to the place, we drove to the town house of the Chieftain. From the outside this looked none too welcoming. Grim walls, loopholed, frowned down upon us, but once inside we were very comfortable.

From Peshawar, the last city before the border on the North West Frontier we took the Afghan highway, our destination the Free Land between the British Empire and the Kingdom of Afghanistan.

The road ran through the Khyber Pass. The great rocks, towering boulder upon boulder to heights ranging from 600 to 1000 feet, strike a peculiar terror in the traveller. In some places the pass is so narrow that four camels cannot walk abreast. At the actual frontier there is a 'turnstile' through which one passes into 'No Man's Land'. That turnstile looks unimportant. It should be massive to stand for what it is, the gate leading to what is one of the least known and most remarkable countries in the world – a strip of land inhabited by clans who owe allegiance to none but their own chiefs, and live in loopholed towers, always armed and sleeping with their rifles at their sides. Some of the greatest empires the world has ever known have tried to conquer them, in vain.

Into this land of mystery I passed, through that insignificant turnstile. Certainly, I must confess, I felt a little that there might be some truth in what I had been told in far-away Edinburgh. I stood for a few seconds in wonderment at it all. Was it a dream? Would I awake to find myself back in Scotland again?

I looked back at the last outpost of my own people and knew there would be no possibility of my return if the odds went against me. It is a moment I do not wish anyone to experience, unless they are certain of their ability to face confidently what lies over those hills.

My husband I think sensed my feelings. 'Welcome,' he said, 'to the land of my fathers.'

It broke the spell. It reassured me. 'Syed,' I said, 'I trust you. You realize I am friendless here and have only you.'

'You and I are together always, Morag,' he answered. 'So long as I live, I promise to protect you with my life.'

Thus we started on our journey. As we passed finally out of sight of the last British post Syed said, 'There is still time to go back if you regret your decision. Time for *us* to go back.'

'We are not going back,' I told him; 'at least not yet.'

MEALS AND PRAYERS WITH THE HILL-MEN

It is one thing to read about the land beyond the Khyber and another to be actually in it. Compared to it, the grim Khyber Pass seemed friendly. Here I felt at the mercy of anything that might be lurking behind those grisly boulders. It was as though I had left something behind at that turnstile; I could only hope it was not courage! Certainly there was no welcome in the bare hills themselves. But we had not much time for meditation, for we were soon met by a party of my husband's clansmen who had been sent to greet us as soon as we were fairly into the Free Land of the Pashtun – as they style it.

They were all young men, tall, lithe, straight. They embraced my husband, bade us both welcome, and fired a volley into the air, calling in their melodious Pashtu, 'Welcome to the land of the free. Welcome to the wife of our noble Chief's son.' These men went ahead of us to clear the road, so to speak, while our ponies made their way slowly behind. The terrors of which I had heard and read in my now almost-unbelievable homeland seemed far enough away. Even if any courage had been needed one could depend upon these stalwart warriors to provide it.

On we went: the rocks seemed never-ending. Never had I imagined mountains like these. On and on until it was time to stop for refreshment. It was difficult enough to imagine where one would be able to get food, until just around a corner we came upon the house of a Khan. One needs to be sure of hospitality when one's party numbers thirty, and it was with not a few misgivings that I saw we were about to throw ourselves upon the kindness of the Khan.

As we approached the walled fort – still about thirty miles distant from my father-in-law's – the sentries challenged us. 'Friends or foes?'

'Friends, and peace be upon you!' our men replied.

'Welcome, and peace be upon you too!' heartily (and probably with relief) responded the sentries. The gate opened, and our guards stood back while our ponies entered, then came immediately behind us and closed the gate. Two sentries, I noticed as we dismounted, were on guard at the gate.

The Khan, a huge, jolly stout man, armed, and dressed in baggy trousers, long embroidered coat, and a tremendous turban, gave us a real Highland welcome. It was not a time when one wanted to receive an address of any length, but it was the correct thing here, and the old Khan was a master at receiving people in the proper manner. A woman servant came and carried Margaret, our little daughter, while two others asked me to follow them. We crossed the courtyard and entered the house. Here another welcome awaited us, when Margaret and I were taken to the women's apartments, whilst Syed stayed outside. These rooms were thick-walled, with small windows. The floors were spread with Persian and Bokhara carpets, and against the bare, whitewashed walls immense bolster-like cushions rested. We were evidently in the sitting-room of the family. The absence of pictures, ornaments, and furniture gave me a feeling of restful content.

I removed my all-enveloping veiled cloak, the *burqa*, and breathed a sigh of relief as we sat on the great bolsters. The women of the household – the Khan's wife and three grown-up daughters – had never seen a Western woman before, and were obviously delighted. They gathered round me, the maidservants in the back-ground, examined my clothes, wound my watch, and would not be happy until I showed them everything I wore! They asked the price, and talked so much and so quickly that the little Pashtu I knew deserted me, and I sat silent and almost overwhelmed.

Margaret was playing happily with one of the daughters, and making up her own language. Peeping out of the window I saw the men were praying, kneeling on their carpets with their faces turned in the direction of the Holy City of Mecca.

The maid now placed a large white cloth on the carpet in the centre of the floor, and on spotlessly clean plates we were given huge helpings of deliciously cooked rice – such as we never see at home – and little discs of roasted meat. The men evidently ate apart. With the name of Allah on our lips we seated ourselves cross-legged on the carpet and ate with our fingers. Margaret asked for a spoon which luckily I had with me, and without further *contretemps*, I had my first meal in the 'Free Land'. I noted it was not etiquette to speak or look at anyone during the meal and felt grateful for such a desirable point of table manners.

The women were so delighted to have me there that they could not disguise their disappointment when we had to leave. Again they tenderly fingered all my clothes, and gave me gold slippers as a parting gift, making me promise that any time I passed I would be sure to 'bring light to their household' by my presence.

Donning my *burqa* again, I joined our party with my daughter. The women chattered like magpies behind the latticed wall, and the Khan gave us a great send-off, thanked us for the great honour we had done him by coming, and ordered an escort, ten of his men, to see us well on our way. Finally he gave us two beautiful chargers, exquisitely saddled. Large tassels hung from their ears and silver crescents from the blinkers, while a broad red band encircled their necks. Tassels hung also from the saddles, and the bridles had many tiny jingling bells. This equipment had been presented, the Khan told us, to his father by the Amir of Bokhara. It looked to me as good as new and must have been kept carefully as only people who have few treasures know how to care for them. As I mounted I longed for the old freedom with neither saddle nor *burqa*, but I obviously had to follow the custom of the country.

Our escort was worthy of an emperor. Knives and guns dangled from them, and I wondered when these arms would be required in this land of seeming hospitality and remote aloofness. It was not to be long before my enlightenment! It was the duty of this smaller chief to protect us against the warring clansmen in his part of the country, and the guards were to show that we were important travellers.

Off we went; our men called back messages of peace and farewell which echoed in the distant hills, and our second welcome was over.

I now began to take stock of our cavaliers. Even the greatest coward might have felt safe when surrounded by them. Some wore big fur coats, *postins*, fastened with silver belts over their embroidered waistcoats. Each man carried a rifle slung on his back, a long knife at his belt, and a cartridge-filled bandolier across his chest. They were taking no risks! Their black hair was bobbed, and most of them had beards that did not disguise their youth. Each man looked a trained and fearless fighter. They reminded me of eagles. Two of them played wild, warlike chants on reed flutes, others beat small drums as our procession passed from deep gully to deep gully of the parched hills.

At one time we were amongst great boulders; at another we were passing through scrub woods with scarcely any visible vegetation – a partridge would start up into the air, or a hare dart away, roused to sudden anxiety by the noise of our party. Then the reed flute and the drums ceased, and there was a deep silence broken by our horses' hooves echoing slightly in the rocks as they struck a stone.

After a few hours we felt hungry in spite of the food our good friend the Khan had thought worthy of us! We alighted for a meal. Being a woman I was allowed to sit where I liked. It looked as though this meal were going to be a lengthy business: but no. A rough fireplace was constructed and a wood fire made and lighted. Newly killed fat-tailed sheep were roasted whole in their skins on the improvised camp-fire in an incredibly short time. Tin plates appeared from the luggage. Rice was juggled in some marvellous way in the gravy.

For the first time in my life I witnessed the great unity of the clansmen, who sat together, without distinction of class. Among them, according to Muslim custom, at mealtimes, in wartime, and at prayer-time all men are equal.

I was bewildered. I might have been seeing a film in a comfortable cinema. It may have been hunger, it may have been unfamiliarity, but until that day I had never tasted such delicious meat. Savoury and juicy, done to a turn, it had a distinct flavour almost like the nutty taste of really fresh country butter. The meal proceeded in silence, for it is considered bad manners to speak after the name of God is uttered in the grace until one can thank Him again for having given such good food and the health to eat it.

Not once did any of these men turn his head to look in my direction. I was their guest and could sit quite comfortably with my *burqa* turned back, without being stared at. The simplicity of that meal made me decide that tables, chairs, table linen, and cutlery were an unnecessary luxury.

My husband, being the honoured guest, gave the cue for the end of the meal. It was understood by all that when he finished all must finish. He was obliged here to give the others a handicap, for his appetite was not equal to that of the clansmen. He therefore took as long as possible over his food, for it is also etiquette to see that a guest's plate is never empty.

It amused me to see Syed eyeing the other heaped plates. I could imagine what was passing through his mind – whether he could continue eating until they finished! Nevertheless, slowly as he ate, he was finished before the others, and he began to nibble a crust of

bread. The rest of the clansmen at once stopped and took crusts
too. I did exactly as they did. Our crusts were eaten, two men
poured water from goat-skins over our hands, my husband now
raised his hands, then turning the palms upwards he slowly
repeated a prayer of thanks to Allah, the Giver of all good. The
men folded their hands over their faces and repeated their thanks
to the one God 'Who brought kindness and food and peace to all'.
The feast was over – the most simple, moving, and thrilling one I
had ever shared. We rose from our carpets, for all Muslims carry
their carpets with them on such treks, and drank water – this is
done only when the meal is finished.

Mounting our horses we started again in and out of the winding
passes. Some of the defiles were indescribably bleak and inhospitable, and I could easily have believed that any of them led to the lair
of a brigand. Now we passed out of the high-walled pass, to be
spellbound by the depth of the gullies round the corner. Stones
knocked over fell down, down, down, striking less and less loudly
against out-jutting rocks. Now we came to the rocks again.

Our next halt was for prayer. Muslims must pray five times daily.
My husband led the prayer, I joined in. One needed prayer in this
bleak country. So-called civilization being left behind, one thought
more of the Creator of it all, and felt thankful for such blessings as
health and strength and safety. We knelt on our rugs with our faces
towards Holy Mecca, and thanked God in all simplicity and reverence and sincerity for our safety so far. This religion gave me a new
feeling. There was no loud organ, no bag in which we had to
deposit whatever 'coin we could most easily silence our conscience
with, no wondering whether our clothes were passing muster with
the occupants of the seats behind. This was the simplicity of prayer
which made it the powerful thing it was. Near me knelt a mule-
driver. At that moment we were both equal, for prayer here
humbled my usual conservative ideas of class and position; yet
later on the mule-driver resumed his old status without taking any
advantage of the level to which prayer had raised him.

Again we started. I at least was tired, but was only dimly aware
of it.

From time to time we saw little forts of clansmen who lived in a
state of perpetual war with each other. Some ancient feud made
life a precious possession. Men who pursued each other and would
kill each other at sight would yet, had I required shelter of any one

of them, have guarded me, respected my person, and ceased warfare until my departure. Hospitality is sacred.

Shots were resounding somewhere near us, daytime though it was, and a shot in 'No Man's Land' is not an ordinary event. Once we were held up while two rival snipers tried their skill at each other across the road. Neither touched us; it was a private war. Eventually one of them fell off his rock, the other wished peace upon us – this struck me as being particularly appropriate – and waved his hand for us to pass.

It was an everyday affair with him and I expect one day some other sniper got him. The strange thing to me was that the women of these rival clans go about their usual duties, carrying water, driving cattle, and are never shot. No brigand, however infamous, would kill a woman. Women, these rough warriors say, are sacred. They wear scarlet trousers in order to be easily seen in the distance. These women, nevertheless, can shoot as straight as any clansman, and at a later date I had experience of their marksmanship. They can take to the loopholed towers with unfaltering courage, and more than one man has missed the inheritance life would have brought but for the unerring aim of one of these warrior women.

These clansmen were always willing to give us water or sherbet – a sweet drink made of fruit juice – and could not do enough or offer us enough when they knew who we were. Their hospitality reminded me of home. Yet one would have excused inhospitality in a place where fruit was almost a luxury and often had to be brought many days' journey from India or Afghanistan.

Again we halted, for the Asr or afternoon prayer, just as we had performed the Zuhr previously.

From time to time we saw men ploughing the inhospitable land, trying to wrest a living from a country which seemed ever to resist their desires. All had rifles slung over their shoulders; all around were black boulders, frowning down upon them as though in anger and perpetual defiance. In other stretches there were mulberry-trees clustering over the sides of the mountain.

Several times shots were fired in our direction as a challenge; a voice, sounding almost unearthly between the high rocks and the stillness, shouted, 'Friend or foe?' and always we called back, 'Friend! Peace be upon you'. I listened eagerly and excitedly for the reply, 'Peace be upon you too'. Our escort then fired two blank shots, in case the voice assuring the clansman of our peaceful intentions did not reach him. At any rate there are occasions when it is as well to make assurance doubly sure. Sometimes when the occasion demanded it one of our guards would wave his sword in the air to denote that we belonged to the family of a chief, where-upon the raider up in the hills would fire three blank shots, giving us salutations and welcome to that part of the land and his assur-ances of good feeling towards us.

Thus we journeyed. Dusk began to fall just as we reached the friendly haven of another Khan, with whom we were to spend the night. The next afternoon would see us at our destination.

This Khan was known as a deeply religious man. Our arrival coincided with the evening prayer, after which, washed of our travel stains, we were given a feast of *palao* – a delicious dish of rice with aromatic herbs – and roast chickens. The hill air makes appetites keen, and we enjoyed the meal heartily. It seemed quite an easy matter to eat four square meals a day. Mutton and rice appeared to be the staple diet, but there are so many ways of cooking the sheep that it never tastes twice the same.

After the meal the clansmen danced round the camp-fire with flashing swords. We women got the best view, looking down from the latticed windows. Suddenly, in the midst of the dancing, shots rang out. As though the wand of a fairy had transformed the scene, the men turned from dancers to soldiers. There was no 'scene'. The women drew back into their rooms, the men shouted orders to each other. A rival clansman was raiding the Khan's fort. Word was somehow sent to the enemy by lighted torches that guests were being entertained. More shots meaning retreat were heard, and the dancing was resumed. The women crept back to the lattice. To them, looking down again on the gleaming steel and whirling figures, the interlude might have been part of the dance.

That night my husband and I slept in a windowless, heavily barred turret; the fort was guarded by thirty armed watchmen. I wondered, as I fell asleep exhausted after the excitements of the tiring day, whether I should yet wake up to find myself back in Scotland. Dawn, however, brought back the reality. We awoke to the 'changing of the guard' with a long exciting journey still before us ere we reached our destination.

Looking at each other . . .

IN THE WARRIOR CHIEFTAIN'S FORT

We had breakfast and left the kindly shelter of the Khan's fort. The ten men forming the guard lent us by our previous host now started homewards, and their place was taken by ten belonging to our present host. These men would accompany us until we reached the safety of my husband's home, where if all went well we ought to arrive late that afternoon. The nearer we approached the more apprehensive I was feeling.

The way became bare and desolate. It was indeed a wild land. It only required a terrible storm with thunder and lightning to turn it into a nightmare. Yet the heavily armed men who surrounded us were enough to absolve the most chicken-hearted from fear of personal violence in any case. I began to enter into the spirit of the land. It had appealed to me from the first. Here I would never require to look for adventure; it would find me. It lurked everywhere.

The very stillness was mysterious, gripping. Some of the men sang songs, others recited couplets from the ancient Pashtun poets, others remained silent, but all seemed in the best of spirits. If they were not looking for trouble, I thought, there was no reason for me to do so. I watched their faces from time to time, expecting them to turn their heads as we passed suspicious-looking rocks and crevices, or gaze up into the boulders, but they plodded steadily ahead.

The way became wilder still, though here and there in the terraced uplands more cultivation appeared, and later on in the afternoon when we were yet some distance from our goal we saw on the surrounding hill-tops great blazing bonfires. These my husband explained were a welcome to us by all the surrounding chiefs.

'You will see something round this next corner,' said my husband. 'Guess what it is?'

'Brigands!' I replied, fearing the worst.

'No, home.'

'Home!' For a moment the very word itself sounded foreign to me. As we slowly made our way to that corner I thought of the peaceful home I knew, the quiet ordinary safe life I had led, my brother, the day I hooked the salmon . . .

The cavalcade had stopped. 'What do you think of it? Wonderful, isn't it?' The words came to me hazily. My husband was beside

23

me looking away up into the hills. 'There is your new home, Morag.'

My new home! I looked up and saw a grey loopholed wall, neither welcoming nor inspiring: unless it were with awe. It was hung with bunting; a huge bonfire burned near it on another hilltop. My eyes grew misty as I looked at the distant welcome. These people were doing their utmost to make me happy. Up and up we climbed. What would my new relations be like, I wondered. Would they like me, and I them? Suppose they did not like me! My tortured thoughts came to an end. I had arrived at my new home.

As we, my husband and I, entered first the courtyard, a very tall, dignified man approached us slowly, giving us time to dismount before he reached us. My husband helped me to alight and turning round I saw him kneel before the tall man and kiss his hands.

'My father,' said Syed. I kissed the Chief's hands too, and he bent low to kiss my forehead. His dignity and height were so great that I suddenly felt small and speechless.

'Welcome, my son, and welcome to you, my daughter, to this your home! We are proud today to welcome you. You must now be tired after your long journey.' He picked up our little daughter and turned towards the house. We followed. Syed squeezed my hand reassuringly as my knees knocked together, and, amid a volley of shots fired into the air by the clansmen gathered to greet us, we passed along the beautiful carpets laid down in our honour into our new home. The fort itself was a huge black building with high grey loopholed towers at each corner, obviously built to resist attack. Today it was hung with bunting which softened its military-looking coldness.

Servants stood all along the corridors as we passed to the harem or women's part of the house.

My mother-in-law and her daughters were awaiting us expectantly, and came forward at once as we entered the room. The old Chief presented me, and his wife at once embraced me warmly, kissing me on both cheeks. She was a tall, remarkably young-looking woman, with lovely dark flashing eyes and the fair skin of the women of that tribe. Ceremoniously she bade me welcome, and was so courteous and charming that I liked her immediately. Her daughters now came forward with Margaret clinging to their hands. They resembled their mother both in looks and manner, and their long three-quarter tunics, gauzy head-veils, and gold-

24

embroidered slippers made them look like fairy-tale princesses. This welcome over, they led me to my rooms on the first floor and insisted upon helping me in every way possible.

The low-ceilinged room was long, with whitewashed walls. A thick plush curtain hung over the main entrance. The long, narrow window was placed high in the wall; rugs covered the floor and a large low bed like a divan occupied one corner, with a low brass-topped Indian table by its side. On a shelf over the bed lay a copy of the Holy Koran covered with a silk cloth, for the Koran must never be placed under any other book or on the floor. Another curtain hid a number of shelves where clothes might be kept.

Before my arrival I had imagined servants who would probably watch me round the edge of a door, and leave me to do all the unpacking for myself. But here were two women who had never before seen a Western one, yet now, without displaying any obvious interest in me, were unpacking my clothes as though they had never done anything else in their lives. It gave me the feeling of being insignificant and unimportant. The coats, skirts, and frocks they were putting away suddenly seemed drab, uninteresting, and unromantic. I remembered having worn an Eastern dress once at a party at home; when it appeared too colourful and even bizarre. Here it seemed the only suitable dress.

Overcome by curiosity, I opened another door and saw men-servants putting Syed's luggage into a room similar to my own. My first fears were stilled. After all, there seemed to be no harem as I had imagined it. We were to be allowed rooms to ourselves and would not be obliged to crowd in with the rest of the family, as well-meaning friends assured me would be the case; moreover, we each had a separate bathroom.

My sisters-in-law interrupted further comparisons by asking from the door whether they might come in. Their arms were full of garments of every colour of the rainbow, specially made for me by them on the strength of measurements Syed thought would be suitable! Eagerly they watched me transform myself into a chieftain's daughter. When I had put on the heelless gold-embroidered slippers they laughed at my faltering steps in the unaccustomed shoes. Then they amused themselves by putting on my coats and skirts. They both kissed me affectionately and were so unaffected and vivacious that I liked them immediately; we might have known each other for years. The misery I had gone through at the thought

25

of meeting these relations of my husband seemed to have been the misapplication of much hard and distressing thinking. Yet here we were, in spite of the language bar between us, perfectly happy and at ease in each other's company.

The blue satin trousers were certainly comfortable; peg-topped and cleverly draped, they looked like a skirt. The three-quarter tunic and gauzy veil added a touch of mystery. By the time I had negotiated a few rounds of the room even the slippers had lost their terrors, and I felt one of the family.

The girls clapped their hands and laughed at my anxiety about my appearance. Each took one of my hands and we passed along the balcony to where shouts of glee and a great splashing of water proclaimed that Margaret was not having any difficulty with either language or environment.

From the windows I could see nothing but stretches of wild hills. They thrilled me, and I promised myself future exploration; when I later found that this was strictly forbidden, it of course seemed all the more desirable.

Down below, the vast courtyard looked like a fair. Hundreds of stalwart clansmen who had trekked from the Kohistan [Highlands] were arriving in a stream. Thirsty and tired like ourselves they must have been, but they were not going to let that mar the occasion. Every now and again a volley of welcome rang through the courtyard. Some came on ponies, some on camels, some on donkeys, but all were well and truly armed. How, I wondered, in my Western way, were all these people going to be accommodated?

Selima and Halima, my sisters-in-law, told me they were having the feast of welcome that night. 'But not for all those people?' I asked. 'No, there are yet more to come,' they replied, 'and there are many tents put up for them.'

They pointed through the latticed balcony wall to where the tents were still going up in the gardens. It looked already like a vast city of canvas, dwarfed by the towering hills. What a welcome to give a foreigner, I thought! The hospitality of the hills is the same everywhere. My heart warmed to these people, many of whom, judging by their travel-worn appearance, had come long distances to greet me. The past for me was now dead.

I was Morag Abdullah, and must live up to the name.

THE WOMEN DEFEND THE FORT

Not long after my arrival, the engagement of my sister-in-law, Selima Khanum, was announced. What an event that proved to be!

Thrill followed thrill. Presents arrived in a continuous stream. The news that two powerful clans were now friends caused mixed feelings. There were those who were glad, and those who no doubt had cause to be less so. The presents from the bridegroom-elect's people were composed of everything from humble household cooking-utensils to exquisite jewellery. The clothes alone would have been sufficient for fifty brides and then might well have caused comment, for every clanswoman gives at least one garment to a newly engaged girl.

Gifts were sent to the bride's fiancé, and news was spread of the marvellous saddles, guns, heaps of gold coins, ammunition, and swords he was receiving. The most wonderful gift was a perfect Arab horse, supposed to be the finest specimen ever seen and greatly desired by all. The owner, an uncle of the Chief of Killa Fort, was old and wanted to see the horse disposed of as he desired before his death.

Invitations came for the womenfolk of our clan to go to Killa Fort to a feast in honour of the occasion and by this 'eating the salt', as it is called, to show we were reconciled and friendly.

We packed all our smartest clothes, our best gold slippers and jewellery, and were to leave in three days. These days were crowded with excitement. Messengers were arriving with orders from the fort of my father-in-law, the chief; while our own messengers were continually on the run with our replies. There must be no hitch in these preparations, no cause for the clan's name to be ridiculed! I was afraid some quite innocent act of mine might give displeasure, but my mother-in-law with her unfailing diplomacy supervised all my endeavours to do my best, and for two afternoons put me through the different salutations to be given to the clanswomen when we met.

Each night instead of going to sleep I rigged up in my bedroom an imitation reception-hall, with boxes against the wall representing Killa Fort clanswomen, and practised until I was salutation-perfect. Being the son's wife I came after his mother in status,

27

and my being a *farangi* [Englishwoman] made it even more important that I should avoid mistakes.

At last the day of the departure came. Our luggage would have
taken us twice round the world. My mother-in-law went first on
horseback, I followed, behind came the excited Selima Khanum
and her sister. Armed guards were in front, behind, and on both
sides. An hour before we left a bonfire was lit so that the Killa Fort
people might know of our departure. No sooner had its smoke
been seen by them than they lit an answering fire on their peak. We
left in great style, being given a ceremonial salute by our fighting
men.

The three-hour journey passed without mishap, and our arrival
at the Killa Fort was welcomed with a salvo in which every man
must have joined. Bunting was everywhere, strings of roses and
cut-paper foliage in all colours made by the deft-fingered villagers.
Someone with more than the ordinary love of gaiety had even
stuffed coloured paper into the loopholes.

We dismounted and were shown at once into the women's
apartments, which were hung with decorations. The Killa Chief's
wife was past middle age, with greyish hair, fine eyebrows shading
soft brown eyes, and she had given much thought to her clothes;
but I think not more than we had given to ours! From head to foot
she was dressed in cloth of gold, shot with shimmering blue and
pink. Her little gold cap was massed with small artificial roses, and
over it her sparkling golden veil hung gracefully.

'Welcome and peace be upon you, bearer of so honourable a
name,' she began. 'On this great occasion it is my pleasant duty to
be, by the will of Allah, well in health to give you a welcome
appropriate to your clan. The honour is all the greater on account
of your respected daughter and the wife of your noble son, who
comes to share our gladness of heart. To her too we give greetings.'
My mother-in-law bowed, I followed with the proper salutations.

'Peace be upon you, scion of so worthy an ally. It gives me the
greatest pleasure to join you in this feast of welcome. May Allah
give us all his blessing!' With a low bow my mother-in-law walked
into the room towards a group of girls and women. I bowed twice
and then kissed the hand of the Khanum; she then kissed my
forehead and I passed next into the room.

Selima Khanum and her sister followed with greetings first to the
Khanum, who joined us as I reached the group. Then followed

introductions, brow-kissing, hand-kissing, bowing and more hand-kissing from the youngest girls, and we were taken to our apartments. From our balcony we could see the bonfire at my father-in-law's fort, and below in the courtyard great displays of shooting, jumping, and wrestling between the men of the Killa Fort clan. Our warriors were not with us. It is customary for only the women to attend the engagement feast.

Servants were supplied – four to each of us – to wait upon us, do our hair, and assist us to dress. They put scent on my wrists and behind my ears, a thin film of the secret face-powder, a little rouge – and all four vowed they had never seen such perfection. The maids in the other rooms were probably saying just the same to my relations! My sisters-in-law certainly looked lovely. There were fifteen girls there to welcome us, daughters of the fort and nieces from another stronghold some two miles distant.

We feasted for quite three days, and paid each other compliments, saying practically the same thing in different ways.

After the feast we girls were allowed to exchange confidences in our own rooms; we gave each other charms, heard the latest the stars foretold for us and the speculations made for the future of Selima Khanum, and looked at each other's jewellery. I was asked many questions about my country. They could not believe the stories about the traffic and said the policemen must really be magicians if they succeeded in keeping so many cars and people going in the same direction without being killed by the dozen! They marvelled at the description of the shops and at Western women being allowed to mix with men shoppers who dared to look at other men's wives! Nothing, they all agreed, would persuade them to travel in an aeroplane, which their men called a 'devil machine' and which must have been invented by the Devil himself. Among them I began to feel almost as much handicapped as the man who was suddenly shot into the country of the blind. I had to unlearn a great deal, and quickly.

After the evening meal we were sitting on the balcony sipping sherbet and eating sweets when we saw a stranger arrive. He was a travelling blacksmith with veterinary skill who examined horses' feet and treated them if they required it. He produced references from other chiefs speaking of his abilities and was at once engaged to go the round of the horses in the Killa Fort. He seemed a very efficient and painstaking man and would not even leave his work to go to the evening meal, saying he preferred to work until finished and then to travel on, as he had to reach another fort before nightfall.

The men left him, praising his skill, and were in the midst of their meal when we heard a furious galloping, and running out on to our balcony we saw a fast-disappearing horse and rider at full gallop. The guards fired, the watchman shouted, 'The Arab! The Arab!'

The courtyard was full of excited, half-stupefied men. The guards exclaimed that the blacksmith had galloped past when they were unprepared, for as it was meal-time only half of their number were on duty. Who was the blacksmith? Which direction did he take? Questions were called without being answered. Pursuit parties were soon mounted and rallied outside the courtyard. The Chief of Killa Fort was directing twenty men in one direction, twenty in another, and so on. Sending farewells to his wife and daughters he galloped off and disappeared from sight. The sound of thundering hooves, the *thud*, *thud*, on the hard rocks, peculiar to that part filled the air. We were astounded at the unexpectedness of the event.

Still standing there waiting as darkness began to fall we watched in vain for the return of either clansmen or Arab, or both. At bed-time they were still absent and we women decided to lie down on our beds and rest. The excitement of the day and now the anxiety overcame us. It was a sorry end to the engagement feast. I lay awake wishing the men would return. Suppose they were set upon by hill-brigands and killed, shot by men who knew the hills perhaps better than they and who would take their lives for the guns and ammunition they carried, and counting themselves in luck would ride off to their fastnesses. I got up and hastily wrote a note to my husband:

The Arab has been stolen. The Killa Fort fighters left hours ago to search. Am afraid something has happened. For heaven's sake have help sent.

Calling a servant I asked for this to be sent immediately to my father-in-law's fort, where Syed was staying during my absence. With relief I heard the gate open and the courier's horse galloping at full speed, sure-footed along the hill road. The feeling of foreboding depressed me. I went to Margaret's room – she and her nurse were both sound asleep. Tiptoeing to Selima's room I saw she was praying – I crept away. Would the daylight ever come? Would the men ever come back again? Why had none of the parties returned? Had they been ambushed? It was now eleven o'clock. Perhaps the men were back after all, I comforted myself. I would have one more look and go to bed. This was a strange country with strange ways and I was a coward, I thought.

Stepping out on to the balcony I was surprised to hear distant rumblings of thunder. A flash of lightning gashed the darkness, rain poured in torrents, but through the storm I caught the crack of rifle-shots. Thank heaven! It must be the returning clansmen.

But our few guards, snipers, and sentries suddenly replied. Orders flashed quick as the lightning. To the loopholes! Selima Khanum was beside me.

'A raid! The clansmen are away. There are only a few men left. Can you shoot?'

'Yes.'

'I'll bring my rifle. Get yours, and as much ammunition as you can,' she said quietly and slipped away.

Running in, I brought out my rifle and two belts of cartridges which everyone carries. The storm was terrific. The raiders must have been soaked through. How many were closing in on us in that awful darkness? The lightning flashed repeatedly, the thunder rumbled and crashed, every now and again the flashes caught the barrels at the loopholed wall. My sisters-in-law and the girls who could shoot joined us. There was no fear shown. Through my mind went the words of the Chief of our clan to his son in far-off Edinburgh: 'Would she be able to defend the fort if required?' The fear was banished; my own clan was as courageous as this or any other!

'Let's get to the loopholes,' someone said. Selima, the elder girl, led the way. The shots were nearer; to judge by the fusillade there must have been at least a hundred attackers. Our replies were weak. 'One woman to a loophole and remember the honour of your clan,' called Halima Khanum as we found our loopholes.

The rain was not so heavy now, but the storm continued. The lightning-flashes glinted on the knives and rifles of the men approaching. The girls fired steadily and determinedly. The lightning showed the raiders now crawling like snakes towards the fort wall. Once they reached it, our poor defence would not hold long.

Shouts and the groans of the wounded outside the fort began to reach us. Our few snipers inside the walls would soon be overcome.

Suddenly fierce yells rent the air. I felt like flight back to my room, but the girls held firm. I suddenly felt strong again. This was probably our last hour in any case: nothing seemed to matter. The hand-to-hand fighting outside was furious, yells followed yells; by the lightning flashes we saw men struggling together, but our snipers inside the wall who were practically our last defence were mercifully still at their posts. There had been a check, and the whirling fighting mass seemed to me to be retreating. Another flash showed men lying on the ground. I crept to Selima Khanum's side.

'There is a check,' she shouted, 'so the Killa Fort clansmen must have returned, and attacked the enemy's rear.' Then my recollection of the note to my husband! It must be our warriors who had come to help search for the Killa Fort men and the Arab! My husband must be out there in that nightmare scene.

I must go. The suspense inside was terrible – I doubted that anyone could survive that hand-to-hand fight. They would all simply kill each other ... I stumbled in the darkness down to the courtyard clutching my rifle and cartridge belts, but the sentry would not let me pass. Climbing through a window I got to the women's open courtyard. The storm was over, darkness was now blacker than ever. Shots were flying in all directions, bullets whizzed past my head. I crept, as I thought, round to the front gate of the fort. Our snipers were calling, 'They retreat, they retreat.'

I ran back, fearful of what would be carried through the gate. Thankful for the mercy of the darkness, I groped my way back to the loopholed wall. The girls had heard the call passed round and were now showing signs of restrained anxiety as to who had been wounded. 'Wounded,' I thought. 'What about the dead?' Who could have survived such a raid? The fort gates were now open. Flares were lighted and lanterns held high as men were carried through.

Shouts of victory rang through the air. I stood looking on the scene from inside a doorway on the ground floor. They were carrying the wounded to the big dining-hall. My teeth chattered. I found I was still grasping the cartridge-belts.

Looking at each other . . .

'Dead,' a man said as four clansmen passed carrying an inert figure. 'He was a great warrior. God is great, on Him the salute!'

How long the weird procession lasted I did not know. I felt as though all my life had been spent watching the terrifying spectacle. Two men walking now I recognized as from our fort. I wanted to call, but no word would come. My husband must be there! But where? I crept round to the archway near the dining-hall where I could see each man being carried in. My eyes glued themselves to the passing figures.

My sisters-in-law and the other women now came down, unveiled as was their privilege in the circumstances, and walked into the hall. I followed. They began to attend to the wounded men. Friend and foe lay side by side. The dead were carried to another room. Bowls of water were brought and rolls of cloth. No preference was shown to any; each man took his turn. Some lay unconscious, others called for water. I walked among them looking for a face I feared to see. Why had I sent that note?

'You help me here, light of my eyes,' came my mother-in-law's voice. Daylight came and we were relieved by other women. The dead were buried. Many still lay out where they had fallen.

It turned out that my husband had not been present at the fight, having been away at another fort. His father had sent for him, but luckily by the time he arrived the enemy was retreating.

The Killa Fort clansmen were dangerous foes, yet merciful to their enemies. The raid was forgotten as they helped the wounded on their homeward way. The seriously hurt were afterwards collected by their friends.

Later we discovered that the blacksmith was not such at all, but a notorious outlawed brigand chief, who had stolen the Arab as a ruse, so that the defenders of the Killa Fort might be weakened during the resulting search and he and his men might attack the fort, to steal its large stores of rifles and ammunition. They had been attacked and routed from the rear by the returning Killa Fort men, who in turn were aided by our clansmen arriving to help in the search for the Arab.

The horse found its own way back to the fort of the bridegroom-elect's old uncle, and had to be presented, with ceremony, once again.

HOW TO FIGHT AFGHANS

The Pashtuns of the Frontier (whom the British, following an Indian mispronounciation, called 'Pathans') have never acknowledged any rulers but their own. During the British imperial period the Empire never subdued them. General Sir Andrew Skeen's book *Passing it On* – from which these extracts come – is a classic of the wars when as many as 40,000 troops were thrown into battle against a single clan. Perhaps they had not heard of the Pashtun curse: 'May you live to become a taxpayer!'

THE COUNTRY

'What is the North-West Frontier like? The country and its fighting men?' Not easy to answer. Though I have footslogged or ridden most of the frontier from Mastuj to Kalat, I can only tell you that no short stretch of it is like its neighbour. You will never find ground of the same nature for twenty miles on end.

Miles of cliff and stony slopes giving way to open fans of cultivation backed by steep and sheer cliffs; narrow river gorges opening out of fir-covered mountains which drop to swelling bush-covered hills... through wooded Maidan, deodar forest, strips of open downs. Most dangerous of all, the bush-tufted, stony plains and ravines where the dashing tactics of the Mahsud find their fullest scope. In no one place are conditions a guide to what may be found in another.

34

Looking at each other . . .

THE FIGHTERS

The people differ less than do the parts they live in. All are men to reckon with. I place the Mahsud highest as a fighter along with the Mamund. But all are apt in war, and taken all in all are probably the finest individual fighters in the east, really formidable enemies, to despise whom means sure trouble.

They come down hillsides like falling boulders, not running but bounding, and in crags they literally drop from foothold to foothold. To deal with such mobility on their own lines is impossible. These men are hard as nails; they live on little, carry nothing but a rifle and a few cartridges, a knife and a bit of food, and they are shod for quick and sure movement.

Their power of moving concealed is astounding, not only in moving from cover to cover, but in slipping from light to shadow, and background to background. It has to be seen to be believed.

RAID ON A PICQUET

A picquet of some 60 men held a hill overlooking the Tichi River, securing a big stretch of road near Miranshah.

Days passed, quiet and deadly dull; standing to at dawn became a neglected duty.

Then, one morning as the day party reached the dead ground, a blast of fire downed it, while another swept the *Sangar* (breastworks) and for ten minutes kept its occupants firing blindly and intermittently, while a bunch of the enemy dashed into the dead ground, secured the rifles and most of the ammunition of the day party, and legged it. The occupants of the picquet issued to find the enemy several hundred yards off, and ten of their own comrades dead.

I take off my hat to that bunch of raiders. They deserved what they won.

HOW TO DEAL WITH THE PATIENCE OF THE PASHTUN

The solution – never relax any precautions: devilish hard to apply because it is not natural to keep nerves and imagination on the stretch when there is apparently nothing to justify it. That is the trouble – day after day you will see nothing but bare hills or rock or bush – quiet as the grave.

Remember the enemy is always there, and looking for you to make a mistake.

A lightly equipped 'floating' platoon ceased to stay mobile. The first night, nothing happened. There were two parties of the enemy: each had taken steps to protect itself from being seen by building thin stone walls at their backs, and were crouching in the open. The platoon was completely wiped out by the tribesmen in ground dead to the piquet.

One can't help admiring these folk, and if we don't take lessons from their doings, we deserve all we get.

EVIL DODGES

There is no need to become discouraged with tales of fiendish cunning and inescapable disaster. Think out evil little dodges. Lay booby-traps. A gun-cotton charge is attached to a long string. To secure a really stout material for stringing the family bed, if our friend runs merrily along coiling up a quarter of a mile of usefulness and jerks the string, he will himself be jerked noisily across Jordan.

Another is an ammunition box with gun-cotton for contents, realistically dropped on withdrawal. A stout group will certainly gather round this best-of-all loot to share out, *et voilà*! Cad trick, but all booby traps are more or less that . . .

DESPERATE ATTACKS

Distribution in depth has the advantage that you are strong to resist assault, and this may come.

Look out for it coming from men lying up a little distance in front of the main position.

These will be men who have accepted the fact that they will not return and make a desperate surprise dash so that their try for Paradise may have a better chance of taking some of the attackers with it.

Once I saw this happen, when six Bunerwals, ages from sixteen to sixty, suddenly leapt out as the front line was fixing bayonets for the final assault on the enemy's defences.

They came out from a mere furrow of rock and went slap through three of our lines before the fourth bayoneted them.

Armed only with knives and axes, too, stout fellows.

Looking at each other . . .

THE AFGHAN SNIPER

The accuracy of these people's shooting is sometimes astounding. At Makin I saw four men knocked out by one sniper, known to have been fifteen hundred yards off. Shortly before that, taking up camp at Marobi, one man, who was bagged before he could do more damage, got two men and two mules in five shots, at a range of not less than five hundred yards.

WITHDRAWING IN GOOD ORDER

Make sure that the men carry food. A phenomenon of every campaign in which the British soldier takes part is that he will throw away his food rather than carry it, trusting to a grouse to get more when as a rule there is none to be had.

In withdrawing, the commander has two great responsibilities. The first is to make his decision to withdraw as early as he can. It was the delay in withdrawing which caused the nasty incidents of the Saran Sar, and it was the memory of that which made me move back when the entrance to the Ahnai Tangi was almost in my grip.

The second is to direct the main lines of the withdrawal and not leave troops to find their own way.

Look back from time to time, to see if a comrade has been hit, and to see if the enemy swordsmen are not rushing along behind. I have watched a couple of men struggling clumsily down a steep ravine, and behind them two Mahsuds bounding in pursuit from rock to rock, nothing in their hands but knives.

LOOTING AND LIGHTING

Never set light to anything as you pass unless ordered. A stack of fodder will put up a dense smoke and in a moment all chance of visual signalling is gone. You will often find that someone puts a light to something, out of pure devilment.

When collecting fodder, do the work as quickly as possible, with a party on guard. At Nahakki in the Mohmand show of 1908 three greybeards, ripe for Paradise, dashed from hiding on a few pioneers and took five with them as a passport.

Drive your men all the time. Taking other folks' property is so new an activity that they will waste time if you do not check them. Stop looting. Korans in houses are holy books and family bibles; they are no good to the despoiler and taking them is a dirty trick.

One area cleared of whatever you were set to collect, move to another, piling stuff as gathered in some handy central place.

In demolition, you are not collecting supplies from a comparatively quiet locality. You are going out to set your mark on a stubborn enemy, to punish him for years of accumulated evil-doing. There is usually an outcry about this form of punishment, with good reason. I dislike it intensely, but after the enemy's will to stand and take punishment is broken, there is no other way to make him watch his step in the future. If there is a way, we have not found it in eighty years.

Unless the enemy is completely crushed, he will rally to defend his property or revenge its loss, and you will find him fully as fierce as a wasp in a harried hive. During the destruction of Makin in 1920 this was very marked.

Fifty-one towers and over four hundred and fifty main dwellings in various hamlets in the cultivated area were destroyed. Here I would say that it is far better not to attempt destruction unless it can be vindictively thorough.

Some of the infantry prefer the method of blowing out corners of houses and lighting the debris. Grain, if not taken away, should be heaved into water or heaped in the open with a good lacing of oil and left to be lit at the end.

More dangerous and equally necessary work is in the open, pulling out key-stones in the retaining walls which hold up the terraced fields. The knack is soon learnt: out comes the stone, and several feet of the wall comes down with a roar, with earth following – a year's cropping lost – during which the sinners pay for their sins.

When the houses are all ready for firing, be careful about the problem of smoke. At the signal of a Very light, the houses are systematically fired. Each house should be fired and all piles of grain. Look out for bees. A Highland battalion saved their faces by covering them with their kilts when the bees of Maizar resented the burning of their homes.

Hot, dusty, dangerous work, but frequent, and therefore you should be prepared for it, by sound training in the principles of advance and withdrawal and by constant thought over the most time-saving methods of organizing for work.

AFGHAN LESSONS FROM A BRITISH INVASION

Colonel Ghazi Hatim of the Afghan Cavalry prepared these notes for the Sipah Salar (Commander in Chief) just after the Second Anglo-Afghan War over a century ago:

Captured officers from the attacking forces have confirmed that the superior firepower of the artillery of Sardar Ayub Khan was one of the decisive factors in our victory on the field of Maiwand.

Subsequent events during and after Sir Frederick Roberts' attack on Kandahar show that avoidable things can make the difference between defeat and victory.

Roberts complained, when he entered Kandahar, that the troops were disheartened. This was due to the lack of their accustomed comforts and such things as the death in battle of Brigadier-General Brook and many others in an unsuccessful sortie against the Afghans outside.

Again, out of the enemy force no less than 12,000 men were Indians, while only 4,000 were British. The British were less afraid of our cavalry and equally (with us) ready to use sharp arms. Our swords were matched by their bayonets, which they even used against our cavalry.

It might be remembered that our cavalry training and equipment were better, as were our heavy guns and marksmanship. This caused great surprise as well as success. On the other hand, less than a quarter of our men possessed rifles and their marksmanship, though second to none, was limited by the poor quality of antique weapons and a severe shortage of ammunition. The British are always over-supplied with stores and war materials. This adds to their troubles on the march, but gives them great defensive and attack ability. As for us, we often had to obtain our supplies from the invaders by *Jan-Nissari* [self-sacrificing] attacks.

Our leaders are conspicuous in dress and mounts. This makes them easier targets. English troops are taught to recognise them and seek them out for killing by a mass of attackers, to deprive our fighters of their leaders. This is a difficult matter: for the duty of a leader is to be seen on the field of battle, and to be always in the forefront.

In the War of Shah Shuja (40 years before) the commercial and private areas of Kabul were looted by order of the military chiefs. This meant that English soldiers have a great incentive to attack and to win, as they get the loot as their reward: in Kandahar, even ordinary foot-soldiers became rich from plunder.

On the other hand, our troops falling on the British baggage after Maiwand prevented them from their main task of destroying the enemy. I am aware that our *Ghazis* [heroes] have said that they were forced to do this in order to resupply themselves with arms; but there may have been other reasons, too.

What they lack in artillery skills, horsemanship and accurate shooting, the English make up in very well-drilled infantry work. They stand and fight, generally, in an excellent fashion. We should learn this skill. The abundance of supplies which almost obsesses the English is, again, a great help to them; for they seldom need to fear that they will run short of necessities.

They are brave, but not trained for mountain terrain. Heat and inaction do not increase their fighting power. The men are of good quality; so are the officers, when their hearts are in the matter.

The wonder of the world is that the Afghan people, dispersed as their armed contingents are among so many chiefdoms, are able to reach the battlefield and carry on concerted actions as well as they do.

Of course their faith, and the defence of the Realm Given of God, are decisive factors against an adversary who, when questioned, seems not to know why he is invading us.

AN AFGHAN IN ENGLAND TO MEET THE KING

'I went to England to meet the King.
But first I had to see something of the place.'
An Afghan's first impressions of England,
some of her people, and her monarch.

'Show us your hearts!' said an American tourist to his English
guide, as I sat in the hotel lounge.

I shared in his request: for a visitor to London wants to see both
the museums and art galleries, and something more important.
The living, pulsating picture of the English folk which is perceived
abroad and which – at least to an Oriental – helps us to form that
almost Utopian idea there is about them and their ways.

To be candid, I tried in vain to tally my ideas about this country
by walking through the London streets. Beyond the fact that the
high buildings awed me (it felt at times like walking between
mountains of stones) I could not see what might seem the life of the
people. Finally, a kind friend advised me to go to the English
countryside where I would see people in their real setting: and then
trek back to the heart of London.

I hied forth to a village. And I was in luck, for the people were
enjoying themselves at the fair. It wasn't at all like hurrying,
scurrying, stone-faced London. Fascinated, I joined in the fun.
'Lovely food, lovely food!' called the man offering to dole out a
pennyworth of eels set in jelly. A labourer standing near the booth
recommended it to some passing women. Two youths, after a
dazing ride on the dragons of the roundabouts, came to celebrate
the spirit of the fair by quaffing two glasses of lemonade each. In
England, I noted, lemon juice and even lemon squash may indeed

be made from lemons. 'Lemonade', though, is only carbonated water with sugar added...

But there were slices of lemon floating in the glasses. One of the youngsters even thought that this addition authenticated the liquid: but an elderly woman jeered from behind the counter, and advised them to stop wasting her time, to go to the love birds and the gypsies.

Round the corner of a tent on the village green, a man wearing a pyjama suit and a top hat sold three large boxes of chocolates for a shilling: the broad red ribbons on the boxes alone looked worth more. The man wanted me to believe that, precisely on that spot, 330 years before, Queen Elizabeth had dined. Being imbued with the festive atmosphere, he added, he was practically giving away his wares.

Again and again, the roar of a caged lioness attracted the attention of the children – and their nervous parents.

Winding in and out, between the gypsies' caravans and carts, the people trekked to the switchbacks and bumper-cars, all aglow with tiny lights in many colours. Even on the way to the allurement of the coconut shies and the shooting-gallery, many could not resist the hazards of the numbers game and dart-throwing challenges. A beautiful silver bowl could be won, simply by lodging a penny here, or getting a ring right over the broken spout of a teapot there. It all looked so easy.

Then, as I watched, the tents and canvases, the flags and the pennants were rolled up, the merrymakers had departed. Hefty men were heaping coconuts and clown-suits onto their donkey-carts; great wheels and shafts were piled onto traction engines. Noisy men covered all with tarpaulins, gypsies played mouth-organs and everyone leapt onto their transport – and the cavalcade moved on.

Sadly, I turned back to London, to solve the mystery of how the people lived there, and what they felt. Walking down some basement steps, I saw the microcosm of a world. The sales were on; and it was war.

Around a stack of silk remnants a slim and a stout lady were working in double harness. The one wriggled her way towards a piece which was marked ridiculously cheap, while the other impeded the progress of a rival. Her tactics were what the theoreticians of war call Impositional Deterrence, impeccably performed.

Hats, frocks, all manner of garments and fabrics, each had their devotees; for the military complexion of the scene also resembled religious fervour. From a vantage-point on the steps (until swept away by a fresh tide of enthusiasts) I could even identify the elements of the rugger scrum, the snatch-and-run thief and the anarchist revolutionary.

Still they came. The warmth of the basement increased with each horde of what the papers call bargain-hunters. And hunters they were, as well as everything else. They arrived ready for the fray, sensibly dressed and shod, equipped with large, sometimes metal-bound, bags which had a dual purpose: to thump the opposition and to carry away the loot.

They had seemed on the whole, a quiet people, these English: but not here. The silent ones were those who had fainted from the heat, and perhaps from indignation, for there was much of that.

Yes! The ways of the English are indeed strange.

Strangeness is fascination, of course. And, if I had seen something of the standoffishness, of the rollicking, and of the specialised mass-behaviour, I was now due for a closer look. I was about to glimpse the very heart of what people call – England.

THE COURT

On being presented at His Britannic Majesty's Court, I soon learned two things. Firstly, that colour and pageantry do not reside only in Asia. Secondly, that King George had a breadth of knowledge almost equal to that of the best-informed people I had met. Was the Empire, as people said, falling down? If the grandeur of it all was any guide, no: not yet.

Here was the Royal Command to present myself at Court. Beyond being magnificently printed, the summons did not differ from the gilt-edged invitation cards which many other people send. For us Easterners, though, there is always something beyond the outward aspect. The mighty command of a monarch lay behind those cold letters; the voice of the world's greatest empire throbbed and echoed there.

In the days of our own great empires, such as that of the Moguls, the arrival of such a document was celebrated by weeks of rejoicing by the people: 'So that our own lord might also see,' would sing the bards of the Nawab's villages, 'the radiant face of Allah's Shadow on the Earth.'

Yet I did not feel at ease. It is a peculiarity of the men of the Afghan mountains that they would rather face a hail of bullets – or would slash at all comers with a long razor-sharp *shamshir*, with nonchalance. That is their training and their instinct, the path of honour, the Way of the Saracen Knight.

This is not because we feel lacking in sufficiently polished manners to face the glitter and ceremony of a Court: many of us have courts of our own, with centuries-old traditions, reaching back beyond recorded history. But I realised, examining my feelings, that I was measuring the impending visit with what I had gone through on several awe-ridden Eastern occasions. Then, your limbs might freeze, but you dared not move a hairsbreadth, lest the King's gaze fix you, and at such times any head might quickly part company with its shoulders.

The limousine drew up at the gate, then at the door, and we went inside Buckingham Palace.

The hall where we had to wait seemed crammed with tapestries, flags, blazons and arms. My seat was next to that of an old country gentleman. Mercifully, he did not talk. His daughter supplied the deficiency. Try as she might, she could not read my name on the card: I was holding it upside down, she complained in a stage-whisper.

From my robes, she guessed loudly, I must be an Eskimo prince; or perhaps I was only a Polish general.

A tall, blond, aristocratic equerry flitted about. Their Majesties would soon be in the Throne Room. The young lady sprayed her bouquet with water, fiddled with her hat. Someone, talking to a man behind me, said, 'Put that monocle away, if it won't stay in your eye!'

The rich melody of *God Save the King* struck upon our ears. It came floating along the long corridors from a distant room. All were now on their feet.

We were moving to the Presence; I heard my new shoes squeak, '*Chaar . . . chaar; chaar . . . chaar*'. The sound filled the narrow passage until I felt like taking them off. We passed through an antechamber.

My card was taken from me by an officer and passed from hand to hand by half a dozen dignitaries until it reached the one standing just before the King.

I waited for the usual mangling of my name; then I realised that it was being called out with perfect diction, the cadences just right:

'Sayed The Sirdar, Ikbal Ali Shah'.

I advanced. A firm grip from the King's hand; my nervousness gone. A benign smile lit up the face of the Emperor. His naval uniform and fresh-faced look enlivened the atmosphere.

It was later, at one of the Garden Parties, that I had more time with their Majesties. Both the King and Queen walked about among the guests, mixing and talking to anyone. Little clumps of people collected around them as they moved about, so unconventionally.

Standing with a teacup in his hand, and smoking a cigarette, the King started a conversation. Afghanistan? He knew that the Helmand River had changed its course three times. He was interested in the towering, ancient rock-carved Buddha figures of Bamiyan. He knew, too, about the Topes of the Khyber region: the 'pyramids' of Afghanistan.

His voice was mellow, perhaps a trifle hoarse. Above all, it was his unconventionality which captivated me. Unlike a king, and yet so kingly.

Talking to King George, in the sunlit vistas of his glorious lawns and gardens on that afternoon, I thought of greatness. It does not, need not, shroud itself in mystery. If ever a king reigned, it was King George, ruling not least the hearts of his people.

'Show us your hearts!' the American had said in the hotel lounge that day, I recalled, as we drove away. And I had just been in the presence of the heart of these people's own hearts...

Sirdar Ikbal Ali Shah

AN ENGLISH ENVOY MEETS
THE AFGHAN KING

In the early nineteenth century, the English
Envoy, the Hon. Mountstuart Elphinstone,
led a delegation to the Court of Shah Shujah,
Ruler of the Durrani Empire, at his Winter
Palace. The Chaush Bashi, Chief Herald,
struggled hard to familiarise himself with the
English names, then:

He now explained the ceremonies to be observed in a very courteous manner, and entreated us to whisper our names to him when
he should touch us. He then conducted us up a sloping passage and
through a gate, after which we passed behind a sort of screen, and
suddenly issued into a large court, at the upper end of which we
saw the King in an elevated building.

The court was long and had high walls, painted with the figures
of cypresses. In the middle was a pond and fountain. In a high
building, supported by pillars and Moorish arches sat the King on a
very large throne of gold or gilding.

We thought at first the King had on armour of jewels, but on
close inspection we found this to be a mistake, and his real dress to
consist of a green tunic, with large flowers in gold and precious
stones, over which were a large breastplate of diamonds, shaped
like two fleurs-de-lys, large emerald bracelets on the arms (above
the elbow) and many other jewels in different places.

In one of the bracelets was the Koh-i-Noor, known to be one of
the largest diamonds in the world. The crown was about nine
inches high – the whole so complicated and so dazzling that it was
difficult to understand and impossible to describe.

The walls on each side were lined with the King's guards three deep, and at various places in the court stood the officers of state, according to their degree.

The floor was covered with the richest carpets, and round the edges were strips of silk, embroidered with gold, for the Khans to stand on.

The view from the hall was beautiful. Immediately below was an extensive garden, full of cypresses and other trees, and beyond was a plain of the richest verdure: here and there were pieces of water and shining streams: and the whole was bounded with mountains, some dark and others covered with snow.

On coming in sight of the King, we all pulled off our hats and made a low bow. We then held up our hands towards heaven, as praying for the King, and afterwards advanced to the fountain where the Chaush Bashi repeated our names, without any title or addition of respect, ending, 'They have come from Europe as ambassadors to Your Majesty. May your misfortunes be turned upon me!'

The King answered in a loud and sonorous voice, 'They are welcome', on which we prayed for him again, and repeated the ceremony once more.

HOME TO AFGHANISTAN

Extracted from an unpublished diary of the
Sirdar Ikbal Ali Shah are these experiences
and prophecies of change . . .

Bonfires blazed on the hills, and constant fusillades of joy-firing
into the air went on day and night. I asked Mihrban Khan to calm
things down since there was no point in it. I heard him say to one of
the heads of welcome-contingents, 'It is ordered that silence and
discretion be observed.'

The other man asked, 'Why?'

'Why? Obviously because Hazrat [the Presence] does not want
Kabul to fear that he has *Khiyal-i-Padshahi*!'

I, wanting to become king? I immediately told Mihrban never to
say any such thing again, even as a joke. 'It is not only dangerous to
talk like that, putting ideas into people's heads,' I said, 'but in our
family, we do not have kings. Besides, I am a loyal subject of our
sovereign Lord. It is a command of Islam that one should be
obedient to those set in authority over us.'

After that, (no doubt briefed by Mihrban Khan) scarcely suppressing a smile, the heads of groups bringing the gold-coin *Nazar*,
offerings, more and more often addressed me by our ancient title,
Badshah – King. 'This is the custom of Paghman,' said Mihrban,
'and you are correctly so styled: even at the Court of Kabul this
title is used for your family.'

At a gathering of black-turbaned Mullahs, when we had had a
great feast, with fireworks, one of the senior clerics said, 'In
Afghanistan, four things count: money, lineage, descent from the
Prophet (Peace upon him!) and the hearts of men, who will go into
battle or perform any other service.'

48

I said nothing. He went on, 'Someone who has the lineage will have the hearts, and can have the money which he will use wisely.'

'There are many such people in our country,' I told him, 'and I am sure that they all play their part honourably and well, under our benign and sagacious Monarch.'

It is a very old tradition among us, as in Europe in the past, that people are constantly testing whether a new power-base is coming into existence – or an old one being revived – for opposite reasons. They may wish to 'get in on the ground floor': or they may want to report trends to existing centres of power, in hope of reward.

It is not really possible for one to gauge Afghan thought and speech from a Western point of view. Something, for instance, which would be innocent in the West may be regarded as dangerous thinking among the Afghans: and nothing you can say will convince them that their interpretation of your words is not the right one.

This has been sufficiently well tested in international relations. Similarly, what Afghans say and do is just as frequently misinterpreted by Western people; as I have myself often enough observed. So, on the whole, it is not wise to pronounce on political matters: one or the other will assume that you have sinister motives...

Partly to avoid further talk of this nature, I went into the northerly mountains to visit the castles of our kinsmen there. Everywhere we saw sword-dancing, heard ancient tales, inspected warrior groups, and ate great meals.

Halim Jan, as my henchman, soon saw to it that from among the many who came to offer their services, a regular household was formed: pages, messengers, heralds, musicians were among them. When I protested, they only said, 'It will blacken our faces if the most noted and senior of our family were to appear, as you did, like a wandering dervish.'

This gave me an idea. Forsaking my robes and fur cap, I donned a simple white garment and took to the turban; with the consequence that, though treated with great respect, I was recognised as having no temporal ambitions.

Afghan techniques of communicating what is in the person's mind, however, continued to be used. A story-teller, in the middle of a tale, would suddenly go into a long description of some fictional figure: and to a purpose. One of them, for instance, said something like this: 'Many years ago there was a man. He traced his ancestry from the Koreish; in fact he was a Hashemite Amir. Because of his lineage and his accomplishments, when he returned to his own country after living abroad, people flocked to his banner. You see, he had supporters among the Pushtuns and the Tajiks, among the Hazaras and the Nuristanis, among the Farsi-wan of the West and the people of Badakhshan and Wakhan . . .'

He looked attentively at me, then, and I had to say, 'Yes, yes. But get on with the story'.

It is an Afghan custom that people do not plunge straight into any subject without preliminaries. These usually take the form of a fairly long recapitulation of what has led up to the matter under discussion. This part of the proceedings takes place whether or not the facts being recited are already known to the other party.

So I was treated to discursive descriptions of Afghan history, manners and customs, and even potential events.

I had been first, on my arrival in Kabul, to pay my respects to the King, to thank him for his favours and to recall the opportunities which I had had of serving his great father in the international field. Only after this had I made my way to my own ancestral Paghman.

The word of this had preceded me to Paghman, and everyone wanted to know the substance of my 'discussions' with his Majesty. Nothing of importance had, in fact, been said, so I confined myself to generalities, and spoke of my meeting with the King of England as the discursive background.

The chiefs of communities in the Koh-i-Daman [foothills] area, some of them great magnates with land, mines or large stock-raising establishments, were concerned about the lack of cohesion among the various ethnic groups. Turkestan, for instance, was quite recently the domain of a viceroy: the people were not sympathetic to the Afghans, as they called the Pushtu-speaking adminis-trators set over them. In other parts of the North, such as Qataghan and Badakhshan, the old ruling families, princes, were not forgotten, and there were separatist tendencies. Did I not think that the people of the flatter lands to the north, the Uzbeks, might not be induced to throw in their lot with their fellow Uzbeks in the Soviet Union?

No, I said; Godless communism had no attraction for Moslems.

Well, then: Herat was a Persian kind of place, and many of the people were Shiahs. So were the Hazaras, the Mongolian people of the central mountains. The Iranians had been spending millions, in gold, in trying to persuade these people to mount a separatist movement. Could that not happen? I thought it would not.

Again, what about the strip of land touching China to the North-East? The Wakhan Corridor might go to China: if the Soviets were to offer it to the Chinese in return for non-interference in Afghanistan. I knew nothing about this.

Now, said the leader of another deputation, from near Kunar, the people of Nuristan were one of the newest provinces of Afghanistan. They had been conquered by Abdur-Rahman within living memory. They had always been enemies of the Afghans, and were a completely different race. Would they be swallowed by Pakistan: or even India?

I denied the likelihood of this.

Finally, according to a greybeard chief from the southern borderland, there were the Pushtun people. The present regime in Kabul were Pushtuns. They were from Kandahar and Peshawar. The latter city was now in Pakistan. Much of tribal territory was now in Pakistan. What if the Yaghistani [Rebel-Land] people joined Pakistan, seduced by money, prosperity and opportunities?

What, said I, if the moon were made of cheese?

'Our Sufi leaders and teachers,' said the man, 'always know what is for the best ...'

I told him, 'What is for the best is a strong, enlightened and united Afghanistan, which we must all work to create and maintain.'

There was general approval of these words: or, at least, a general murmur of approval.

After a tour of the country – most of the areas mentioned – I decided to make my base in Kabul, rather than Paghman, even though the Paghman is a nicer place, with a perfect climate and my own kinsmen.

The pace of modernisation in Kabul was rapid; the face of the place was changing very fast. Among the intelligentsia, my books on the country, both historical and otherwise, were well known. Living simply in a pleasant enough house, I busied myself with a definitive work on our country, and left other considerations to look after themselves.

If there were enough opportunities for ambition and energy – never lacking among the Afghans – the old power élites would die out; of that I was sure. In the meantime, with relatively few outlets and ways in which to achieve their optimum self-realisation, people would continue to seek political, military or other forms of authority.

Afghanistan was emerging into cohesive national statehood with an abundance of talent and unrivalled material resources. It would become one of the great countries of the world, I was sure: just as it had been one of the axes of culture and imperial glory in former centuries.

What worried most people was the question whether the Afghans would be left in peace while they effected this transition. That was the external picture. The internal one was no less clear. Afghan institutions, whether commercial or otherwise in the private sector, would have to expand at a phenomenal rate if they were to absorb the talent and energy of the young people impatient to improve their lot.

Students flooded back from the West, and found, sometimes at least, that opportunities did not match their expectations. The administration sometimes had difficulty coping with the pace of change. The land was unbelievably rich, but a faster pace of development was needed, with only limited finance available. The old stresses in the country had not disappeared.

These stresses were due, in part, to the very fact that there had not been an unified national power structure for very long. The result had been that talent flocked towards smaller groupings: towards the Khans, the Mirs, the Sayeds and others who offered rewards for service. Ability and energy were not always at the disposal of the centralised State.

Again, one of the reasons for the localised power-groups was historical. They came from so many differing communities. The Pushtuns, the Mongols and Turks, the Tajiks and others, had come with successive waves of conquest and settled: each with their own leaders and administrations, their own traditions, often their own languages.

Afghanistan, though truncated, was more like an empire than a nation. There was a furious national spirit, but there were separatist influences as well; some of them, at least, supported by foreign interests.

This 'empire' was not entirely unlike England in Anglo-Saxon times, when a monarch might be King of the English: but there would be various other independent sovereigns, some with the kingly title. In some ways there was a resemblance to the German or Italian States before unification. In other ways, modern Afghanistan was somewhat like the England of King John: when local lords considered themselves sovereign in their territories.

As time went by, more and more people began to talk, almost openly, about the *musibat*, the calamity, which was sure to come. Listening to this talk, without venturing any opinion, it became clear to me that something would happen. This happening might be triggered by any one of a number of causes. It was a matter of which one would mature first.

And, I was sure, when that thing did come to pass, people would seize the most conspicuous feature to explain it, not realising that many of the factors in the story were connected. If certain things were stabilised, certain others would not be able to happen.

Afghanistan was an organism with many elements in it. How it went in the future would depend upon which feature combined with which others; and which of them, seen to be destructive, could be attenuated in their potential.

When I decided to leave Afghanistan because of family illness, there was trouble in the southern border area because of the Pashtun minority in Pakistan. The outcome of that could be very grave. At the same time, the Eastern and Western superpowers were competing here, (mostly with aid programmes) as in the case of other non-aligned States. If either were to drop out of the race, there could be a vacuum, which the other would fill.

If the Russians dropped out, Third World people might think that Soviet co-operation was impermanent. If the Anglo-Americans dropped out, the Russians would try to take over. If the Russians took over, they would besmirch their name in the developing countries and the Islamic world, unless they could devise some scheme to make the takeover seem legitimate, as they had tried to do with the old Khanates of Central Asia, which they had swallowed piecemeal.

Today, in late 1959, the likelihood is that the West will withdraw their co-operation from the Afghans, since the West tends to support the Pakistanis: who, it is said, are being needled by Kabul over the border question.

There are many steps which can still be taken to effect reconciliation between Pakistan, Afghanistan and the Pushtuns. If the powers of the West make the over-simplified decision to withdraw their interest from Afghanistan, we may see the greatest catastrophe since Genghiz Khan.

PART TWO

WANDERINGS . . .

A PERSIAN: WHAT AM I
TO SAY?

An Iranian student travels to Afghanistan,
explores its legends, and loses his heart to the
place . . .

What shall I speak of, in Afghanistan? Its snow-capped ranges,
like the Hindu Kush or the high mountains of Badakhshan, in
whose folds hide the fabled ruby mines? The walnuts of the East,
as large as a man's fist; or the grapes as big as a plum? The priceless
carpets of intricate design, or the humble rugs of the nomads,
woven with love and skill? The conquering armies of the great
war-leaders, who overturned proud India, not once but three
score times; the wise sages of Ghazna, of Balkh, of Herat, of
Turkestan?

You see, my friends, I have travelled throughout that happy
land, drunk from its crystal mountain streams, sung with its enchanting bards, watched the wrestling masters of far Khanabad,
slept in the *hujra*, the guest-room which even the smallest village
offers free of any charge. I have gorged myself from the great
platters of the divine palao, tasted the apricots, the melons, the
apples and the pomegranates which are without compeer. And I
have shared the hard-boiled egg and dry flat bread of the mountain
shepherd in his hut.

How shall anyone who has had such experiences ever hope to
bring them to you, hope to choose something which will sum up –
Afghanistan?

Before I went there, I had heard – as you, too, have heard – of its
fierce highlanders who practise the blood-feud; the harsh deserts
of Registan where our own brave Rustam of the epics fought and
won; heard of the giant killer-bears of the Hazarajat, of the men –

57

descended from Genghiz Khan's warriors – who fear no foe. Like you, I had heard of the valleys of danger, the robbers who levied tolls without mercy; the Afghan who would die as readily as he would live. Of course I was afraid.

But I was intrigued; for few Iranians cared to travel from the domes and minarets and the delights of Isfahan, from the bustle of Tehran, from which we see the reassuring, glistening peaks of Demavand, to that unknown land whose troops had marched against us under ruthless conquerors, even under Tamerlane.

I was right, and I was wrong; as all who rely only upon report must be. Afghanistan is, above all, a land of irreconcilable contrast. In summer, you bake in Kabul, but, just a short journey North, you revel in the bracing upland cool of Kohistan. You may die of thirst not far from Kandahar: but you will think that you have found the rivers and gardens of Paradise in fair Paghman, nestling amid the ranges below the Hindu Kush. You will be robbed by a bandit if he takes a dislike to you. But for every such man, you will find a hundred honourable, dignified, God-loving grandees: and grandees they are, these Afghans, whether they are rich or poor or in between.

Journeying from Holy Mashhad, in our own Iranian Khorasan, I could already taste the air, feel the spirit and hear the beauty of the tongue of the Afghan. Herat is our first important halting-place. Here, the great mosque and amazing buildings, treasures of the earth, from the time of Tamerlane, dominate the fair city of orchards and of trade. Here, too, is the tomb of Ansari, Prince of Thinkers, the great Sufi divine.

Southwards and to the East lies Kandahar, in the less Iranian-feeling territory of the warrior Pashtuns. Here Sayed Sabir Shah, the Kingmaker, crowned Afghanistan's first King: Ahmad of the Precious Pearl. Here, too, reposes in a stately building, beauteously surrounded by water and gardens, the Cloak of the Prophet and his banner, which are taken out only in time of peril or of war. If I were to tell you of the profusion of fruits, of nuts, of vegetables and the delights of the lamb dishes – you might not credit it, so I shall pass on.

From Kandahar I made my way northwards to Kabul, through country of startling beauty, forested or bare, valley or upland, through fields of ripening crops and past the ancient imperial city of Mahmud: Ghazni, Jewel of the East, with its great, frowning castle. There, in his tomb, I saw the giant war-mace and banner which the Emperor carried into battle. There I paid respects to the memory of his galaxy of knights and philosophers – not least the great Firdausi who wrote our national history for Mahmud himself, in the *Book of Kings*.

Kabul, whose history is lost in time, but which legend says was first built by Cain who slew Abel, lies between mountains which, with the Kabul River, bisect it. Here the people from all parts of the country – Tajiks, Pashtuns, Turkomans, Kafirs and the rest – meet and mingle, in commerce, in study, in administration and in their leisure.

The city is fair, well set out, adorned with graceful buildings. The great Arg, the Palace, is a splendid sight; and the Bala Hissar, the High Castle, on the hill dates from such very ancient times that no-one knows who built it.

I struck north from Kabul, across the Hindu Kush to the lands of the Turkestanis. Here I found Balkh, Mother of Cities, from which the great poet Rumi came. This city, now ruined, must have been one of the largest on earth. The remains of palaces and mosques, of colleges and minarets, of gardens and wells, of markets and parade-grounds, are so numerous that it is unlikely that anyone has ever counted them – or, probably, ever will. What treasures must lie buried in the ground there, whose owners, at the approach of the Mongols of Genghiz, hastened to bury their gold, their jewels, their wealth – and then died on the spears of the attacking hordes . . .

In Turkestan, too, I saw the Holy City of Mazar-i-Sharif [the Holy Shrine] with its immense mosque and university, which must, with its blue-glazed tiles, be a wonder of the world. Here the Faithful come to pay their respects to the memory of Hazrat Ali, the Prophet's son-in-law and successor.

The whole of the northern territory, which abuts the Oxus River, the Amu Darya, is filled with plains on which are bred the beautiful karakul lambs for their skins – black, white and even golden; where rugs of the matchless Turkish kind are made, and where are found some of the very finest horses ever to be seen. There are, too, fields of melons, the best in the East; of cotton and a dozen other crops. These Turks are first-class husbandmen and well-disciplined soldiers. Some of the best fighters in Afghanistan hail from Turkestan.

And what shall I say of Khanabad, the Town of the Khan, from which caravans ply between here and China, along the high passes of Wakhan to the North-East? Only that here I met wise Sufis, rich or poor without their making a distinction between them, and sipped of their wisdom. Here I found rare artefacts from the time when it had a vast Grecian temple complex, with plodding pilgrims from far and wide. Here I ate the best mulberries I have ever tasted, drank green tea flavoured with cardamoms and topped with pink *Qaimaq*: the cream, which only the northern people know how to make. I relaxed in their fair gardens and listened to the music of their many orchestras, accompanied by poetry and the legends of long ago, recited by long-bearded bards, sometimes singing to the music of the sitar, the dol and the oud.

My journey took six months. How did I live, a scribe and student from poor parents? I was passed from one hand to another, given letters from a Sufi to a postmaster, from a cleric to a merchant, from a farmer to a horse-breeder. And I did not spend a farthing.

There are many poor Afghans, but there is none who will not share his meal, his house or his room with you. I went to a mosque if I had no introduction, and told the Prayer-caller that I had arrived. He would inform the Mulla, who would announce it to the congregation after his sermon. Then I had a bed for the night: when, that is, I had survived the jostling of the people competing for the honour of taking in a guest. 'Travellers are the guests of God' is one of their sayings.

I saw Jabal as-Siraj, founded by Alexander the Great, and the Buddha statues carved from rock in the immense and beautiful valley of Bamiyan. The colossi are 50 or so metres high: an amazing sight; with thousands of caves dug out for the monks who lived here before the advent of Islam.

I lived in the glorious mountains of the Koh-i-Daman north of Kabul. Here, relations of Rumi and descendants of the great Abu Bakr welcomed me. I saw mighty wrestlers, sword-dancing, horse-racing and all the sports for which the Afghans are famous throughout the world. There, as elsewhere in Afghanistan, the people have high-walled castles with loopholes which are generally the strongholds of the Khans who rule the tribes or territories.

These, even more hospitable than most, gave me rich presents and accorded me honours more befitting a man of great importance. They sent me to the land of their kinsmen, the Lords of

Paghman, the most renowned Sufi teachers and warriors. Paghman, which is near Kabul to the North, has to be seen to be believed. It is a land of plenty: of abundant crops, of unexcelled fruit, of staunch patriots and scholars. In the most ancient times, it was the spiritual centre of the country under every successive faith.

Paghman is the place where may be seen the great castle of Jan-Fishan, the Hashimite Saiyid of a century ago, in a line of illustrious leaders who held the title of *Shah-Saz*, Kingmaker. Blessings upon them and their House!

O fair Afghanistan! O peerless people! You have given happiness to a poor traveller. A negligible person, cast in your land, was made to feel as someone of account. But it is, rather, the other way about. By honouring me you have shown your own greatness and my own lack of humility. For I am not – who is? – humble enough to appreciate your qualities to the full.

What shall I say about Afghanistan? Brother, any attempt is bound to fail; that is what I shall say. And to the Afghans?

> Once we were like you.
> Once more, God willing,
> We may be like you again.

A RUSSIAN: COLONEL
GRODEKOFF'S RIDE

I was given permission in Autumn 1878 to travel overland from Russian Turkestan, through Afghanistan to Herat. To save time, a courier was to be sent to Kabul, asking for the Amir Sher Ali Khan's leave to make the trip through his dominions to be sent for me inside Afghanistan. I proposed to pick up the pass at Mazar-i-Sharif, the administrative capital of the Governor-General of Afghan Turkestan. I set out from Tashkent, with an open letter signed and sealed by the Russian Governor-General himself. With me was my servant and interpreter, Mustafa Rahmmatulin, from Gulistan near Meshed in Iran. He spoke Persian, Turki and Russian. The second was Ibrahim Mulla Hasan, a Persian born in Samarkand. The third was a Kirghiz groom, Urazali Kojanbergenoff.

Our armament consisted of a cavalry Berdan with 100 cartridges and a Smith and Wesson revolver with twelve cartridges. Later, at Mazar-i-Sharif, we acquired two Afghan knives, and at Meshed, a double-barrelled gun.

For transport we had four riding horses, two pack horses and one reserve horse.

I did not have recourse to disguise, travelling in my uniform. Any masquerade I might have adopted would only have impeded my movements; my knowledge of Oriental languages was unsatisfactory and I was ignorant of the Moslem ceremonial observances.

I received an excellent reception from the Amir of Bokhara. It was to be different in Afghanistan.

The Afghan Ambassador at the Court of the Amir of Bokhara

had sent three men with me to accompany me to Mazar-i-Sharif, the capital of Afghan Turkestan. On October 17, I arrived at the bank of the Amu Darya [Oxus] River, which has to be crossed by boat.

Nobody was visible on the Afghan side. After about two hours, however, a body of horsemen were seen. They pitched two tents; I was informed that these were for my reception, and that the horsemen were my escort to Mazar-i-Sharif. I believed this.

I sent a man to shout to the Afghans, asking if I could cross in the morning. They agreed. The following morning I crossed to the Afghan side with my men and horses. I was met by the Chamberlain and the officers and cavalry escort, and invited to enter one of the tents.

I approached the nearest, and a guard flashed his sword over my head. I asked the Chamberlain why he had done this. He replied that that entry was prohibited because it contained prisoners. Entering the other tent, we sat down on a carpet.

After the customary congratulations on my safe arrival and enquiries respecting my health, the Chamberlain asked me who I was, where I was going to, and the object of my journey.

I handed him an open letter, which contained, in Russian, Persian and Turki, the following announcement:-

'The bearer of this, Colonel Grodekoff, accompanied by his servants, is proceeding to Russia, with my permission, *via* Afghanistan and Persia. On that account I beg all officials who may be found along the route traversed by Colonel Grodekoff to accord him assistance and protection. September 21 (OS) Tashkent. The Governor-General of Turkestan, commanding the troops in the Turkestan Military District, Adjutant-General Von Kaufmann lst.'

The Chamberlain said that I would have to wait on the river bank about two days, until I received the permission of the Luinaib, the Governor-General of Afghan Turkestan, to proceed to Mazar-i-Sharif.

I protested, saying, among other things, that Afghan subjects were allowed to move about freely in [Russian] Turkestan. He replied that in Russia there was one law and in Afghanistan another.

He would only keep me waiting a few hours, he said. He would give orders to kill a sheep and prepare dinner for me. I refused to have dinner except at the next station.

I allowed myself to speak in this sharp manner believing that any concession on my part would only be interpreted as a sign of weakness. Moreover, my high rank of Colonel and the friendly relations between Russia and King Sher Ali meant that the Chamberlain would not dare to endanger himself by using force against me.

He discussed the matter with himself. Getting up off the carpet he said, 'Good! Let us go. But you must understand that they won't let you proceed beyond Mazar-i-Sharif without the permission of the Amir.'

'That is no concern of yours,' I replied. 'At Mazar-i-Sharif I shall have dealings with the Governor-General and not with you.'

I talked with the Chamberlain as we passed along marshes and sands, with tamarisk trees. The sands extend for twenty-four miles, to the ruins of the city of Siyahgird, which extend for nine miles.

To my question 'Will the English Embassy be allowed to enter Kabul?' he replied, 'Not for the world.'

'But if the English declare war against you?' I said.

'We'll manage them,' he replied, 'just as we have managed them more than once before today.'

We halted at Siyahgird for the night, and were lodged in a house adjoining the Chamberlain's. One of the sentries exclaimed loudly as I passed on the way to chat to the officers, 'If I had my way, I would cut that Kafir [infidel] into pieces!'

These words were uttered in the hearing of two officers, but they took no notice of them, although they knew that even if I did not understand Persian, my interpreter did, and he would translate it for me.

The next morning Mustafa told me he had overheard the soldiers talking together. One suggested that they should go and kill me. I do not know whether this dialogue really took place.

We rose late to start the journey to Mazar, which is about fourteen miles away. I went into the courtyard and the Afghans gathered around as I did my toilette. When I was cleaning my teeth one Afghan asked Mustafa, 'What is that brush made of?'

'Pig's bristles,' replied Mustafa.

The Afghans fell back in horror, spitting violently to express their disgust. I immediately retreated to my room, inwardly resolving to perform my ablutions in future in my tent or chamber.

At the end of an hour's ride we saw four blue minarets of Mazar. One road led to the shrine; but, on approaching the town we left the track and turned off across fields. It was obvious that the Afghans did not wish me to pass by the sanctuary.

When we reached Mazar-i-Sharif the Chamberlain ordered the soldiers to draw their swords. We entered the town in the following order: in front rode three soldiers, then followed a bugler, playing the advance; afterwards came myself and the Chamberlain, side by side. And, finally, my interpreter, Mustafa and the escort.

'Why did you order the soldiers to draw their swords?' I demanded of the Chamberlain, as we rode along the streets.

'For your security,' he replied; 'our people are wild and unrestrained. One can't tell what might happen.'

'Am I right, I would ask you,' I said, 'in ascribing as the true reason your desire to expose me to the town as your trophy? Don't you wish the people to believe that I am your prisoner?'

'Think what you like,' replied the Chamberlain; 'but I must give you up whole and uninjured. I have to answer for every hair that falls from your head.'

At last we reached the house assigned for my residence. It was the one in which members of our Embassy had lived in July 1878, waiting for permission from King Sher Ali to proceed to Kabul.

We, myself, the Chamberlain, two officers and one Dafadar (an underofficer in charge of ten men) entered the lodgings. The Chamberlain announced that two rooms were wholly at my disposal. We sat down on the floor and tea was served by my attendants. I offered some to the Chamberlain and the officers, but they all refused it. When I had finished one cup my companions rose and said goodbye, expressing their warmest wishes respecting my welfare.

I thanked them for their attentions on the road and begged the Chamberlain to inform the Governor-General that I wished exceedingly to see him that day if possible.

In reply, he observed that I was a most restless man. However, he would give my message to the Luinaib, Khushdil Khan, although he doubted whether he would consent to receive me before tomorrow.

On being left alone I took a walk in the courtyard to examine my residence. The court was about 150 paces long and 75 broad. Along its whole length flowed a broad canal, with, on its bank, six magnificent Oriental plane trees. On the opposite side of the canal was an artificial elevation, covered with alabaster. Above this rose several peach and apricot trees.

The court was sprinkled with sand, and kept in excellent order. The whole of the buildings, in one of which was a bathhouse, were empty.

Having examined the courtyard and the buildings, I thought I would inspect the enclosure where we had left our horses. I was stopped at the wicket by an Afghan officer who courteously informed me that I could not pass. I looked, and saw the doorways of the other courtyards guarded by infantrymen with rifles. I understood the officer now. I was under the charge of sentinels.

The Secretary of the Governor-General arrived, with men who carried two leather-covered armchairs. He announced that he had been deputed by the Luinaib to pay heed to my desires. He would visit me daily to see that my commands were properly attended to. He then said that the Governor-General, knowing that Russians were not accustomed to the Oriental way of sitting, had sent me armchairs for my use.

He presented the individuals appointed to look after my comfort, seven in all. There was a footman, who served tea and looked after the water-pipe; a cook and his assistant; a scullion; a watchman; and an attendant to take charge of the bath.

'From this moment,' said the Secretary, as we sat side by side on the chairs, 'you are the guest of the Amir, Sher Ali.'

The questions he then put to me were like those which the Chamberlain had asked: who was I? And so on. I showed him my passport, which he put in his pocket, saying that he would show it to the Governor-General.

I asked him when I should be granted an interview. He said that he did not know, but was going now to ascertain the Governor-General's wishes.

He then ordered tea to be brought. This was given to him in a different teapot and cup from those presented to me. After this, Muhsin Khan always ordered tea to be brought when he paid me a visit. But his tea service was always kept separate from mine. The vessels used by him were clean.

The Afghans never used my tea service; and, following their example, my servants the Kirghiz and the Persian now also refused to make use of my utensils.

The dinner consisted of *pilaf* with aniseed and mutton, mutton soup and sauce, and mutton with cabbage. The whole of the repast was excellent. After dinner the attendants brought me sweet melons and watermelons; and finally tea.

After dinner my servants came to me in a body, to complain that their mutton was scanty and their *pilaf* cold. One after the other they found fault with the rascally Afghans, for giving straw to their horses instead of clover, and for forbidding them to go into town to worship God.

The Secretary came to tell me that the Governor-General had consented to receive me the next day, at eight o'clock in the morning. I informed him of the complaints raised by my attendants, and he called Ali Raza whom he roundly scolded: threatening, in the event of another complaint being made, to cut off his ears.

The Secretary appeared the next morning at half past seven. I put on my uniform and we set off for the palace of the Luinaib, as follows: in front, two soldiers, ten paces in advance; then myself, afterwards the Secretary, and finally ten infantrymen.

The road had been sprinkled with water and police were stationed to prevent anyone passing during the progress of our little procession.

My lodgings, I found, were some 600 paces from the Governor-General's residence. At the entrance to the palace grounds a sentry in red uniform presented arms to me as I passed. The escort received orders to leave and I entered the grounds.

At the cross-roads of the extensive palace grounds were stationed sentries. I counted fourteen during our advance. The Secretary made gestures to them that they should salute me.

Opposite an open gallery where the reception was to take place was drawn up a company of infantry, the palace guard. They wore red cloth tunics with yellow facings, white cotton breeches, shoes and a felt cap with a metal star in front of it. All the men were well developed and had a good appearance. Their faces reminded me greatly of the old soldiers of the Russian Guards. The officers wore dark blue single-breasted tunics, black breeches and a felt cap with a blue muslin cloth attached behind.

I passed along the front of the guard, but the men did not salute me.

I walked up some steps to a broad gallery on which were a number of leather armchairs, like the ones which had been sent me. The floor of the gallery was covered with carpets.

The Governor-General was attended by the Mirza Nizam, corresponding to our Chief of Staff. We shook hands.

Khushdil Khan was very young for such a responsible appointment as he had: the largest Governor-Generalship of Afghanistan, comprising all the Uzbek states lying between the Oxus, the mountains and Badakhshan.

He was scarcely thirty years old. In appearance he was remarkably handsome, tall, well-built, possessed fine features and had a short, dark beard. He wore a double-breasted tunic with bone buttons, blue breeches, patent leather boots, a felt cap and wore white cotton gloves. Around his neck was tied a yellow silk handkerchief.

Most of the Khanates of the north have been subjugated, or their rulers made pensioners of Kabul. Some Turkestan states are still independent. At my interview with the Governor-General I enquired about the health of the Amir Sher Ali; but, to my surprise, received no reciprocal enquiry respecting the health of the Sovereign Emperor (the Czar) and the Governor-General of Turkestan.

I expressed my desire to push on as quickly as possible. Khushdil Khan said that I could not go on to Herat without the permission of the Amir in Kabul.

'In the summer,' he replied, 'a messenger might go and return in six days. But now it is winter in the mountains, large snowfalls have taken place between here and Kabul and so your letter has, no doubt, been delayed.'

He said that I would have to wait at Mazar for perhaps fourteen days.

'Of course you will allow me to go freely about the town, and visit the vicinity, while waiting for a reply?'

'No, I cannot allow you to do that. I cannot permit you to leave your quarters.'

'Why?'

'Because I fear your safety may suffer. You do not know the people here. They are a wild lot . . . I must therefore take care that they do not murder you. I cannot explain to you how much you have disquieted me by your arrival. I cannot sleep at night, because you are the guest of the Amir, and anything unpleasant might happen to you. It is only just now that I have received intelligence of another Russian officer (Colonel Matvaeff) proceeding in the direction of Badakhshan.'

I told him that in that case I should return to the Bokharan side of the Oxus and await the Amir's permission. He said that he could not allow me to return, but must await the King's instructions.

I asked him why he would not let me return to the Bokharan side.

'Because no one asked you to come here.'

For several minutes I did not know what to say. I felt I was a prisoner, and my thoughts kept running on the best way to escape.

'It seems, then, that I am your prisoner!' I exclaimed at length. 'You say I am your guest and yet treat me like a captive. Your people in our country go where they like and do what they wish . . .'

'You have your law: we, ours,' calmly replied the Governor-General.

'I shall write to General Kaufmann. The letter, I presume, will be forwarded to its destination.'

'The letter will be forwarded.'

I then rose. The Luinaib begged me to sit down. 'Do you find my company dull?' he asked.

I took these words as a piece of mockery, and remarked, angrily, that it was disgraceful for him to mock me, in the position in which I found myself placed.

The Governor-General turned red with confusion, saying that I had not understood his words properly, and that he meant that it would be pleasanter for me to be with him and his people than to sit alone in my lodgings. He added that he would that very day send off an express to Kabul, and if I cared to write a letter to the Russian Envoy there, the man should take it with him.

Harmony being restored, he began to question me about my medals and decorations, and the campaigns in which I had served.

At my request the Luinaib gave orders for the guard to go through their exercises in front of the palace. The men performed them very well, and the bayonet drill was done excellently.

After this I was escorted back to my lodgings, where I wrote to General Razgonoff, [Charge d'Affaires at Kabul] begging him to obtain, as soon as possible, permission from the King to ride to Herat.

I sent the letter by Yar Mohammed to the Governor-General, and summoned my men, telling them what had taken place at the interview.

Ibrahim, the Persian groom, offered to take a letter to Samarkand. I told him that if it became necessary to flee from Mazar it would be better to escape all together. Before seeking safety in flight, it would be best to see whether Khushdil Khan would send my letter to General Kaufmann.

The next day the Secretary, Muhsin Khan, came early in the morning to ask if I would lend the Governor-General my uniform, which had pleased him so much that he wished to have one made like it.

The uniform was given to the Secretary and returned the next day with the Luinaib's thanks. When the English entered Kabul they found a Russian uniform. This caused an immense sensation and alarm throughout India and England. It is as likely as not that this uniform was the one which the Governor-General of Afghan Turkestan had had made for himself.

I prepared my report for General Kaufmann. The Secretary refused to take it. I should have to wait until the post arrived from Kabul, when my letter would be sent on to its destination.

This made me explode with anger. I could not but now recognise that I was a complete prisoner in the hands of the Afghans, and they did not want my condition known to the authorities at Samarkand. The guard over my residence had been increased by five men. A sentry had appeared at my door. Yar Mohammed had started to sleep outside my door.

And, independently of all this, the Secretary had decoyed into the Afghan service my interpreter Mustafa, offering him an increased salary and an honourable post at the court of the Amir Sher Ali.

I gave full vent to my anger. I denounced the Afghans as a lying, treacherous, fickle lot. I declared that I would find my way to the Court of Sher Ali and would then see if he approved of the measures taken against me by the Governor-General.

I told Mohammed Muhsin Khan to be off, saying that I did not wish to see his face any more. Without saying a word, the Afghan Secretary left my presence, maintaining a quiet demeanour.

I summoned my people, asking their opinion. They declared that they would follow me wherever I asked them to go. We decided to wait for an answer from Kabul until the end of the longest period required for the journey: fourteen days. If by then no answer arrived, we should consider ourselves prisoners. On the following night we would break through the guard and escape to Bokhara via the ferry of Karkeep. In the meantime we would try to get hold of firearms and, if that were impossible, some cold steel weapons.

We got the steel weapons – two Afghan knives – through some Uzbek smiths, who came to shoe the horses. The men refused, however, for any amount of money, to bring us firearms.

We began to study the topography of the locality. The stream flowing through my courtyard came through a wall eighteen feet high. The opening for the stream was large enough for a man to crawl through. In the next courtyard lived a family of a man, his wife and two children. A wall about six feet high was then the only barrier to the street.

The only dangerous obstacle was Yar Mohammed, sleeping outside my door.

On reaching the outside of the town, we meant to proceed north-west and hide the first day among the sandhills near Mazar. We would start again at nightfall, and if we found a Turkoman encampment we would steal some horses.

Early on the morning of the 25th of October (nine days before the proposed escape) Yar Mohammed, with a shining face, appeared and informed me that the night before a courier had arrived from Kabul. Today the post would be sent on to Bokhara. If I had a letter for General Kaufmann the courier would take it to Samarkand, whence it would be sent on by Russian officials to Tashkent.

I gave him the letter, without hope that it would be sent on. I imagined that the Afghans wished to deceive me.

On the 27th of October the Governor-General invited me to visit him in the evening. He had heard, he said, that I was dull at home, and would I like to hear some Afghan music?

The band played slow, ordinary and quick marches; during which, at my request, the infantry guard company marched in time with the music. This was all the musicians knew, my host informed me. The band had only recently been formed, and the bandsmen played by ear. What they did know they certainly played very well, and in harmony. I did not hear a false note during the whole of the performance.

After a conversation about the recent campaign with the Turks and assuring me that the Afghans would never receive a British Embassy at Kabul, the Governor-General asked me whether I needed anything. I kept my promise to my men by asking that they might be allowed to go to the mosque to pray.

'I cannot allow them to do this,' he replied.

'But why?' I urged, 'my men are dressed as Musulmans, and if I attract danger by wearing my Russian uniform, the same is not the case with them. They have nothing about them to show that they are Russians and belong to my suite.'

'Impossible,' answered the Luinaib emphatically.

The days dragged heavily. Not wanting to carry too much baggage, I had not brought a single book with me. I read, over and over again, the bits of old newspapers wrapped around my things. Every morning I observed the marks made in the gravel by the sentry marching up and down.

I asked that some public dancers whom I had heard of should be brought. In reply, I was told that they had all gone to a wedding at Tashqurghan. I then requested that performing serpents might be sent to amuse me; but was informed that at that period they were always in a dormant condition. In the end I had to content myself with the stories related in turns by my followers. The food supplied to me and my men was very good, and in this respect we had no complaint.

Ibrahim, bringing his usual report about the horses, said that they were exceedingly lively, as though they had a presentiment of a ride before long.

The next morning, when I put the usual question to Yar Mohammed: whether the courier had arrived from Kabul, he replied in the negative.

Towards noon, however, came Muhsin Khan. In a calm, matter-of-fact tone, he observed that the long-expected courier had just arrived from Kabul. I had permission from Sher Ali, and I should leave the town at four o'clock. He would return soon to tell me what arrangements the Governor-General had made for the journey.

He returned, saying that I was the guest of the King, and all expenses would be paid by him. A lieutenant, Mir Ali, would be appointed to take me as far as Herat. Thirty troopers would escort me as far as Maimana. Beyond Herat I would have 300 men, for protection against the Turkomans.

Finally, on account of my rank, an *Ajutan* [Lieutenant-Colonel] would be permanently attached to the convoy. I was strongly advised to listen to the wishes of the chief of the convoy.

I expressed a wish to see the Governor-General before leaving, but the Secretary said that this was impossible, as Khushdil Khan was ill. On my afterwards repeating the request, he replied that the Luinaib was too busy counting money to receive visitors.

Thanking Muhsin Khan for his attention towards me, I gave him, as a present, a large stock of quinine. Bidding him goodbye, I saw him no more. Remembering him now, I make my peace with him. He was a faithful servant to his sovereign, and fulfilled his orders with exactness.

Shortly before four o'clock the Adjutant appeared: Ahmad Ali, Adjutant of the Abbassi Regiment.

Mounting my horse I rode into the street, along which formed the escort, composed of two Jamadars, four Dafadars and forty troopers.

In the Afghan Army, the relations between the officers and men remind one of those in the Turkish Army. If an Afghan officer drinks tea, a number of soldiers are sure to sit around him. If he smokes a water-pipe, all the soldiers gather near him and await their turn. If a soldier smokes a pipe, the officer asks him to let him have a draw at it.

During the whole of my ride through Afghan Turkestan, I met only one officer who kept himself aloof from the soldiers. This exception was the Adjutant Hamid Khan, by birth a Sayed or descendant of the Prophet. It was not his military rank that kept him aloof, so much as his descent: for Ahmad Ali, the Adjutant who escorted me from Mazar, was on terms of the utmost familiarity with his men.

I did not observe that this mutual freedom of manner had any detrimental effect on the discipline of the troops. The men obeyed the commands of their officers with docility, and never displayed insubordination.

Our horses had stood so long in the stables at Mazar that they were exceedingly lively. It needed all our strength to control them.

We rode from Mazar south of Takhtapul and Sherabad. Further on, we halted for the night in the steppe, near the ruins of a Ribat [halting-place] alongside a stream.

During the halt I was struck with the attention and foresight which Muhsin Khan had shown in the preparations for the journey. Besides the Jamadar Mir Ali Khan, he had given me two cooks, a scullion and a groom. The escort had been supplied, for my comfort, two tents, a portable cooking stove, several rugs, mattresses, a fur cloak, a candlestick of prodigious weight and size, tallow candles, a toilette set, a metal teapot shaped like a pitcher, and a number of plates and dishes and teacups and saucers sufficient for the whole of my party. All these items were carried on three pack horses, with two extra ones in case of accident.

From the outset I experienced the beneficial effects of being the honourable guest of the Amir. Every individual attached to the convoy did his very utmost to anticipate my wants and execute my wishes.

The Afghans fed my horses entirely on clover. This spoilt my men to such a degree that they regularly demanded clover, even in barren places where no sum of money could possibly have secured a supply. This compelled Mir Ali Khan, in despair, to come to me to complain. My grooms no longer looked after my pack horses, letting the Afghans tend them, and rode alongside, now and again indulging in an encouraging cry.

The road was perfectly level, to the left were irrigation canals and cultivated fields. Seven and a half miles from Didadi the road was crossed by the River Balkh, known as the Band-i-Barbari. 'Band' means dam, and 'Barbari' is applied to the wild people living among the northern spurs of the Paropamisus and the Hindu Kush.

We stopped at a shrine, where a brother of the Imam Raza is buried. The soldiers prayed very attentively, some of them being excited to ecstasy. Around the sanctuary were flower beds and a garden. The guardians of the tomb were five monks, who wore their hair extremely long and were nearly naked.

A monk came up to me, saying that he was a native of Lahore, and asked if I was an Englishman. It transpired that he had never heard of the Russians. 'Have they as much money,' he asked, 'as the English?' Were they as powerful?

We passed through well-irrigated land, with water of excellent quality. At Salman the Uzbeks begged us to halt for the night. They brought out wheaten cakes, watermelons and sweet melons. When I said I could not stay, they brought me a sheep.

We passed through two mountain passes and a valley, whose floor was too poor for cultivation. We came upon a herd of white antelopes, but the troops were unable to kill any.

Across a mountain, along a valley, we came across excellent pasturage used by Turkomans for their sheep. Beyond, for more than two miles, it was sandy, growing saksoul and tamarisks. Along a perfectly level road we came to Salmazar.

This is a village of forty houses, everywhere there is water and it has the tomb of a saint. We rode in at sunset. I found awaiting, in a garden, a double tent and inside it tea, dinner and a soft couch. For these comforts I was indebted to the Governor of Shibarghan, General Kadir Khan, the commander of the Afghan military force which had taken Maimana four years before.

Here the cavalry of the Abbassi Regiment returned to Mazar. Now my escorts were men of the Husain Regiment. The new convoy, under the command of Major Ghulam Mohamed, awaited me and immediately relieved the former guard.

We journeyed to Maimana, en route for Herat. Attached to the squadron for the last leg of the journey was Colonel Hamid Khan. He was a Sayed by descent, and a man wholly unlike the Afghans in features. I could not help observing to him that he had not the appearance of an Afghan: upon which he proudly replied, 'I am an Arab'.

As a descendant of Mohammed, everybody paid him great honour, and even the officers kissed his fingers.

During the change of escort at Maimana, the soldiers appointed to accompany me to Herat had greatly interested themselves respecting my military position. My man Mustafa, to increase my (and his) importance, exaggerated it. By the time I reached Herat it was commonly believed that I was a commander of ten thousand men.

AN ENGLISH BOY: LOST
AMONG MAGICIANS

In the 1840s, the British Army, trying to maintain Shah Shuja as a puppet king in Kabul, was destroyed in the resultant uprising. A child of two was found among the slain, with his Muslim nurse, who claimed that he was the son of a British officer. Named by the Afghans Farangi Bacha – the Frankish Child – he was adopted by an Afghan nobleman, related to our own family, in Kunar.

He lived the life of an Afghan of good family, learned the arts of the pen, of war and of survival in an almost medieval land: and finally set off, in his early teens, to become a soldier of fortune, seeking his own people.

Farangi Bacha tried to reach India, but the way was barred by the Sikhs. He travelled with slave-traders over the high Pamirs, lived in Kafiristan, Land of Infidels, struck north for Turkestan, became the favourite of kings and a colonel in the army of the ruler of Herat.

Finally he reached Persia, where he was cruelly treated, but made contact with a Major Taylor, in the entourage of the British Ambassador en route for Herat. By now it was 1857; he was sent to India, renamed John Campbell by Lord Elphinstone, went to England with the famous Captain Raverty and was placed in the care of a Mr Fry in Brighton, where he learned English. Hubert Oswald Fry wrote the story of the English Child's adventures. The following is the story of his interlude with magicians, on his journey to find his fellow-countrymen. He has just emerged from a forest in Central Asia . . .

In the evening, to my great surprise, I came suddenly to a queer-looking little hut, outside which I saw some naked people

76

squatting on the ground, with their faces buried between their knees, which they were clasping with their arms.

There was something weird and ghastly in their appearance, so that I felt an instinctive dread, and laid hold of my sword.

At this the creatures lifted up their heads, and said, 'What are you about, young man?'

'Who are you?' I asked. 'And what do you do here?'

Without heeding my question, they merely said, 'Come down and rest.'

I dismounted, and approached these strange beings, wondering who they could be, for their nails were like great claws, and long hair was on their bodies. They had hidden their faces again, and they sat motionless, hugging their knees.

I half doubted their humanity, and again took hold of my sword, just to see if they knew what pain was: but though they could not possibly see me do this, their faces being turned away, they immediately lifted up their heads, and said, 'Young man, what are you about?'

'What sort of people are you?' I asked. 'You squat there, and won't speak.'

Then they said, 'Sit down and rest;' and again resumed their extraordinary position.

I sat down, and waited to see what they would do. I was very hungry, and hoped they would offer me food. When it got quite dark they rose, and I followed them into the house, where they all sat down again as before.

Presently a man brought in a candle. This fellow was a proper human being, the first I had seen for some time, and he had clothes on. Suddenly he fell down before one of the naked men, crying aloud, and kissing his feet. Then he arose, wiped his eyes, took the light, and motioned me to follow him.

I went after him, and he led me to a room in which was a carpet and various household things. The servant left me here, and went into a little garden near the house, and gathered some vegetables or herbs. In the middle of the room was a fire between four large stones. The servant put over this fire a round shallow iron pan. As soon as this was heated, he put the herbs in, having chopped them up, and he fried them with butter, pepper and salt; and he brought flour and water and mixed a cake, which he cooked in the pan with the herbs.

77

When all was done, he brought it and set it before me. I asked him to eat with me, but he refused to do so. I was too hungry to stop to ask what the food was made of, so I began eating, and never, in my life, tasted anything so good. When I had finished, I asked where I should keep my horse, and the man said he would take charge of him. I said I would go too, and look after him; so we went, and as I felt sure no-one would touch the animal, I left him tied up outside the house, and went indoors to rest. I lay down to sleep, and soon found myself alone in the room; the man had gone away with the light, without saying a word. I rose and tried to open the door, but, to my astonishment, it was locked; so I lay down and went to sleep. I dreamed that a beautiful girl was by my side. I looked at her face, she was very lovely, and I kissed her; but the moment I touched her lips, a sudden pang shot through my teeth, and I awoke. I felt very unhappy, and began to cry; the girl had vanished, but my teeth were still in great pain. The door was open, and there was a light in the room, and on looking round I saw the servant standing by my side, offering me something in a cup.

I said, 'Thank you, I do not want to drink.'

He replied, 'If you do not drink, your teeth will continue to pain you.' So I took the cup, and swallowed the contents, which tasted to me like some sort of wine.

In a little while all my limbs began to feel very heavy: my hair seemed like trees, my arms and legs like mountains, and I laughed excessively at nothing at all. Then the man brought some bullock's dung and burnt it in the fire, and while it was smouldering, he laid three eggs upon the embers; gradually the fire faded, and at last went out, leaving the blackest darkness in the room; thick, and it seemed to me almost palpable, was this darkness.

Presently I saw something moving in the ashes, and the three eggs appeared glowing with a red light, like rubies. One of them rose in the air, and gradually expanded, opening out into a large ardent ball, in which I saw many countries, and kingdoms, and peoples.

I gazed attentively on this wonderful picture for a time, and then it gradually faded. The egg remained for some moments, still burning in the air, and revolving rapidly, and at last fell down on the ashes. Again the same thick darkness filled the room, but soon the second egg rose from the fireplace as the first had done, and burned with the same red light. It expanded, and I heard a fearful noise as of loud thunder, and in the luminous ball I saw again many countries and people, but the latter were all dead. Suddenly they all arose, and began to dance; some of them thrust out their tongues, others looked very angry, and others were crying. I was all this time unable to stop laughing.

Then I saw scenes of war; all the people in the mysterious landscape began to fight, shooting and stabbing one another with great fury. This picture vanished slowly, and the egg, after turning for some time in the air, fell down and left me in the terrible darkness.

Once more the red light appeared in the ashes, and the third egg rose and expanded as the others had done. Another scene presented itself. I looked upon the most beautiful jungles and gardens, just such forests as I had passed through, and suddenly the landscape was enlivened with troops of beautiful girls dancing and singing together, and drinking wine: amongst them I spied the same damsel of whom I had dreamed.

She moved as if to speak to me, and I heard her companions ask her who I was.

'He is a poor stranger boy,' she answered, with an accent of pity.

I sprang forward to embrace her, but the servant man seized my arms and held me back. I struggled hard to get free, but he cried, 'Take care, if you go near her you will be mad till judgment-day, and never leave the jungles.'

'Who are these beings?' I asked.

He told me they were creatures summoned by the arts of the naked men; and if any one touches these beings he will be mad until the end of time. 'It is best,' said he, 'to turn away from their enchanting looks, or you will love the spirits and lose your reason.'

By this time the scene was beginning to fade; the beautiful maid slowly retired, bidding me adieu as she went. I felt some pain to see her go. The globe then began to revolve, and finally fell, leaving me in deep darkness.

Soon the door opened, and the servant came with the light, and asked me how my teeth were.

I told him they were well, quite well, and asked what time it was. He said, 'It is nine o'clock.'

I was astonished, and thought the night was very long indeed. I was already feeling hungry again. Then, in the wall behind me, suddenly a door opened, and a curtain came before it and bars of iron. The man sprang out through this door and left it open, and I saw that it was bright sunshine outside. The door shut to, and though I tried very much I could not find it again to open it.

Presently, the man sprang in again by the same mysterious door and began to cook me some food, just like that which he gave me before.

I asked him to eat with me, but he said, 'No; I cannot do that.'

I said, 'You must eat. How can you live without food? I won't begin my meat until you join me.'

I looked to see if my pistols were right, and as they were all near me, I took one up and cocked it, intending to fire at the roof of the house; but the man cried out, 'Oh! don't do that, or we shall all die directly.'

I said, 'I want to go out and to look after my horse.'

The servant then came and sat near me, and cried very much. I felt sorry for him.

He said to me, 'Those four men are very clever in mystical crafts; and when any wanderer comes here they never let him go away again. I, like you, missed my way, and fell into their hands.'

'But why do you not run away?' I asked.

'Ah!' he replied, 'would that I could! I have tried to do so, but a fearful burning came in my bones, and I was obliged to return. They will keep you here shut up for ten days. Then you will be like me and many others who are in this place.'

'How long will you be kept here?' I asked.

He said, 'Till judgment-day.'

I said, 'If I were to run away now, should I feel that burning pain?'

But he said, 'No; you have not been here long enough.'

'Do you know any wisdom,' I asked, 'by which one may break this charm?'

He answered, 'I do: the mystery lies in those eggs which you saw. All those beings who appeared in the landscapes are about the house all day, but invisible; and if you had fired your pistol just now we should all have perished at once, and have been burnt up. If you are a good shooter and can hit those three eggs, the spell will be broken, and we shall all be free: but if you should only hit one or two, the charm will remain, and you will be fearfully punished till judgment-day. If you succeed we will kill those four old men, and all be at liberty. But many have tried in vain.'

'But,' said I, 'how is it that among the many who you say inhabit this house none can do this thing?'

'Well,' replied the man, 'they did not all come like you with a horse and gun.'

I inquired how it was that the eggs were so wonderful, and the man tried to explain it to me, but I could not make any sense of what he said. He told me something about burning the fat of some animal, and other mystical things. I could not believe him, so I said, 'Give me an example of it, that I may understand more clearly.'

'Well,' he said, 'how does the silk come?'

'From the worm,' I answered.

'How?' said the man. 'All worms cannot make it.' So he left the subject, for I could make no sense out of his speech. He told me if I wished to shoot the eggs I must wait until night; and he related to me some tales of horrid witches who lived in that place, whose eyes were set perpendicularly in their heads, and whose breasts were so long that they used to put them over their shoulders. 'These vile creatures,' he said, 'delighted in killing people and tearing out the entrails of their victims.'

I asked how the witches came to belong to the old magicians, and the man told me that they knew some mystic words to repeat, which make the witches ready to obey their summons, and they had only to ring a bell to bring these terrible beings into their presence. The servant also told me that his masters knew of a kind of food which would cause wings to grow on those who ate it. Besides this, he spoke of many other things which the four naked men could do. At last, he rose up, and said, 'I must go now. I leave you to decide whether you will venture to shoot at the eggs.' Then he sprang out by the hidden doorway.

I felt very miserable and afraid, for the room was quite dark.

I was kept prisoner in here for a time that seemed, as near as I could reckon, about three days and two nights. Then I heard a bell ringing very loud, and many voices outside the door, as of children, and old men, and women. Mingled with these was the sound of drums, and cymbals, and the cries of many animals. Afterwards came the most beautiful singing. Then all my bones became very painful, and I resolved to shoot at the eggs at the first opportunity; for I thought, 'If I miss I will shoot myself, and be free by death from this wretched place.'

That day I heard many curious noises.

At night the man came again with the candle. The thought often crossed my mind that perhaps this fellow was as much of a rascal as his masters. However, I was still determined to follow his advice in one thing, and have a shot at the eggs.

I sat down and thought, 'I don't know what is the matter with me; whether I am dead or alive, or whether I dream or am intoxicated.' I tried to collect my senses and understand my condition, but I could not.

The servant began to prepare the same sort of food for me again as he had done before, and though I did not wish to eat, I was so hungry that I was obliged to take it; and soon after, I fell asleep. When I awoke, I was alone, and the room was quite dark. Suddenly I was startled by a loud noise as of cannons. This came three times, and then the place began to shake as if there was an earthquake, and I felt myself moving up and down like a ship. The servant came in with a candle, and I began to vomit. He held a cup like the one he had offered me before. I refused to drink, but he said, 'If you wish to go straight down through the earth, you will not drink.'

So I swallowed the draught, and the earthquake stopped. The house seemed to grow larger and larger, and I felt a pleasant sensation of great comfort, and was inclined to remain where I was, and forget all my former life. I noticed that my gun and pistols were gone. I began to laugh, and laughed extremely at everything – at anything – at nothing.

The man came, and said, 'Someone calls for you.'

I said, 'No-one calls for me, for I know no-one here.'

He replied, 'Oh, yes; someone has called for you.'

So I tried to follow him, but fell down three times. Then he took my hand, but still I could not get along; so he put me on his shoulders. All this time I was laughing very much. As I was carried along, my face was towards the ground, and I could not see where we were going. When the man set me down, I found I was no longer in a room, but in the fields, and it was broad day. I saw before me a beautiful tower, exactly like the one I lived in at Konnar, in my childhood.

I was astonished, and thought, 'I will go to my home, and will say, "I have been for change of air, and now I am come back."' So I began to walk, and came to a room where were all my old friends, but no-one would speak to me. They looked very angry, and I was afraid they might kill me. There was one servant-girl to whom I used often to speak, for we both felt that we were obliged to remain at Konnar against our will; and to her I now went, and spoke, but she only laughed.

I said, 'You are my friend, speak to me. I want to leave these people, who wish to kill me.'

Then she gave me a book, and pointed to it, and signed to me to flee. So I understood that the book was to read in, if I felt pain or unhappy. I took the little volume, and went away until I came to a village. I began to read, and many people came to hear, and laughed at the words of the book.

Then came one who looked like a stranger, and he said, 'Come with me, I will take you to my country, that my people may hear that book.'

'I will go with you,' I replied, and I rose to follow him; but all the people were angry, and looked fiercely at the stranger. He, however, held me by the wrist.

Then I saw a number of soldiers mounted on white horses; they were dressed in red, and looked very terrible. At their approach the people all ran into their houses.

Just at this moment the servant of the naked men came behind me, and touched my shoulder, saying, 'How are you? How do you get on?'

'I am very well,' I replied, 'and very happy.'

He then gave me a round white thing like a marble, telling me to eat it. I refused to obey, but he told me if I did not take and eat it, the soldiers would shoot me.

'No,' said I, 'they won't do that.'

But as I spoke, they all cocked their guns and gave me a most menacing look.

'Oh,' I cried, 'I will eat the ball.' So the servant gave it to me; and when I had eaten it he gave me another, which I ate too; and he gave me something to smell. When I smelt this thing, the earth-quake came on again, and I began to vomit, and fell down.

The man brought the cup again, and offered it to me with an insinuating smile, saying, 'Drink,' just as he had done before. I would not take it, but he said if I did not I should go down into the earth. So I drank, and got happy again. The man then brought a cup, into which he poured something like vinegar. Then he took out a chain like a watch-chain, on each end of which was a triangular piece of gold. He put these triangles in the liquor, and then applied one to each of my ears. Immediately I began to burn all over, and I cried out; 'Oh! don't do that, I shall die.'

'There is no fear,' said the man; but he took the pieces of gold out of my ears, and suddenly vanished.

I stood thinking for a moment; then, on looking round, I perceived the stranger standing near me. He took my wrist again, and said, 'Read your books.'

I did so, and we laughed very much.

The stranger said, 'Come, I will take you now to my country.'

I tried to follow him, but I fell down three times; so he took me on his back and walked into the desert. We came to a bank, and I saw many of those soldiers who had appeared so terrible to me before; now they were all ranged in a line and looked very fine.

They spoke to my bearer and said, 'Have you brought him?'

And he answered, rather knowingly, 'All right; this is he.'

I then mounted on horseback, and followed the soldiers, who marched on in front.

I felt rather afraid, and asked where we were going; and my conductor replied, 'We are going to a place where you will see many officers of Government, and with them is a prince who takes taxes from this country. We are not far from the camp now.'

Soon we came to another bank, and my guide said:

'Look, there are our encampments;' and I saw many snow-white tents, all striped with gold, and very symmetrically arranged. I was glad, for I was tired of riding, and felt very much heated and in a great perspiration.

I said, 'I am very thirsty and hot;' but my companion said, 'Never mind, you will soon be where it is cool, and you will be able to get plenty of water; but you must mind and be very polite.'

When we came quite near the camp, I saw a row of soldiers standing. They were three times as tall as ordinary men, and were very powerful-looking and beautiful young men; they had ornaments of gold on their foreheads and golden medals on their breasts and knees; they all held their guns straight up, and these were very clean and bright.

As we approached I heard some music and singing, and the tall soldiers faced about and marched, we following behind. I began to laugh, for I could not think where I was, or whether I was asleep or awake. When we arrived at the tent of my conductor I came down from my horse, and I saw an officer and heard him read the list of the soldiers' names. I sat down, and they told me to read from my book. I said, 'Tell me where I am, and what has happened to me;' but they answered, 'Tomorrow morning, early, we shall start on our march to our own country; and when we arrive there you will be where you want to go.'

It soon became night, and I got very hungry. Suddenly the servant came with a candle and touched me, saying, 'How do you get on?'

I replied, 'I am very well, thank you.'

Then he brought me a large 'kuncha', or dish of pilaw, which is rice and meat. It looked as if some one had been eating some from the dish; so I said, 'Who has been having their dinner from this?' for I did not like to take it after it had been handled.

The man said, 'I am servant to this prince, and it is the custom here for his highness to take his food first, and what he leaves is given to the others.'

So, as every one else had begun to eat, I joined them, and made a good meal. When I had done, I seemed to be in a house; there was a light in the room, and several persons were with me. I read to them, and they were much pleased with the book. They asked the man who had me under his care not to take me away to his country, but to leave me with them. But he said, 'I am afraid God will be angry with me if I do not take the lad; he must come with me.'

In the morning I heard many bugles sounding and beautiful martial music, and the man told me they were about to march. I saw all the tents taken down, rolled up, and packed on camels; then all the people became silent and looked unhappy. The animals all stood loaded, ready to start, and the soldiers were in marching order; but an ominous stillness was in the camp. I asked the man who had charge of me what was the matter; but he only motioned to me to be quiet. I was very angry and struck him a blow in the side. He took it quite quietly, but my fingers immediately gave me great pain, so that I cried out with the torture.

Then the servant of the naked men came with the cup, which he offered to me with the same bland smile as before, saying, 'Drink'.

Again I refused; but he said, 'Very well; your fingers will continue to hurt you.' So I drank the dose, and the pain passed.

I began to cry very much, and someone asked me what I wept for.

I said, 'These people all seem so unhappy: why is it?'

They said, 'Because we intend to go away; but we wait for two men-servants, who are away; we are looking for them. We have heard the noise of the bugle. It is time to go, but they are not found. When the bugle sounds all must be ready; but these men are not found. We still wait.'

The men who were lost were *furrash* (servants of the king). Presently the bugle sounded, to let us know that they were found. They were taken before the prince, who was in the open air, seated on a handsome throne. The people and soldiers stood round, with their hands crossed on their breasts, and I was amongst them. The prince was very fair, and was a fine, strong young man, with long moustaches. All the people were from the same country and dressed alike.

The prince asked his servants where they had been.

They said, 'We have been to a village, buying eggs and other food for the journey.'

The prince said, 'I gave orders, two days ago, that you should be all ready this morning at the call of the bugle, and now we have been kept waiting for you for some time.' Then he ordered that their beards should be plucked out. They prayed for mercy that their honour might not be taken from them before all the people. But the prince ordered them to be carried out of his presence. So the soldiers dragged them away, still crying for mercy, and the sentence was carried out; and the prince ordered that they should walk, and not ride, during their march home.

Then I heard a noise louder than the loudest thunder, and my heart failed me for fear. I saw an immense train of cannons drawn by horses. Next to these came the foot soldiers; after them the horsemen; and last of all were the camels and the baggage of the army. Again I heard the noise of firing many cannons, and afterwards was played most beautiful music, when suddenly the whole grand pageant vanished, and I was alone in the wilderness. I was much frightened, and wandered about to try and find the soldiers; but all was solitude and silence, and I was soon tired of my fruitless efforts.

I stood still under a tree to think what I should do, and a man touched me on the shoulder. I looked round and saw that it was the servant of the magicians, and I was not standing, but lying down in the same little room which was my prison, and it was dark, for the servant went out with his candle. At first I was very unhappy. I thought I could go with the soldiers and escape from my tormentors, and I lay some time wondering at the manner in which they had disappeared; then I felt a pain like diarrhoea.

When I returned to the little room where I had been so long shut up, I cried very much.

'What have I done?' said I. 'I am sure I have wished no-one any harm, and why am I here imprisoned?'

The servant answered, 'It is your own fault, why don't you shoot at the eggs?'

I said, 'If I do not hit them, I shall be worse off than I am now; and I cannot believe your words, I am afraid you are also deceiving me.'

Then the servant went out, and soon came back with another man, who walked monotonously up and down the room, but would not speak a word. I asked the servant why the man was so silent, and he replied,

'Oh! He speaks and laughs with those who know him. You only do exactly what I say, and he will talk to you and joke as much as any one, for he is a very funny fellow.'

Then the servant went out and fetched a basin of hot water, which he handed to me, telling me to empty it over the silent man's head.

'No,' said I; 'it will scald him and make him angry.'

'Only take my advice,' said the servant, 'and you will see if I am a deceiver.'

So I poured the water on the man's head, and he fell all to pieces. I saw that it was only a clever piece of mechanism covered with paper, underneath which it was made of wood, and the joints were of something like india-rubber. I was much amused at this unexpected dissolution of the silent man, and the servant said, 'Now, will you have confidence in me, and shoot at those eggs?'

I promised to do so at the first opportunity, and I asked who the four old men were.

He replied, 'They are called "Munnajum" or "Sahar". They always live in the wilderness, and understand astrology and various wonderful secret arts.'

That night I found my gun and pistols and sword all replaced near my bed. I loaded the gun carefully, and waited anxiously for the appearance of the eggs.

'Now bring them,' I said, 'I am ready – live or die.'

'Don't be in a hurry,' said the servant, 'you need not be so sure of getting free.'

I was very impatient. At last the man brought the cows' dung to burn, and I made ready to have a fair shot. I sat down with my gun cocked, and resting on my knee. Directly I saw the little ruddy-glowing spot in the ashes, I took a steady aim at it and fired. The room was instantly filled with smoke, and I smelt a disagreeable smell. The second egg arose. I was ready for it, and fired again, with the same result. Then the third egg appeared, and I fired at it.

Directly after this last shot, I looked round the room. There was a loaf of bread near me, and the door was open. I walked out into the open air, but there was no-one to be seen. I could find no trace of the magicians. I saw my horse still tied where I had left him. The poor animal was very thin, and was grubbing in the ground for some roots to eat. He had cleared all the grass from the space within his reach.

I went back into the hut, but could find no-one there, which seemed to me very curious. There was only one little room.

My senses seemed gradually returning. I comprehended this one fact, I was alone with my horse in the wilderness. Oh, what a sense of relief, of release, I felt! I could not believe I was really at last free; so I jumped on Zangi's back just to try round in every direction, and see if no horrid spell imprisoned me still. I made a few turns, and every moment was more assured of the reality of my deliverance. I returned once more to the scene of my misery; but I soon remounted my horse, resolving at once to fly from the fright-ful place. I put my hand in my bosom, and then discovered my crowning misfortune – my rings and my money were all gone! This treasure, which had cost me so much trouble in gathering together, I could not bear to part with without some effort to regain it. Five hundred pounds was no trifle to lose. I led my horse into the little room of the hut, and slept there that night.

In the morning I tried to discover some of the other chambers which I had seen in my visions, or whatever those strange sights may be explained to have been by wiser heads than mine.

I was soon convinced that there was no other room in the place, except the one where I was, and my money I could not find any traces of.

'Well,' said I, at last, 'what is gone is gone;' and taking the loaf which the villains had had the heart to leave for me, I mounted my horse and rode away into the desert.

This account by the Farangi Bacha may seem the wildest nonsense to the reader; perhaps it is. Two things make it interesting. First, his account of his upbringing in Afghanistan rings true, and is correct in all details which can be checked, including much circumstantial fact. Second, very similar tales of encounters with magicians in Afghanistan have been reported again and again. Although Afghans and others seldom believe them, the inexplicable feature is that these stories are always very similar. Yet they are not similar enough to be derived one from the other. The framework of the tale is usually just what one would expect if the events had really happened, though there are often astonishingly detailed accounts of the minutest details of the 'magicians'' doings...

AN IRISHMAN . . . A
MYSTERIOUS JOURNEY

I rendezvoused with my old friend Mirza and three young 'Seekers' at a prearranged spot, well away from the Pakistan-Afghan borderline. Mirza had given me a complete *Mullah's* outfit to put on: baggy trousers, a very long shirt, the tail extending beyond the knees, worn outside the trousers; an undershirt, scarf, diminutive turban, cummerbund, and *chapli* sandals. All of these were well-used, and the white shirt looked as if it had once been dipped, for the merest fraction of a second, in pale blue dye. A huge blanket completed the rigout, being placed on the shoulders and then one end whipped over the left shoulder. Thus prepared, with a small amber rosary in my hand, I rehearsed various expressions (mostly scowling) before my bedroom mirror in Karachi.

I was obviously not supposed to be a completely out-of-this-world Moslem ecclesiastic, in that although I had a fairly good beard I also wore a wristwatch and a pair of socks. In my sack, which was carried over one shoulder, I had a selection of necessary items. A cheap compass was for determining the direction of Mecca for prayers; a small amulet tied in a piece of red cloth was a relic of some pilgrimage to a shrine. A well-used copy of the Koran, lithographed in India, was carefully folded inside a large bandana handkerchief. There were also supplied a bag of pine-kernel nuts in a coarse cotton bag, a pair of scissors, a toothstick and a few other odds and ends.

I had no writing materials, because I was almost incommunicado. This was a *mullah* who was on the verge of Sufihood. In order to discover, by established religious practice, whether I was to enter the company of the dervishes as a member, I had taken a

90

vow. This story was to protect me against too much conversation. The vow that I had taken was to repeat certain formulae an illimitable number of times, in accordance with the instructions given in a very famous book of magico-religious practices, the *Jawahiri Khamsa* [Five Jewels] which may have been heterodox but was nevertheless held in sneaking regard by very many people.

Mirza's idea to make me a sort of expert on this book was a good one from the point of view of helping one's free progress into and through the Afghan-Pakistan borderland and beyond. Many versions of the book exist, almost all of them being in Persian, but some are in Urdu. They are invariably lithographed, not very well, on rather indifferent paper. The entire work is ultimately derived from the medieval Arab works of the Moroccan Al-Buni and the Arab Ibn al-Hajj; some people spend years collating their own copies, in the hope that the mixture of magical processes and religious formulae will yield the results which the Moorish magicians are positively known (through stories at any rate) to have achieved.

The book's reputation rubs off onto people who are students of it. Not everyone wants the name of being a dabbler in the occult, and hence the experts on the Five Jewels are not often met with or will not admit to their secret vice in public. Mirza remembered a man who gained and sustained an enormous reputation for years through his reputed mastership of the Jewels. So I was appointed to the rank of follower of this marvellous treasure.

Not everyone in India, Pakistan, the Pathan land and Afghanistan knew or understood Sufis. The natives of these countries might often be against one another. But who had not heard of the marvellous Book of the Five Jewels? Whoever had not would soon have his ignorance repaired by information supplied by some at least in any average crowd.

So my role boiled down in the main to acting as though I was a semi-magician in a semi-trance, accompanying (or being accompanied by) companions with similar and Sufi interests. The only phrase I really needed to know, in answer to a question was *'Qasam Khurdum'* [I have taken a vow]. In tricky situations it would be up to the rest of the party to get me out. My knowledge of Persian was good enough to understand most of the things that were being said, and that should help in planning my reactions.

Mirza told me, as soon as I arrived at the caravanserai and

91

introduced me to his friends, that we were not going by the ordinary routes. We would merely stray across the border by night, and take our chance: a very good chance indeed, of being able merely to walk across without meeting anyone at all. I doubted whether any of our party had ever seen a passport, and everyone seemed equally anxious to avoid official contacts. The three Seekers were very completely under Mirza's orders, and not for one moment did I gain the impression that they thought me to be anyone unusual in their midst.

We were just over ten miles from the border, at a spot chosen to coincide with other routes further along the road. This meant that, as far as anyone knew, we had taken the right-hand fork instead of going straight ahead, and had headed back into Pakistan after visiting a small shrine situated conveniently by the wayside. This would be the explanation of our movements if by any chance anyone asked about us. I thought at first that it was intended to deceive the owner of the teahouse in the caravanserai, but was soon undeceived. As we sat reclining in a bare room, our backs against the wall, padded only by our bundles and waiting for evening, Mirza called the proprietor in to have tea with us.

'How much money have you, Mullah Saheb?' I stopped muttering my *wazifa* and scowled. I was not sure what he meant, but took out the twenty-five hundred rupees which I had brought with me, and handed the bundle to him. He gave it to the other man, to my dismay, for this was quite a large sum of money. 'We collect it on the Other Side,' he told me. The proprietor placed his hand on his heart. No receipt, no counting of money. This was the way to do one's banking – if it worked.

No details, as they say in some circles, are available of the precise course which we took after that, until we found ourselves on the Other Side, heading for the first of the settlements of the Sufis which were named after a Central Asian river. But more of them in a moment. There was one incident. An army lorry with desert tyres crunched up to us as soon as we had left the road that night, to strike across a fairly bare patch of hard sand in an area where we should not have been. Before the headlamps had properly picked us up, Mirza and his companions were circling round in a frenzied dance, hooting and cheering like anyone's idea of a dervish. Taken by surprise, I froze in their midst. The Pakistani driver pulled up beside us, then drove off, shouting: *pagal log* – madmen.

Amu Daria is, of course, the name of the immense river which forms four hundred miles of the northern frontier of Afghanistan: beyond it lies the Soviet Union and the lost territories of Turkestan, once the site of ancient Sufi strongholds. Russian penetration into the Central Asian khanates is no new thing, and faced with the encroachment of the 'West' in the form of Czarist advance, and the need to develop Sufi teachings further in order to coincide in some way with modern technology – the Sufis started to move into the hinterland of Afghanistan during the early part of this century. Some of the oldest foundations were already established in the Hindu Kush area. Those who migrated into Afghanistan began to use the name of Amu Daria, run into one word, as the designation of their teaching. Thus they perpetuated the crossing of the river and the tradition of their trans-Oxus origins in their name.

The River Amu (Amu Daria in Persian) appears on most maps as the Oxus. It will be convenient to refer to the emigre Sufi groups as *Amudaria* ones, because such a phrase as 'the Oxus Sufis' does not sound anything like as felicitous. They are also known as the *Samoun* (a code-word for 'bee', a reference to one of their exercises).

Although the Sufis do not like to engage in historical or geographical discussions of their cult, there seems little doubt that the Amudaria elements concentrate upon practices and ideas which differ from those found elsewhere, with the exception of the Old Afghan Orders. In some ways their rituals and methods are quite like those of other Sufi Orders, but more organised. As an example the habit of compiling multiple words taken from the syllables of other words is a fine art with them. The concentration upon the belief that the Sufi way is the only suitable one for propagation throughout the world is another characteristic. Then there is the teaching that it is from here that the Sufi message must be diffused, and that it will have to be naturalised in each community.

I spent one week in each of four Amudaria communities. The organisation of the monastery, according to this group, is ultimately a spiritual entity: the building or the location is secondary. Thus two of the 'monasteries' actually had no premises of their own. Meetings were held in the open, or in houses. In one village when the gun which marks noon was fired, virtually the whole population started repeating formulae under their breath. This was a 'meeting' of the Amudarists: no monastery, not even a physical meeting.

This principle is carried even further in Afghanistan. Although monasteries exist and *halka*, group, meetings are held, and discipleship as I had seen it elsewhere was carried on, the whole community is considered to be in a special kind of *rapport*. This means that the constant spiritual communication between the members is thought to continue, especially at designated times.

The four leaders of the trans-Oxus communities, Sheikh Jalal, Ahmad Baba, Ishan Ali and Pir Turki, all accepted the authority of the Naqshbandi chief of the Hindu Kush Sufis. This is the representative of the Studious King, who is the overall leader, and who may be 'found in disguise, in almost any country of the world'.

Ahmad Baba showed me the method of sewing the patchwork cloak which some Sufis wear, and which was until quite recently the uniform of those who were going through a period of retreat from the world. It is not known when this custom started, but I was reminded of the 'coat of many colours' and wondered whether the robe originated in Syria, where it is also to be seen. Ahmad was about seventy years of age, but might have been older. He was in astonishing health for a man who could clearly remember pre-Revolution Russia, and attributed this to his carrying out the longevity exercises which are a part of Sufi training. 'Nobody,' he said, 'would get feeble if he carried them out regularly. Certainly they would live, as the Sheikhs of our Order do, up to a hundred, or twice as many, years of age.'

In addition to most of the usual Sufi exercises, the Baba's community practised healing, and Sufis came from various places to receive this part of their 'enlightenment'. 'Of course,' said the sage, 'we can also send it out to those who are ready to receive it. You see, we only have a portion. It is like having a *karez* (underground water channel) connected to the source. But we cannot transmit to those who are not ready. If they are only slightly developed in the requisite ways, then they must come here.'

I was interested to know what these Sufis felt about the possibility of making their cult known in the West. Ahmad was not to be drawn. 'That is a matter for the Studious King.'

Ishan Ali was a Turk, and half the age of the Baba. His ministry extended through the wild north-east of Afghanistan, right up to the Chinese border in the thin tongue of land which sits astride the Pamir mountains. He was forthright, greatly loved, and yet difficult to approach. He received me in a Western-type suit, with a small karakul lambskin hat on his shaven head, something like a kalpak cap, but more stylish. 'You must not force the pace,' he told me so many times. 'You are anxious to learn a great deal of things about us. That is good enough, and there is sufficient reason to tell you. But you must remember that if you allow yourself to be blinded by curiosity – by the collecting of facts and snippets of information – you may write a good book, but you will slow down your spiritual progress.'

I saw him apply this teaching to a party of young men, not long out of the Army, who had come on a pilgrimage to meet him. 'Remember what I say,' he admonished them, 'for you will not be told again, but sent home. What you have learned in the Army will be of inestimable value to you, although you are still cursing the day the *pishk* (conscription) caught you, and blessing the day you were discharged. Both are wrong: but I cannot expect you to understand this yet. Pay attention to everything that you are told, and do not take an interest in things that you are not told or shown. At your stage your so-called human abilities can often be a curse to you. Plenty of time for changing back when you get to the outside world again.'

Pir Turki, who in spite of his name was not a Turk but of Indian extraction, ran the strangest school of all. Everything was based upon gymnastics. Pits had been dug in the circle which had been marked out around his miniature castle. In these depressions, some twelve feet deep, disciples had to wield heavy clubs, often to music, sometimes accompanied by the voice of the teacher. They were reputed to develop occult powers; and I heard many tales about how they could make things float on water, see at a vast distance, and so on.

It was said by local villagers that one of Pir Turki's teachers had, by the power of his glance, held up an army for three days in the passes of the Khyber. Be that as it may, Pir Turki the ascetic was a martinet. Shunning over-eating or loose talk like the plague, he provided plenty of food for his disciples, though nobody knew where the money for it came from. He did not make collections. There must have been a source of his income, of course, but it was never visible. One of the first things that he said to me was: 'If you revere any man, forget him; for all that matters is the Work.'

I have never seen anyone who impressed me so much. When I told him this, he took hold of a beautiful lamp which stood on his desk-table and smashed it. 'I have destroyed a thing of beauty. Do you respect me less now? I hope so.'

Then he called a disciple, accused him of theft, and sent him to wash out the assembly-room. 'Must he suffer so that I can see that you have defects?' I asked him.

'I hope that you think that I have been unjust in making him suffer,' was the answer.

Unfortunately for the lesson's permanency in my case, I learned later that the disciple who had been unjustly treated had committed some grave breach of regulations and merited punishment in any case. 'You don't understand,' said a disciple, when I mentioned this; 'the lesson has sunk in where it counts. That is all that counts.'

Yet punishment was something which seemed to happen very rarely among the Sufis. I would not say that they were immune to it, but as they had been taught that personal dignity was sometimes a grave disadvantage, they were not able to suffer much through being made fun of in front of each other. Manual labour on the three farms which the community owned gave many opportunities for exercises in self-development. All the income from the farms was collected by an administrator and sent to the women's welfare association, so the Sufis did not benefit directly. And yet the Sheikh, as I have said, did not seem short of cash.

Sheikh Jalal was a feudal-type chief, a man of towering personality within a slight and delicate frame. He lived in considerable style from the income of vast inherited flocks of some of the best sheep in the country. He smoked a little, but did not seem to eat much. He always wore similar clothes, the robes and turban which old-fashioned judges assumed in Afghanistan. He was about sixty-five years old. Although surrounded by servants and a great deal of luxury, he personally partook of it little. When, for instance, we went out shooting and felled several hundred wild duck and grey geese, none was served at his table. The birds went as gifts to the surrounding villages.

Jalal, it was rumoured, could neither read nor write. This idea must have gained currency because he was never seen with a book or a pen. His teaching was done in the normal Sufi way: through short addresses, exercises, meditations. Going with him several times on long walks, which he embarked upon without any prior notice whatever, I realised that he spent a great deal of his time in silent communion and commemoration (called *Zikr*) and that this had become almost second nature to him. He had several sons, all of them, I believe, in the Army.

He often showed small signs of a sense of perception which is repeatedly mentioned in Sufi writings as a sign of 'saintship', but which would not have been noted except by an attentive disciple or someone else very close to him. One day, for instance, he picked up a cooking-pot and took it on a walk on which I accompanied him. Stopping at a poor small house he saluted the occupant and handed in the pot. The old woman was amazed. She said that she had just broken the earthen dish in which she cooked. Again, he handed me a box of matches when I had come out without any, in spite of the fact that I could not be sure that he realised that I had left them at home. It should be mentioned that he could not have observed that I brought none with me, for I had met him in his garden, on the way from my quarters to his.

I mentioned these small indications to him. But he would not discuss them, merely saying: 'Would you make me a saint, and rob me of the power of *becoming*?'

There were many of these instances. Some were observed by me, others reported by disciples. It was interesting to note that among the disciples stories were never exaggerated; they would often hinge upon the smallest event. This indicated to me that many of the wilder tales current among the countryfolk and others outside Sufism were elaborations of actual happenings.

It was Sheikh Jalal that I questioned on this subject.

'These are normal, not abnormal, developments,' he said. 'They are of no value in themselves, partly proved by the fact that the experiences seldom have practical value. For every happening of this kind that is a warning or can be turned to practical use, there are a hundred which are not of any use. Why is this? Materialists would say that it merely proves that the power is fitful, partial, something of little account. What they do not know is that these are signs. They are encouragements, they show that the recipient has a real chance of developing his 'gifts'. They are signs that the time has come for self-work. Most people cannot use them, because they do not know that this is the *alif* (letter A) and that the *be* (letter B) follows, until there is a *iaa* (last letter of the alphabet).'

I entertained all the four Amu Daria sheikhs at one time or another by describing to them something of the life and thinking of Europe, even going back as far as I could to the days of the Middle Ages, when the East and the West had been closer together in so many ways.

Pir Turki's reaction to this information was interesting, because it showed me that there was something in his mind on this subject. 'A century and a quarter has passed,' he said, 'since the message of the Great Khan about this subject, but the work has gone on uninterruptedly.' The Great Khan was Jan-Fishan, the chief of the Hindu Kush, who was a descendant of the Prophet Mohammed, and in whose family the leadership of the Sufis is believe to reside.

'The Great Khan was the first to be in touch with the West since the time of Sultan Yusuf Saladin. He actually went to India and settled there for a time. His message, which was given out just before the War of Shah Shuja [1838], was concerned with the West. From what I have heard from you and otherwise, it is still as fresh today.'

He did not revert to the message of the Great Khan for some time, and we discussed other topics. Then he told me that the Khan had said that the West was material, had lost the force of religion. This materialism was not the materialism which we understood, but was acquisitiveness pure and simple. There would be a growth in sceptical philosophy. There would have to be a great deal of suffering in the West. 'And the rule of logic and intellect will have to become so severe that there is almost nobody who will listen to truth.'

When that happened, he said, people would start to look for truth. Then the message of the Sufis would be heard. 'But the people in the West are Christians,' I objected.

'So are we!' He turned sharply to me. 'In the West they are materialists, but of the worst possible kind. They are free, free to destroy themselves; but they should not be allowed to destroy themselves, any more than a child is allowed to do so. If I insult Jesus in a Moslem country, I shall be punished by law and by the people. But you have told me that people use the name of Jesus lightly, even in swear-words in the West. Is it true?'

'It is true. But I still think that there are good people, and well-meaning ones.'

'No doubt. They will probably be considered stupid by the others. And many of them will be stupid; they will follow anyone and think that he is a prophet, because they will not be able to discriminate as to what a prophet is.'

'They are very self-critical,' I hazarded.

'Self-criticism is useless without self-work. And who is to teach them?'

I tried to turn the conversation into more illuminating channels. 'Can you apply your concentration to the problem, in the way which you were telling us yesterday,' I said, 'and tell me, as one who has come from the West to learn, whether there will be a growth of a community of Sufis in Europe, strong enough to have any effect on the evolution of man?'

He did not seem to concentrate at all. 'There will.'

'And will it be led by anyone?'

'It will.'

'And will this be a Westerner?'

'It will not. It will be one who is of the East, but he will make the teaching a part of the teaching of the West, as it once was, in ancient times.'

'When will the activity start?'

'It has started, slowly. Some will come and try to force another teaching into the shape of the original one, and many will follow.'

He cut the conversation short. 'Only the Sheikhs can influence this development; it cannot be discussed. It is a matter of the contact of minds. Some who have fixed ideas may have to die to make way for someone who is younger by many years.'

In many ways, my time with the Amudaria was the most interesting of all my life. There was something un-oriental about them; and they were so obviously intent upon some activity which was not of the rarefied nature which characterises Indian and Far Eastern thought and makes it unacceptable to any but a small minority of Westerners. There was a very great deal that one could get hold of, and very obviously no attempt at mystification.

From *Among the Dervishes*, by O. M. Burke
(The Octagon Press, London)

IMAGES AND REALITY: THEN AND NOW

Henry Sargent lived and travelled in Afghanistan in 1964 under the Royal regime, then returned in 1975; and spent much of 1985 and early 1986 with the Mujahidin.

I suppose that my image of Afghanistan was like most people's in England. A bit of Kipling, with his scrimmages on the North-West Frontier: wild tribesmen, gorges and defiles, treachery and heroism. Then there was the idea that, since the place is in the East, there would be exotic scenes, Muslim fanatics, teeming, poverty-stricken peasants and disease under a baking sun.

That's what I would have written, if I had been asked to do an essay on the country.

By the early 1960s, however, the youth of the West were flooded with accounts of the mystic East: of strange rituals, of stranger knowledge, of people with civilisations which made ours look like nothing.

This conception, fostered by all kinds of idealists and malcontents (and some who were both) filtered into my mind. I was twenty-five years old, and I was ready for the Mystic East.

Heading for India overland in an old car, I met streams of bearded, long-haired enthusiasts coming the other way: Australians and New Zealanders, gripped by the urge to find their roots in the Old Country. Whether it was in Yugoslavia, in Istanbul or in Iran, they were there. For the most part unwashed, often stoned on cannabis, as often exhibitionists, they usually wanted to talk only about themselves. I got no information worth knowing about Afghanistan from them, except, perhaps, that it was the only place in the East with hardly any beggars, and where the people fed you on request.

But Afghanistan was my goal. As soon as I got into the Eastern Iranian province of Khurasan, everything changed. The people spoke clearly and with assurance, they held themselves up straight, the very air seemed different. These were hard people, I could see; but they did have something which I was to find throughout Afghanistan – and I still do not know what it is . . .

Iran, at that time under Mohammed Reza Pehlavi, was something of a grotesque. No expense was spared to attempt the westernisation of a people who needed food, not armies, who lacked education, and did not need prestige buildings, who were riddled with bribery and corruption, and desperately needed something doing about that. Instead, they got an almost hysterical campaign to prove that the Iranians were the best people on earth, had the oldest civilisation, but would have to Americanise themselves as soon as possible.

They couldn't take it, so they listened to the harangues of the clergy, who offered a beguiling alternative: throw it all away and follow us.

Once inside Herat, western Afghanistan's great city, I found that the Afghan solution was different. There wasn't much money to modernise with, but people were trying. In place of grandiose plans, they worked. Instead of propaganda, there was good, sturdy administrative effort. True, the Army looked miserable and people wore cast-off clothes imported from the west. But people were clean, they looked you in the eye, and nobody starved.

Genghiz Khan, in the thirteenth century, had destroyed the irrigation systems of the west and south of the country which had made it the garden of Asia. The result was seven hundred years of desert. That was now being put right, with Afghan expertise, engineers largely trained in the USA, and some aid from the West.

The people, I found, were cheerful and had a sense of humour, something which I had missed for most of the way since I embarked at Dover. Islam, deeply believed in, was yet not onerous. On the whole, a man's conscience was his own affair. The Eastern idea of a public conscience, which allows anyone to challenge anyone else on his thought or acts, seemed foreign here.

The Afghans seemed to have solved the problem of tension between clergy and people.

Wherever I went, I was invited to sleep in the village *hujra*, a room or cottage set aside for travellers; for travellers are sacred guests in Islam. Total strangers on the road would call to me to share their midday meals. Westerners, either from the Antipodes or Europe or America, abused this hospitality shamefully.

I spent time in Kandahar, south from Herat, and found it a city which was soaked in the ways of the Pashtun people: the tribesmen who had fought against the expanding British Empire during the 'Forward Policy', a euphemism whose meaning is quite clear.

In Kandahar, the people were on the whole gruff but friendly. They dressed in traditional turbans, trousers and long shirts, with a robe or blanket on top, shod in Chapli sandals. I made many friends there.

Kabul, the capital, I found in a state of tremendous activity. The whole place was being rebuilt, it seemed, and even natives said that they would wake to find some old landmark gone. Set between the mountains, guarded by a huge fortress, blessed with an excellent climate, Kabul has been a centre of commerce for longer than history records. Some say that its name comes from the ancient Aryan word for 'sheep-fold'.

As the seat of Government, Kabul was the place from which all the planning, administration and education emanated. The Afghans are skilled administrators, and the process of getting factories, agricultural projects, science and hygiene improved to world standards was well advanced.

The whole country is a patchwork of communities, many of whose people are so different one from the other that one can only wonder at it. Successive civilisations (Persian, Mongol, Greek, Islamic and so on) have all left their stamp and their genetic heritage. In Kabul you will see Hazaras and Uzbeks of Mongol or Turkish stock, tall hook-nosed Pashtuns from the south, fair-skinned people from Nuristan in the east – and admixtures of any or all of these.

There was an air of expectancy, of optimism, of 'we'll get there', which reflected the intense vitality of a people who seemed to be easterners only incidentally. The Afghans have tremendous energy. In the past they have put it into conquest, into poetry and literature, even into scientific research as known in the Middle Ages. In the 1960s, it was going into development and an attempt to unify the disparate communities which formed the population.

Wanderings

Ten years later, I returned to Afghanistan. I had been back to England and had built up a business, which gave me freedom to travel once more. And I had no ties, and Afghanistan called me once again.

Some things in Afghanistan do not change at all; but some were different. The relaxation of the firm hand of the government over political expression was one. The Afghans of the countryside were not affected by this, but the cities, especially Kabul, were.

Foreign residents were worried. Afghan youth, lacking access to good information on how political processes worked elsewhere for the good of the country, were listening to irresponsible, often half-baked, theorists who sought to form power systems for themselves, not to produce democracy.

Afghanistan was one of the most democratic societies on earth. Opinion, and hence justice and any necessary change, was filtered through authority figures, no doubt. But, on the whole, nobody could hold onto power for long unless seen to be just and honest. Against this, the muddle-headed theoreticians proposed some of the wildest ideas imaginable. Get rid of the clergy (or the administration) and we will all be happy and rich: that might summarise what passed for political wisdom among the inexperienced.

This tale, of course, is not unusual in the Third World. Russian propaganda experts had assessed the potential and sent specially-trained operatives into the country to advocate change, often violent change.

The government were uncertain as to what to do. They did not want to seem backward, but they could not answer the charges that they were stupid and dragging their feet; even if only because such accusations can never be refuted, especially when repeated by malcontents who gain by believing them.

I was especially interested to note the opinions of the foreign residents, some of them very experienced, who had lived here for years: perhaps they had lived here too long. Most of them thought that the Afghans were too conservative, 'too priest-ridden' as one said, ever to change. Therefore full freedom to advocate anarchy should be allowed.

Some insisted that the Russians were not interfering. Their reason was that nobody spoke of communism, of Marx or of the Soviet Union, in terms of praise. When I pointed out (as did some other people) that it was not the actual words but their effect which

103

the Russians had undoubtedly calculated, I was laughed at – even by very senior diplomats from the Western world.

Military officers whom I met, trained in Russia, had obviously been carefully conditioned. Some told me that, 'Castro in Cuba, with enlightened ideas, had shown how a small country could become the ideological leader of all Latin America: so could Afghanistan lead all of Asia'.

They had been given lessons, in the USSR, which held that the Afghans, with their former great civilisations and past empires, could rise again. All they needed was to follow the Soviet line.

Naive? Perhaps. But one has to know the mind of a landlocked people, frustrated former conquerors once feared and respected by a continent, to get the perspective.

The Russians were so disliked in Afghanistan that almost nobody would openly say anything in their favour. Babrak Karmal, a Russian agent soon to be made President with Soviet military power, was a nobody. In 1967, only two years before the Kremlin installed him, a wise authority, John C. Griffiths (in *Afghanistan*) had this to say about Babrak's political party:

> The smallest and least significant is on the extreme left, and consists of 'Mr Babrak' and no more than two or three sympathisers. The path of natural development into a communist party for these neo-Marxists is completely blocked by the Constitution, whose stipulation excluding all opposition to Islam clearly rules out any atheist party. In any case, there is no evidence to suggest any strong, or even potential, support in the country for such a party, although it has one or two adherents among the students at Kabul University.

A few months after reading these words in Kabul, I was fleeing through the snowfilled mountain passes from the capital, into Pakistan – with the Russians, bringing Babrak as the new Afghan leader, not far behind.

Another decade passed, a million Afghans (out of a maximum of fourteen million) died – and I was in Pakistan again.

Aching for my second homeland, saddened by its agony, I had read and cut out every news item or article on the Russo-Afghan War that I could find. I had been in America, in Germany, France, Spain and Japan. Like the diplomats and international workers whom I had met in Kabul, the media people had, almost invariably, got it wrong.

I not only knew this from my personal experience of the Afghans: that they would resist, would score victories, would endure to the last; I knew it from the press-cuttings themselves.

Looking over them, I saw the first confident predictions (by experts) that the Afghans would be crushed, evaporate and be replaced by successive claims that it would take a year, two years, three years...

Then there were the experts who interviewed the exiled political people in Pakistan, or during their well-publicised tours in the West. Some of these people were nonentities who had prevailed upon Arab and Western leaders to recognise them as important factors in the war. I knew them, either personally or by repute, from Kabul. Their eager interviewers often swallowed everything they were told about their plans, importance and effect on the guerrilla struggle.

I decided to go to Pakistan, to try to get into Afghanistan once more, to see what was really happening.

On the North-West Frontier the inheritors of the British Raj were battling manfully with the problems of dealing with three or more million refugees. The camps covered more than a thousand miles, and were situated all the way along the border, from Baluchistan on the Arabian Sea to Chitral, not so far from China in the north.

Some émigré leaders had transformed their local roles into national and international ones. This is how they did it: relatively small leaders in Afghanistan had collected a bunch of followers and set up movements or offices. These they showed to foreign journalists, who were unaccustomed to smaller people being treated like royalty. They wrote excited profiles of these 'national leaders'. The leaders then took reprints of the articles to Arab and other countries, thus 'proving' how important they were. Impressed, the Arabs gave them money. Some at least of this money went into further propaganda, and sometimes into world tours.

I do not say that this was, or is, the rule. But it has happened; and so far few, if any, of the self-made leaders have been seen for what they are.

Quite obviously, in war situations, this kind of thing happens everywhere. It should not be thought that the Afghans are any less reliable than other people. But the fact remains that the situation, several years after the Soviet invasion, badly needs sorting out.

The next problem I encountered was that the Red Afghans and the Russians had planted informers and disinformation people actually within the guerrilla groups' headquarters. Little that some of them did was unknown to Kabul and Moscow. As a result (one result – there are others) it was generally safer to deal with guerrillas still inside Afghanistan than their 'leaders' in Pakistan, unless one was very sure that there was no leak.

Even inside the country there were Spesnatz, specially trained forces, who masqueraded as Mujahidin [guerrillas] and fell upon various resistance forces. The result was that the world press reported the fighters as falling out among themselves.

There is even a suspicion that some seemingly objective Western writers have accepted money from – or been indoctrinated by – the Russians. One Afghan defector told me that he had seen, in the Kabul Press Department, foreign correspondents being wined and dined, and praised, to such an extent that they fell willing victims to almost everything they were told about how happy Afghans were. 'It is a byword,' he told me, 'that as the Press have a low rating in the West, they fall like ripe plums when showered with compliments.'

Naturally, such accusations are hard to verify.

The tranquility of the refugees was not increased by the rumours that Afghanistan was to be dismembered. The North, so the rumour went, would go to Soviet Turkestan, after a 'plebiscite'. The West would join Iran, and so possibly, might the central massif, full of Hazaras, who have some affinities with the Iranians. The southern portion could be offered to Pakistan: thus ending, it was supposedly hoped, the irritation which cut the Pashtun homeland in two.

All this may have been floated by the Russians. It certainly had an unsettling effect.

Arms, which are admitted to have been bought by Afghan resisters on the world market, are said to be intercepted and substituted (with old ones) by elements in Pakistan. Or, another charge, KGB agents have infiltrated resistance groups and sabotaged the arms, or else informed the Soviets that they are arriving: resulting in their capture.

It is true that several valuable shipments of arms have been seized the moment they arrived on Afghan territory, even when they have been betrayed the moment they entered the country through supposedly secret routes.

The export of Afghan children to the USSR was in full swing, abetted by the Red Afghans of Kabul. It has a certain logic, from their point of view. They have themselves been conditioned; and they want to work with a younger generation which shares their outlook. The pattern is the 'brainwashing' of young army cadets in Russia when training there: these were the cadres which seized power temporarily and invited the Russians in.

Two things are badly needed to make the Western help of the Afghans more effective. The first is that aid for the refugees must be detached from support of the politico-religious leaders who effectively dominate the camps. The second is that contact must be made and maintained with the guerrillas actually fighting inside Afghanistan: many of whom have no time for their 'leaders' in Pakistan.

I went into Afghanistan and spent four months with various resistance bands. They bore little resemblance to those whom I had met in and around Peshawar. Many were deserters from the old Afghan Army. Well-trained, well motivated, they form the real core of the resistance forces. They desperately need help, and they dislike the fundamentalists and politically sectarian spokesmen who have the ear of the West.

Inside Afghanistan, I found that conditions and the nature of the real resistance had not been correctly reported abroad. The largest and most effective guerrilla movements have no truck at all with the émigrés. Very large tracts of land – up to eighty percent of the total, in a country the size of France – are in rebel hands. These people depend upon supplies, including arms, obtained from the Russians. It is cheaper to buy Kalashnikov assault rifles from venal Russian quartermasters than to import them from abroad. These are paid for in dollar bills or in gold.

So poor is security, and so questionable some of the Afghan groups outside the country, that a new initiative, to contact and help the internal fighters, is essential.

Interestingly, one or two of the real fighting groups have tried to make overseas contacts. Sadly, though, they have usually been

referred by our own people to one or other of the allegedly representative bodies in Pakistan. They got their messsage in first. It will
be a devil of a job to reverse the impression they have made – if it
can ever be done.

PART THREE

HOWS, WHYS, WHATS . . .

WHAT SHALL WE COOK TONIGHT?

It is related that, after finishing an enormous meal of spiced rice with chickens buried in its mounds, savoury sauce with meat balls, several other dishes and piles of fruit – his lunch – the Amir Habibullah Khan used to turn to his courtiers and ask, 'Now, Noblemen and Friends, what shall we cook *tonight*?'

Afghans love food, and good Afghan food is one of the great cuisines of the world. Feeding people is essential to hospitality; in range and extent it is almost a mania.

This evening, let's have an Afghan meal of . . .

PALAO (NOT PEELOW, PILAU OR PARLOW)

The main dish must have pride of place, for reputations stand or fall by it. Make sure you can pronounce it: NOT peelaw, pilaf or parlow. Rhymes with 'cull-cow'. If you can't say it properly, Afghans will look at you with suspicion. The strange food, sometimes even containing shredded coconut, you may be offered in Indian and Pakistani restaurants under this name bears little resemblance to Afghan palao.

Here is the Great Recipe of the *Khalifa Ashpaz*, Master Chef, of the Hindu Kush. It was regularly served only to my great-grandfather – and, at times, up to 4000 guests:

Spiced rice with meat or chicken.
To serve 6 people (Afghan-sized portions).

INGREDIENTS:

The Rice: 2lb best rice (Basmati or better).

111

The Meat: 2lb tender lamb,
               2 pigeons,
               1 chicken.

The Onions: 1lb, sliced.

The Broth: The juice in which the meat and birds have been
               cooked;
               6 cardamoms – ground,
               4 teaspoons coriander powder,
               1/4 teaspoon ground white pepper,
               4 whole cloves,
               4 teaspoons salt,
               1 teaspoon aniseed seeds,
               2 teaspoons sugar,
               1 tablespoon vinegar,
               1 tablespoon lemon juice.

The Dusting
(for the meat
before frying): Powdered ginger.

The *Amezish* [Amalgamate] added just before serving:
               1/4 teaspoon saffron, in one cup of hot water,
               1 tablespoonful blanched sliced almonds,
               1 tablespoonful blanched pistachios,
               1 tablespoonful sultanas (preferably green),
               Best quality vegetable oil.

The Method:

Cut up the meat and fowl: no piece to be larger than one inch
square, and half-boil each separately in salt and water.

Put all the meat and bird juice in one pot, add the items for the
broth, and set aside.

Fry the meat and bird, separately, until very well done, after
dusting lightly with powdered ginger. Set aside.

Fry the onions until very dark and crisp. Set aside.

Prepare the Amalgamate and set aside.

Put the meat in a large pot over fairly high heat (or cook in oven
at high).

Wash the rice six times or until the rinsing water is clear.

Drain rice and add on top of meat.

Add spiced broth until it is 1½ inches above the level of the meat. Keep some broth for topping up. If insufficient, use chicken broth. Cover well with top and cook.

Test occasionally, to see if rice is *dana-dar*: take a rice grain or two, rub between finger and thumb. Dana-dar is when rice crumbles slightly, splitting into hard and soft particles, 'danas'.

Until then, top up with spiced broth as needed.

When dana-dar, remove from heat and replace top with cloth four times doubled and place pot lid as weight on top. Replace on/in medium heat. This the *dam-pukht* phase, when the steam will be absorbed by the cloth, so that the palao has no excess moisture, with each rice-grain separate.

When rice is tender, turn out onto a very large platter. Stir in the onions, saffron and water, almonds, sultanas and pistachios.

Optionally, any or all of the following may be added:

> Pomegranate juice, 1 tablespoonful
> Ground dried orange or lemon peel, 3 teaspoons.

To complete an Afghan meal, any or all of these may be included (as a side dish):

> Plain yoghurt (*never* fruit-flavoured) with diced cucumber;
> Spiced meat balls (koftas);
> Omelette;
> Ashak (like large ravioli filled with leek);
> Kichri qurut;
> Salan (hot sauce);
> Salad, chopped, with vinegar dressing;
> Naun (bread);
> Immense quantities of fresh fruit in season;
> Fruit salad;
> Halwa;
> Chai-i-Sabz (green tea).

But, for those, you will have to wait for my cookery book...

And please, always remember, all plates must be heaped, and all food must be in profusion. The kind of portions which are sometimes served elsewhere than in Afghanistan can even, in extreme cases, be regarded almost as a deliberate insult...

LAZY MAN'S PALAO

But how do you manage if you haven't got all the ingredients or the means to make a *Great Palao*?

An Afghan scientist in exile, pining for a civilised dinner, carried out extensive experiments in his tiny New York apartment.

As is so often the way in science, he failed time after time. Then, one day, he made the breakthrough. He invited a crowd of other deprived Afghans to taste the result. They raised a few crumbs from the dish to their lips, hardly daring to hope that the impossible had been achieved. A moment later, the huddled mass (yearning to be free) was utterly transformed: 'I felt like a human being again,' one of them reported to me. 'I wanted to laugh, to cry, to do the Attan sword-dance again.'

This is the secret of the triumph of Professor Ibrahim: *Lazy Man's Palao*. You, too, can make it, with less trouble than you would have with many a Western dish:

Take ¼ to ½ lb diced lamb, first parboiled, then fried and set aside, keeping it warm if possible.

¾ lb long-grain rice, half-boiled (to *dana-dar* stage: see recipe above), drained and set aside: keeping it warm if possible.

2 pints or more of broth, brought to the boil, containing:

> The meat juice,
> Chicken stock cubes, to taste (say three),
> Salt, to taste (say 1 1/2 teaspoons),
> 2 whole cloves,
> 4 peeled cardamom seeds, well bruised or ground,
> 1 teaspoon onion salt,
> 2 tablespoons fried tomato puree,
> 1 tablespoon best vegetable oil.

THE METHOD

Put the half-cooked rice into as large a flattish cooking tray as will fit in the oven or under the grill (either should be at full heat). Fill the tray with rice, leaving about 1 inch or more space above: you are going to add the broth, and the rice will expand as it cooks. Pour and stir in the prepared (preferably very hot) broth, until the rice is just soggy.

Now subject the dish to heat in the oven or under the grill; the rice will continue to cook, absorbing the broth. 'Feed' the rice with broth from time to time, as it dries out, raking well with a fork.

When the rice has taken up enough to your taste, and is properly cooked, with each grain separate, remove from the heat.

Add the meat and serve. Surplus broth can be used as a gravy: each person takes as much as desired.

This meal is delicious when served with plain yoghurt and mixed chopped salad, including olives and sliced raw onions. Masses of well-fried onions also add to the delight. If you have time and the resources, you can stir in, at the last moment:

> Sliced blanched almonds,
> Pine kernel (*jalghoza*) nuts,
> Small sultanas, soaked in rosewater,
> Thinnest peel of one orange (none of the pith),
> 1 tablespoon butter or mutton fat.

This dish has also been made as a vegetarian one. Instead of the meat, balls of textured protein with mint and coriander are made and fried or baked. The rice is prepared as before, with more tomato puree and yeast extract to give taste and body.

Now, Noblemen and Friends: *Imshab chi pukhta bekunem –* what shall we cook tonight?

When you serve your Afghan friends, they will say, 'May you live a thousand years!'

Your answer, of course is, 'May you live for ever!'

Idries Shah unpublished manuscript

THE BOOK OF TALISMANS AND GENIES

As elsewhere, magical lore persists here and there in Afghanistan. Most of the books and practices originated in the Middle Ages, and especially from the Arabian magician Ibn al-Hajj. His influence is also found in medieval – and even fairly recent – European texts. I have dealt with some of this material in my *Oriental Magic* (magic of the East) and *The Secret Lore of Magic* (beliefs and practices of the West) which have been bought in large numbers by anthropologists.

Idries Shah

The majority of Afghans, who are devout Moslems, disapprove of thaumaturgical practices, though 'Black Magic' as understood in the West, is not involved.

In the East, 'lawful magic' is permitted because of some sayings attributed to the Prophet Mohammed. An instance is the dictum recorded in the authoritative Traditions [Hadith] collection, *The Mishkat (xxi. c.i)* which lays down that 'There is no wrong in using invocations when you do not associate anything (in worship) with God'.

What may be called the standard magical procedures reached the Afghans through the book of Ibn al-Hajj, and also through the Persian-language *Five Jewels*, the *Jawahir-i-Khamsa* of Sheikh Abu'l Muwaid, which is over a thousand years old.

Magicians use spells to treat ailments, both mental and physical, to compose amulets and charms, and for protection and

116

prosperity. The chief instruments are tables of associated forces, of which an example is given overleaf:

Armed with this table, the magician works with correspondences. Some typical processes:

FINDING SOMEONE'S MAGICAL NAME:

The name is split up into its constituent letters, and the Abjad [numerical] value of each letter added up. Say the total is 265. This is split up into hundreds, tens and units, giving 200, 60 and 5. The numbers are re-encoded into their Abjad equivalents, which are:

```
200 = R
 60 = S
  5 = H
```

This spells RSH. To make the name pronounceable, the letter A is inserted between the consonants: RaSaH – 'Rasah'.

GENIES:

As the table shows, the three genies presiding over the letters are, respectively, Raahush, Fa'yush and Hush. To gain the beneficent action of these in favour of the subject, an amulet or invocation is written or repeated: 'O (naming the genies), aid RASAH, in the Name of The Lord, The Hearer, The Guide' – the three Divine Attributes which govern the genies. The number of times the invocation is to be said corresponds with the numerical value of the Attribute:

```
R = Lord = 202
S = Hearer = 180
H = Guide = 20
```
_____
    402 times.

The Magic Word which is said at the end of the invocation is the decoded equivalent of 402 = 400 + 2 = T + H = Tah.

LOVE CHARM

I once bought a very beautiful inscribed amulet or charm from a Kochi [Nomad] trader. Inscribed on copper, and embellished with

Table of letters of the Arabic alphabet, value of attribute, Divine attributes, meaning of attribute, genies governing quality and Abjad value of each letter:

Arabic Letter	Numerical Value of Attribute	Divine Name	Attribute in Arabic (Angel)	Meaning of Attribute	Genie	Nature of Angel *	Abjad Value
A	66	Allah	Israfil	God	Qaipush	T	1
B	113	Baqi	Jibrail	Eternal	Danush	A	2
J	114	Jami'	Kalkail	Assembler	Nulush	C	3
D	65	Daian	Dardail	Reckoner	Twaiush	T	4
H	20	Hadi	Durbail	Guide	Hush	A	5
W	46	Wali	Raftmail	Friend	Puyush	A	6
Z	37	Zaki	Sharkail	Purifier	Kapush	C	7
H	108	Haqq	Tankafil	Truth	'Ayush	C	8
T	215	Tahir	Ismail	Holy	Badyush	T	9
Y	130	Yasin	Sarakikail	Chief	Shahbush	A	10
K	111	Kafi	Kharurail	Sufficient	Kadyush	A	20
L	129	Latif	Tatail	Kindly	'Adyush	A	30
M	90	Malik	Ruyail	King	Majbush	T	40
N	256	Nur	Hulail	Light	Damalyush	T	50
S	180	Sami'	Hamwakil	Hearer	Fa'yush	C	60
,	110	Aali	Lumail	Exalted	Kashpush	T	70
F	489	Fatah	Sarhamail	Opener (Victor)	Latyush	A	80
S	134	Samad	Ahjmail	Established	Kalapush	T	90
Q	305	Qadir	'Itrail	Powerful	Shamyush	C	100
R	202	Rabb	Amwakil	Lord	Raahush	T	200
Sh	460	Shafi'	Amrail	Accepter	Tashyush	A	300
T	409	Tawab	Azrail	Forgiver	Latyush	A	400
Th	903	Thabit	Mikail	Stable	Wahyush	T	500
Kh	731	Khaliq	Mahkail	Creator	Dalayush	C	600
D	921	Dakir	Hartail	Rememberer	Twakapush	C	700
Dh	1001	Dhar	'Atail	Punisher	Ghayush	T	800
Z	1106	Zahir	Nurail	Evident	Ghafupush	T	900
Gh	1285	Ghafur	Nukhail	Forgiver	'Arkupush	A	1000

*T = terrible; A = amiable; C = combined (A and T)

118

silver – visible when I had cleaned it – were a number of figures and letters. It was a love charm, made as follows:

The man's name, Ismail, and the girl's, Nadima, were written in a diamond shape. Then the equivalent of each, in numbers, was written in a continuous double line around the border of the square medallion.

The word *Ishq* (love) appeared five times around the diamond shape.

Finally, the name Kadyush, the genie working under the Divine Name *Kafi* (Sufficient) is inscribed on the reverse of the charm. Pierced with two holes, the charm is suspended around the neck.

HERBAL LORE OF THE HINDU KUSH

In Afghanistan, agriculturists from abroad have discovered as many as fifty varieties of wheat and at least twenty different kinds of peas. Mixing these in certain proportions obtains quite a different nutritional and therapeutic effect, say the local herbalists, than merely collecting and using one or two varieties.

RHEUMATISM

In order to prevent rheumatic pains and stiff joints, people are advised to eat, regularly, fresh or dried (cooked) wild melon. These grow abundantly in Afghanistan. They are not sweet, are quite small, and should be cooked by boiling in water. In Pakistan a gourd, similar to a pumpkin, is used as a rheumatism preventive. It has been observed that people who eat fresh or dried and cooked material of this kind once a week are singularly free from rheumatic symptoms.

Once, however, rheumatic symptoms have appeared, remarkable cures have been achieved by use of nettle and dandelion leaves, boiled for some hours at a very low temperature, the resultant water being drunk three times a day for a period of a month.

I witnessed one striking remission of rheumatism in Badakhshan (North-East Afghanistan) which was all the more notable because the sufferer did not know that she was being treated for this.

We entered a village and a woman of some seventy years of age, hobbling on two sticks, came to see us at the table which we had set up for the purpose of consultations. She was obviously suffering from rheumatism or arthritis. She did not, however, ask for treatment for this. Instead, she wanted our 'blessing' for her son who was on the point of making the pilgrimage to Mecca. He would not come himself, since he 'did not believe in that kind of thing', she explained.

The herbal practitioners told her to drink water in which garlic had been steeped overnight, mixed with powdered ginger root, one teaspoonful, morning and night. When she had gone, I asked what effect this would have on the intending pilgrim.

'None,' said the physician, 'but I have decided to treat her trouble with the joints. You will see what will happen.'

When we returned that way, a year later, the woman came to thank us. Her son had returned safely from Mecca. Her rheumatics, too, had apparently completely disappeared!

She had faithfully adhered to the recipe, and said that she felt she was better due to the purity of her intention, the *baraka*, which 'had come to her because she had sought something for another, and not for herself'.

I saw the successful use of this treatment again and again, and more than once when administered by a wife to a husband in his food, without his knowing.

In cases where this remedy did not work, I have seen food prepared with red pepper (*murch*), celery, fresh ground, then boiled, and mustard. Although most Afghans do not like 'hot' food like curry, it was widely believed that those who did eat it seldom suffered from rheumatic disorders.

PREVENTATIVE FOR APPENDICITIS

Hakim [doctor] Ghazi Khan explained to me that appendicitis was very rare in the parts of Afghanistan where people sat ordinarily in a squatting position. The condition was found in Nuristan (formerly known as Kafiristan) where the people often sat at tables and on stools. When I asked why it was that this ailment was so common among the Western residents of the country, even though they squatted, I was told that it was also because their diet tended to be too bland.

There certainly is less appendicitis in parts of Afghanistan where people eat wheat, rather than those where they consume large quantities of melons and pulses. There is a strange reversal of ideas about pulses, incidentally. Whereas, in the West, it is often imagined by scoffers that cranks eat quantities of peas, beans and other pulses, in Afghanistan it is believed that pulse-eaters *become* health cranks!

The Indians, who tend to be preoccupied with their health and also have their fair share of cranks and faddists, are pointed out as products of this *dal* [lentil] diet.

COMPOSITE DIETS

We often came across people with a variety of complaints, which were sometimes treated with special composite diets. In typical cases, acne plus depression plus loss of virility was treated with a mixture of sage and onions (for acne), chopped and boiled vine leaves (depression) and nutmeg and cow-parsnip (virility).

This last-named herb is scientifically named *Heracleum sphondylium,* sometimes known as Hogweed. It is of the family which includes coriander, lovage and fennel, all supposed to be highly efficacious for health, especially if drunk as decoctions in the morning on a long-term basis. Effects seem to show after thirty days.

VIRILITY

This, it is said, is increased by grinding celery and paprika, sometimes with cinnamon. About a teaspoonful of each is placed in a mortar and ground until thoroughly mixed. The resultant mash is placed in vegetable oil and left in the sun for a week. The strained oil is then added to the midday meal.

This is what is called *Shah-Tiriyaq* [Royal Elixir] and also seems to provide great resistance to fatigue.

BACK TROUBLES

Often successfully treated with a mixture of cress and sesame oil. The oil is produced by crushing sesame seeds and placing them in vegetable oil for three weeks, in a dark place. The cress is then added (a handful to 500 cc of oil) and rubbed through the fingers. This product is then massaged into the back.

It also seems to have as good an effect if applied like a poultice and then bandaged, to be changed every two days.

Hot baths are another treatment for pain in the back. To a tub of hot water are added nettles (a quarter of a kilogram), hawthorn leaves (half that amount) and 600 grammes of pulverised raw onions. The patient takes such a bath every alternate day.

'Vibration therapy' is sometimes included. This involves finding a large sheet of metal and beating it while standing it 50 centimetres from the back, for about five minutes three times a day. The metal (which is sometimes only a piece of corrugated iron) is beaten with an oak club covered with chamois leather, to produce a dull sound, not a loud one.

HEART TROUBLES

These were treated in a variety of different ways. A very diluted tincture of Persian Speedwell, known in Afghanistan as *Zudkhush* ('Quickwell'), almost a translation of the English name, is taken once in twenty-four hours, in a cup of green tea. The quantity is minute: one bruised leaf immersed in boiling water for ten minutes before being added to the tea, and one might almost suppose that it would have little effect. On the other hand, this herb, whose scientific name is *Veronica persica,* is a relative of the foxglove, also used for heart troubles, and a powerful coronary stimulant, which contains digitalis.

Again, for the *Heart*, there is a gargle which is generally agreed to prevent heart attacks. This is prepared by immersing 25 grammes of nettles, with the same quantity of pink rose petals, in hot water and gargling with the resultant (strained) liquid three times a day.

Coriander in the food is believed to prevent whoever eats it from experiencing heart trouble. This latter remedy is known as the 'Chinese heart-protection tea' by the local medical men.

Certain herbs and spices are so widely used in this kind of medicine that I once asked the chief physician of our travelling medical party why they did not confer immunity to a whole range of diseases. His reply interested me. This was to the effect that not only did the herbs produce immunity, but that the increase in certain diseases in the country could be mapped. This map showed that it was exactly in those regions where people had changed their diets to reduce their intake of this or that herb, perhaps because of expense or through the invasion of foreign eating habits, the corresponding ailment started to appear, and 'got a strong hold before we restored the balance'.

When I mentioned, however, that people in Western countries should therefore show an equivalent increase in health because they were now eating much more foreign food, my informant did not agree. 'This does not necessarily follow,' he said, 'because it is not a balance to consume certain foods from time to time. Herbal health is produced by consistent dietary habits. People in this country who, for instance, sometimes eat potatoes, and who have not made them a regular part of their diet, suffer from all kinds of ailments which are not found among people for whom they are standard fare.'

I then suggested that, since potatoes were a relatively recent introduction into Europe itself, people there must be suffering from complications due to this 'new' diet. 'Not now,' he said, 'for everyone for whom potatoes were really poisonous will have died out since their introduction. We have had them in this country for less than a hundred years, and their ravages are still visible.'

Since I was – and still am – a potato eater, I begged him to tell me whether the ravages of this vegetable could be ameliorated. According to him, the only thing which counteracted their effect was mint or cardamoms, cooked in the same water or dish.

Mint, of course, as in many other countries, is widely used in this area for *Indigestion*, though there are other remedies as well. Caraway seed (*Qaraweea*) are great favourites.

Debility, from whatever cause, is claimed to be removed by drinking a mixture of honey and saffron, left overnight in a pot of green tea, and eaten with the usual Afghan breakfast of nuts, yoghurt and raw cereals. I have seen remarkable results from this treatment.

Lactation, both in human and animal mothers, is made much more abundant by the use of borage, eaten raw.

Many cases of *Asthma* were apparently cured by eating, once a day, a paste made from thyme and honeysuckle flowers. This is also dried and eaten, in the Winter months, mixed with a little water and a green tea decoction.

An Arabian *Rejuvenation* tonic, introduced by the Arabs in the eighth century is *Zatar*. This is composed of equal parts of roasted sesame seeds, thyme and salt. The whole is ground to a powder and then baked into a small flap of unleavened bread. Fed to horses it undoubtedly produces an improvement in their wind and the appearance of their coats.

The yellow orange of the Jalalabad region is one of the most important fruits for all health problems. It is eaten raw or cooked, and people who carry it and make a decoction of the dried form swear that they need no other medicine. I have not seen this fruit, however, outside Afghanistan.

The yellow cherry, native to Paghman, is administered fresh or dried for lassitude, warts, dullness of intellect and weak foot muscles. There is a great deal of folklore about this fruit. Among the beliefs of the people about it is the one that this is where the early Sufis settled when they entered the country from some unknown place, since its presence proves that the region is healthy. It is also said to predispose to 'higher spiritual understanding', but the Sufis themselves would not confirm this.

Mulberries, which form a staple of the diet of the people of some parts of the country, are believed to cure a range of ills. I have seen them administered for the relief of pain, for difficult childbirth, and for improving the disposition of malicious people. But one has to be an expert on mulberries to know which kinds of the great variety are suitable for what; where and when to pick them, and how to administer them.

The Keeper of the Royal Herb Gardens told me, however, that the white, intensely sweet, seedless *Shah-Tout* (Royal Mulberry) was a general tonic; the *Sher-Tout* (Tiger Mulberry) is given for anaemia and certain forms of blindness that even Western medicine cannot handle, and the ordinary red mulberry, mixed with walnuts (the long Herat Afghan type), when a handful is eaten, treats prostate troubles and urinary difficulties.

Afghan women seem singularly free from menstrual problems, of any kind. When I commented upon this, I was told that this was because they all eat the Hussaini grape. It seems to have some sort of balancing power which brings these matters into correct operation. Since everyone knows it, this item cannot, of course, be considered to be a part of medicine as practised by physicians.

The Hussaini grape (named after a remote ancestor of the Afghan Sayeds of Paghman) has a thin skin, is slightly golden and not very sweet. Unfortunately it does not dry well, and people eat as many as they can in the fruiting months, so as to set themselves up for the Spring and Winter. It should be worth analysing this – as well as many other herbs, fruits and flowers of Afghanistan and the surrounding countries – to determine the efficacious content.

In Afghanistan a remedy formerly used in ancient Greece is believed to have considerable effects upon *Gout*. This is colchicum; it is also accepted today by some Western doctors.

Cystitis has been treated on numerous occasions with almost complete success, by an infusion of plantain leaves; though it is understood that this has not yet been verified elsewhere.

Hair Growth is stimulated by the application of a mixture of henna, willow, nettle, and parsley in equal quantities.

A mixture of the seeds of carrots, parsley and melons is used in the treatment of anaemia. This is taken twice a day, in a fairly strong decoction.

Chicory, especially the leaves eaten raw, seems to have a remarkable effect upon the eyesight in many conditions.

Onion seeds are eaten to treat *Piles*.

All kinds of *Sores, Eczema* and other skin complaints are treated with lemon rinds which have been bruised and are applied locally. I have seen conditions clear up which, according to their sufferers, have been raging for several years, in one case over a quarter of a century.

Weeping Skin responds to powdered liquorice, the root alone being used, dried, for this purpose.

Dysentry is treated with a paste made from the fruit of the prickly pear.

Fever is reduced by means of wild chamomile (*Matricaria recutita*). The leaves are made into a tea, which is administered as often as possible.

Coriander (*Gushniz*) and vervain, combined in a salad and eaten thrice a day, seem to prevent insect bites. This preparation is also prescribed for halitosis and for attenuating perspiration.

Colds and *Bronchitis* respond rapidly to violet petals, and a great quantity of this plant is grown for this purpose throughout the area and beyond.

The hollyhock is a remarkable treatment for all kinds of wounds. The mashed leaves are used as a poultice. Within a very few days, especially if the poultice is changed every two days, the wound will be found clean and cicatrised.

One *materia medica* in constant use among herbalists in the region lists no less than 658 herbs and spices, and delineates over 200 conditions said to respond to them.

Najib Siddiqi

NAMES: MR SIR KCMG

The Ambassador briefs me on how to be an
Afghan in England.

How different from the old days! Now, you can order Afghan food
in restaurants whose menus describe the dishes and enable tren-
dies to swot up the ingredients and instruct their captive guests.
You can buy those delicious green, translucent sultanas from
Kandahar, and even pine kernels, in London, without being
thought insane for asking for them.

People who used to gag on our green tea now gulp it delightedly:
the right magazines have assured them of its palatability, even its
health-giving qualities.

When, once, only liverish ex-colonels seemed to know (roughly)
where Afghanistan was, the papers now print maps of it – with,
wonder of wonders, my ancestral Paghman mountains and valleys
actually featured.

Featured, of course, because Paghman figures in one hard-
fought battle after another. Neither the Russians nor our own
people have forgotten the saying, 'Who holds Paghman holds
Afghanistan'.

Listening, on a train journey, to an intense Englishman boring a
lady with a learned (that is, fairly tortuous) exposition of the way to
cook Afghan fat-tailed sheep, I had mixed feelings. The old days,
before Christmas 1979, were somehow much more entertaining:
they had more interest, perhaps because facts were scarce.

Nowadays the once-common English rush of words, 'Afghanistan? Yes, your *dear* little Emperor and those beastly Italians . . .'
is never heard. In fact, people are now doing the same sort of thing
to the English.

Today there is a letter to the Editor of *The Times* in which Mr

128

Foley records that an Ecuadorean official said, after looking at his diplomatic pass, 'Ah, British Embassy. That's Germany, isn't it?'

In those other days, which now seem so far away, I was sitting in the study of our own Ambassador at 31 Princes Gate, sipping cardamom-scented tea, as he briefed me on English native customs. 'First,' he said, 'you will have to get used to the fact that these Franks will butcher your name, and disgrace you with their Misters.'

His Excellency Sardar Faiz-Mohammed Khan, Zikria, in the Afghan way, was probably not really talking to me; after all, I already knew quite a lot about the English. It is customary with us, especially after a meal, to address all present on some subject which is in one's heart, or which is to be directed at someone else in the company.

With us were two Kabul merchants, and it was their first time in England. To have emphasised *their* newness to the country would have been a discourtesy.

'Their Misters, Mr Ambassador?'

'Their Misters. In Afghanistan, as in other countries, everyone is Mister as an honorific. Thus we have "Mr Sardar, Mr Prince", as, indeed, you have "Herr Baron" or "Monsieur le Prince", in Europe. But, in England, "Mr Prince" means that the fellow is not a prince at all, but a mere commoner. Similarly with "Mr Lord", "Mr Duke", "Mr Baron". All commoners.'

The traders were looking at one another incredulously. They had heard of the mysterious West, but this was really remarkable. Downgrading a man by adding an honorific to his name? Amazing.

'Even,' the Ambassador continued, 'even the Americans do it. Over there, "Mr Ambassador" is polite. Here, "Mr Ambassador" would mean that the fellow's name is perhaps "George Ambassador".'

He looked triumphantly around the room. 'But why do they do it, your Excellency?' asked the bravest businessman.

'*Why* is not under discussion. We are dealing with "whats" and not "whys",' the Sardar said. He had been Afghan Foreign Minister, accustomed to diplomatic fine-tuned thought and speech, and was a redoubtable theologian as well.

The Kabuli subsided with a hasty apology and the Envoy continued:

'Now, our own names are perfectly simple. "Sardar" is my title;

but "Mr Sardar" would be the name of a Pakistani grocer, because on the Indian subcontinent they use our titles as their family names.' He looked in my direction. 'They would even call you "Mister Shah".'

'I recently had a letter from an official here which called me "Mr Sardar". I addressed my reply to "Mr Bart" (he is a baronet). What happened? Instead of taking the hint, he had his secretary ring up mine and point out *my* "solecism".'

'But, Excellency,' I said, 'how are they to know how to style us, unless we tell them?'

The Ambassador shrugged. 'That is just the point. They do not know – or, rather, most of them do not. But, among us it is a solecism to tell people: so we are stuck.'

'I can hardly believe that the ornament of the Royal Court of the God-Given Kingdom, steeped in the arts of diplomacy as well as the ranks and precedences of the elite, that is to say your Presence, would be at a loss in dealing with the Franks within their own canons of etiquette,' I hazarded.

'Yes, well, I did ask the Second Secretary, as a matter of courtesy, to reply,' said the Ambassador. He waited three beats for us to chorus, 'Naturally, Mr Ambassador'.

'Our reply said, simply His Excellency the Sardar Faiz-Mohammed Khan, Zikria's correct name and title must, as you will know, be correctly rendered in official correspondence. To do otherwise is tantamount to offering a slight to the Afghan Royal Court, whose representative he is.

'"It has come to my attention that a certain official in this country has either chosen to ignore this necessity, or else has been imperfectly instructed in protocol.

'"In these circumstances, rather than let the matter go forward to my superior, the First Secretary (and thence, perhaps, even higher) I am taking this opportunity of asking you, informally, as to the appropriate course to take should this abuse be persisted in.

'"I have the honour, dear Madam, to profess myself your most obedient Servant, – signed – Second Secretary to the Mission of the King of Afghanistan at the Court of St. James's."'

The Kabul traders looked stunned, searched my face and then, reassured, murmured their admiration.

'Excellent, Excellency!' I exclaimed.

Having absorbed this valuable lesson, I related the tale at a dinner party given by the head of a department of the Foreign Office. He thanked me for the advice, saying that his office (I'll not identify it) was especially interested in correct styles and titles.

We had a useful talk about other matters, too; and the Under-Secretary promised to write to me with some information I had requested.

His letter arrived two days later. It was addressed 'The Sayed Idries, Shah: Dear Mr Shah . . .'

I looked at the carbon copy of a letter which I had written to him earlier. No, I hadn't addressed him as 'Sir Bart'; so he wasn't trying to get his own back. I dictated, to a rather bemused stenographer, 'Dear Mr Sir KCMG . . .'

I am sure that he then dined out on how hilariously ignorant those Afghans were.

Darned clever, these British.

Idries Shah

BECOME AN INSTANT CARPET EXPERT

You can't become a rug or carpet expert in just a few minutes: that's the bad news. But, if you absorb a few facts, act in a certain way, and adopt a particular attitude – you can fool even carpet merchants. How do I know? I've pulled it off with several volunteers: and without any failures.

First of all, note that rug-lore needs aplomb. No carpet man (or woman) behaves tentatively, shows indecision, is fooled by the pretensions – or intimidated by the expertise – of anyone. This is your first lesson: study attitude and posture.

Be warned, however, that phoneys always overdo things. You are not a phoney, so adopt a cool, dignified and firm approach.

The world is full of know-alls, who will tell you all about carpets, providing that they think you are not an expert. Make sure that you get the message across that you know a thing or two, before they go into their act.

Next, get hold of a number of books on Afghan rugs – or books on oriental carpets which feature Afghans. Look at the pictures. At first, do not read the text, beyond the names of the rugs. You are absorbing the basics at this point. You may, later, find that books disagree in meanings of designs, in traditions, in all sorts of things. The absolute beginner must never be exposed to such confusion.

Note the colours and patterns, as well as the designs.

Next see what the books say about how to tell an Afghan from a Persian (Iranian) or a Turkish or a Pakistani copy. Make a list, such as 'Afghans usually deep red ground, feature octagons, thicker, materials of warp and weft . . .' and so on.

You are nearly ready to visit a rug-dealer. Before you do that, though, you have to learn the little things that dealers say to surprise you; not because the information is going to be of much use, but because experts are never to be surprised, and you are on the way to becoming one.

These facts include: Bokhara rugs were never made in Bokhara. They are Afghans, usually; and Bokhara was the place where the dealers went to buy them. 'Golden' Afghans are usually washed (that is, bleached). The octagon, or medallion, is called a *Filpai*; which means Elephant's Foot, and is pronounced 'Feel-poy'. Romanian and Pakistani imitations are common, in every sense. There is no such thing as a 'Pakistan Bokhara'. This is the name given to a rug made in Pakistan, on the pattern of those formerly sold in Bokhara. Many, perhaps most, of the articles sold as prayer rugs are not such at all.

Traders love to produce a rug and say, 'This is a ROYAL Bokhara'. There is no such thing. The answer to that is 'Only in the sense that people call an Afghan rug of really high quality "a royal Bokhara", right?'

A regrettably large number of carpet dealers run a very close second to horse-traders. Therefore, on your first few forays, you must be quite sure not to buy anything at all. The trader tries everything, including attempting to make you feel guilty or under an obligation. He offers you tea or coffee; he implies that you can't afford anything; he pulls down dozens of rugs until you feel that it'll take him all night to get them back into order. Resist these and other ploys. Genuine fellow-dealers (who are an important proportion of his customers, so he won't mind if you are one) gulp the tea and ask for more, claim that they haven't got a penny, and get him to pull down ever-larger piles of rugs. Then, as often as not, they buy nothing on the first visit (or first few visits). In a word, behave like an ordinary customer, and he'll know you're not rug-wise.

On the dry runs, you will not only be looking like an expert, you'll be learning from the dealer. Look at the way he turns the carpets over, how he looks at the underside, the movements he makes as he appraises them. Then go home and practice with your own rugs, in front of a mirror.

There is an interesting sociological (or perhaps anthropological) upshot of the compulsion to sell and to manipulate so often found among dealers. The result of their wholehearted devotion to their art is that relatively few ordinary citizens, whether in Britain or elsewhere, dare even to enter their shops. This means that they sell to one another. Therefore, if you come across as a fellow-expert, you are also more likely to be someone he can sell to. On your behalf I have recently been checking out this fact; and that's what dealers tell me.

Then, you may ask, who *are* the people who are to be seen in carpet shops? The dealers say that they are usually time-wasters, people who have come in out of the rain, or people with the psychological need to prove to themselves that nobody can sell them anything.

When the dealer says, 'How much do you want to spend?' the answer is never in words. All you need to do, if you want to make an impression, is to spread your arms wide, palms upwards, raising them the while. Puckering up the face is optional.

When he says, 'Now this is a most beautiful piece,' you always reply, 'Yes, indeed. Just put it on one side and we'll come back to it later. Show me the top and the bottom of your range, and a few in-betweens, and we'll see if we can do business.'

When he says, 'Rugs are an appreciating asset, they are labour-intensive. Do you know how many man-hours went into this one?' You say, 'WOMAN-hours, you mean. And I'm not looking for assets. I might be wanting to turn over a little capital, as it were . . .'

That is, in the West. In the East, when you are told, 'Rugs are a lifetime investment,' you say, 'Ah, but what is life? As the poet says, "A shout upon the wind am I . . .".' You get the idea.

And never buy a rug from someone who is making a great sacrifice, who is a fleeing nobleman, who wants to do you a favour, and so on. More often than not, they are found easily enough – at your front door. They also generally have a stack of the same kind of stuff in the Land Rover they've parked around the corner.

When you have seen enough rugs (don't forget museums and exhibitions) and heard enough prices, you'll notice one thing. Some traders are actually selling the things at reasonable prices. Not always, but often.

But, I hear you cry, how can this be, after you've run them down like that?

I haven't run them down: it's your imagination working too defensively with my words. It's just that there is this compulsion to sell and this traditional attempt to shift a rug at a great profit. It's like an art-form; the equivalent of the need among Eastern shop-keepers to bargain or else they feel terrible.

And why the reasonable prices? Firstly, because though the dealer may be a bit of an operator, he is still a human being. If, for instance, he has recently made a good sale, he will not want to twist all comers – rather to the contrary. Again, he has to eat as well as you. If he's dealt with too many time-wasters and dealers that day, he'll simmer down and think of the rent, the phone bill or the wife, or all three. That is the moment to strike.

And, final sobering thought: many rugs are cheaper in England than they are in the East. This is because of the self-same over-heads that I've just told you about. Like it or not, the dealer has to sell to live and especially to keep up with the Joneses. To illustrate the difference:

I went into a carpet-seller's shop in a Middle Eastern town. The prices were ridiculously high, and I told the proprietor so. He said, 'Yes, I know, but, sooner or later, some tourist will buy every single one of these rugs, and at my prices.'

I said, 'You'll have to wait a long time. If your prices were lower, you'd shift lots of rugs. Turnover, you know.'

'That may well be,' he said, 'but I've worked it out during the twenty years I've been here. If I just hang on, I make more money from tourists. And, remember, there's the annoyance of having to make trips to stock up again . . .'

As a bonus, I'll just warn you against throwing words and phrases about, even if you get them from an apparently reputable source. I recently saw a woman being greatly impressed (she was giving little cries of delight, anyway) by a salesman who was assuring her that a rug was a real *Pumba-pashmina*. I speak the language and she didn't, so I knew that it meant a 'real wool-cotton' rug.

In Bond Street I once saw a hideously overpriced and sadly poor floor-covering mounted in a frame and labelled 'Guaranteed Kha-lis Baftagi'. *Khalis baftagi* in Persian means 'entirely woven'. Still, by the same token, I dare say that you could impress people in the

East by telling them that you were a Prime Con-Artist. It would sound quite up-market there.

Selima Isfandiari

THE HAND IN THE RIVER

Sultan Mubarak Shah, son of Sayed Khidr Khan, King of Delhi in the fifteenth century, was known for his problem-solving wisdom. According to the annals of our family (King Mubarak was a member of our House) one of his successes was solving the Mystery of the Hand in the River: though some say that the case took place many centuries before, and was solved by a remote ancestor of his, the Caliph of Islam, Al-Mustasim.

One day a fisherman, pulling in his net from the river, found an embroidered bag in it, weighted with bricks. In the bag was – a human hand. On the fingers were rings set with precious stones. The hand, which had not been long in the water, was dyed with henna.

The frightened fisherman reported the matter to the police, who were unable to solve the case, and sent an account of it to the Governor, who mentioned it to the King.

Mubarak Shah was perturbed at such an outrage, and decided to bring his detective skills to bear.

He had the hand put in some preservative material, after removing the rings, which a jeweller testified were not of local make. Then, taking the bag, he visited shop after shop in the city, in disguise, asking for who might sell a similar article.

Finally he found the bag-maker, who, after much indirect and inconsequential talk, mentioned that he usually sold this kind of item to perfume-makers. The King now made a tour of all the perfumeries of Delhi, until he located the one who had bought this particular bag, which the merchant recognised by a mark which he had placed upon it.

Now the Sultan-detective asked who had bought the bag. 'I remember him well;' said the perfumer, 'he is one of my best customers, a grandee of the Family of Hashim who lives in this city.' Sure enough, in his sales book the perfumer had kept a note of the date and buyer.

The King was dismayed: a Hashimite – one of his own relations! After further enquiries it emerged that this man had a reputation for drinking and entertaining dancing-girls at his home. Although advised by his Minister to hush the matter up, Mubarak Shah proceeded with his enquiries.

The King, again in disguise, now spoke to the servants in the Hashimite's house, discovering that the relatives of a certain beautiful girl dancer had called, asking for her. The master had said that she had indeed been there, but had left, saying that she wanted to travel to another city to seek her fortune.

The King went from one house and shop, from one inn and mosque to another, asking who might know about a dancer who had disappeared.

Eventually he came upon a woman, who had long sought her missing daughter. Taking her to the Palace, the King produced the hand and the rings, which the lady, bursting into tears, immediately identified as those of the girl.

Now Mubarak Shah ordered his kinsman to come before him, sending a body of guards, who found him drunk and in the company of revellers.

Confronted by the evidence, the man confessed that he had killed her in a fit of rage when she refused to yield to him; and revealed where the rest of the body was buried, in a disused well on his property.

'Murderer of the innocent!' roared the King. 'The distress of this family and the shame on our House merits only the extreme penalty!'

The man pleaded, 'Lord of the Earth! I am of your own flesh and blood, of the People of the House: and this woman was but a dancing-girl . . .'

The King became so furious that he ordered the murderer to be locked in a dungeon until his temper cooled. In the morning, sending for the miscreant, Mubarak Shah said, 'All your property and goods, large and extensive as they are, are forfeit as compensation for this unhappy, violated family. As for our own dishonour, we can only hope for their forgiveness.'

The murderer was then taken, at the command of the royal detective, back to his own house, where he was hanged.

A WEIRDLY BEAUTIFUL ORIENTAL TUNE

The Amir of Afghanistan, on his visit to India in February 1907, was due to attend a Court held in his honour. British bands were to play the Afghan National Anthem.

General Kitchener, Commander in Chief, was told that nobody could discover what the tune was, and the military bandmasters were much distressed.

The military mind of the General, accustomed to making rapid decisions, produced this order: 'Play two or three bars of something heavy, pompous and slow, and let it go at that'.

A march, from one of the older German operas, was therefore chosen and played upon the entry of the Afghan monarch, and also whenever he appeared on his tour of important Indian cities.

'This was played with such success,' reported the *New York Times (June 7, 1916)* 'that the newspapers of Bombay, Madras and other cities visited by the Ameer printed columns about the "weirdly beautiful strains of the Afghan National Anthem".'

The official diary kept by the Afghan side notes: 'The English Franks are addicted to a certain tune, which is played on the slightest pretext, by musicians who have adopted the style and manner of the ancient Turkish military bands. The sound resembles the shrieking of she-camels. They constantly enquire whether it pleases us, soliciting approval.'

GOAT-PULLING: THE WILDEST GAME ON EARTH

People, even if they have heard of Buzkashi, often simply cannot believe it when it happens. Happening, too, is what it looks like: though the horses are trained to the highest pitch, the men aware of the finest nuances of the game. Buzkashi – Pulling the Goat – has defied short description for centuries.

English people, in their writing, seldom are incoherent; though they sometimes find that they can go no further than the pale simile of 'Rugger on Horseback'. One Englishman, after seeing Buzkashi played in the presence of King Nadir Shah (1929-1933) was properly stiff upper-lipped in the measured tones of his report:

> 'I had often gone to polo matches . . . None of the picturesque formalities of a polo-match precede the Afghan game, which in its speed and roughness makes polo like vicarage garden party tennis.'

He is guilty of very little exaggeration. With a valley, two to four miles long, for a playing field, with as many as a couple of hundred riders a side, beneath the frowning mountains, each man and every horse a seasoned veteran, Buzkashi – as all who have seen it agree – must be the wildest game on earth.

There are not two goals, but one. The carcass of a calf (the 'goat': it never, nowadays at any rate, is a goat) has to be placed back at the spot from which it was first lifted: after it has been carried round the poles at the far end of the field.

Bringing the 'ball' back in this way is a goal. The scorer is a hero, the *Qahraman*, the Champion.

141

Sometimes the game is so fiercely fought that no single goal is scored.

The starting point is a shallow pit, in which the carcass of a calf is laid. The head has been severed close to the neck, the limbs are cut off from where they join the trunk. It often weighs no less than six Afghan *seers*, about 110 lbs.

Around this pit the rival teams arrange their horsemen. At Begram, north of Kabul, there are usually only fifteen to twenty to each team; with as many as three teams competing at the same time.

On the far side of the field, some 1,500 metres away, there are three flagpoles. At a given signal, all the players try to get hold of the calf; one manages to seize it, and gallops full pelt towards the poles, to circle them and return, to complete his run.

Now, of course, everyone else follows in the wildest imaginable pursuit. Anyone who can seize the 'ball' may take his turn.

Nobody, no horse, not at the very highest pitch of physical fitness and training stands the slightest chance. This is no game played for its own sake: unless of winning quality, man or mount is likely to get nowhere at all.

Whoever holds the carcass is set upon by a mass of players: the ball passes from hand to hand: again and again a sort of scrum takes place.

Every now and them someone gets the greased body and breaks away in a hectic gallop, holding the slippery thing, as other riders hinder the pursuit, while some break through the defence line and lash out with weighted whips; not at the animals, however: anyone striking a horse is disqualified by the many roving umpires:

'It was a thrilling enough start, for the Afghan sits on a horse as riders in a horse show aspire to do. I have seen them drop down embankments that a newsreel would come a hundred miles to see them negotiate, and climb another steep slope like a mountain goat, all with the indifference of a debutante and her groom in Rotten Row.'

As the Englishman remarks, even the playing field can be the roughest of mountain terrain.

There are innumerable, carefully practised techniques in this game. Two kinds of horses take part: the heavyweights have to

bore into the other animals, rising on their hind legs in a scrum so
that the rider may grab the prize and throw it to the fleeter
mounted – the 'forwards'. They, in turn, have been marked by the
opposition, who hover, waiting to intercept the throw.

After each interception, a scrum starts again, with the heavies
coming in once more to do their part.

The horses, most of them from the wild North, cost a king's
ransom. As often as not they belong to wealthy landlords or chiefs,
the Bais, who may employ their own retainers as the players, or
even play themselves.

Extraordinary, unbelievable scenes can take place. Men are
wounded, stunned, unhorsed. The 'ball' may break in two, and the
umpires called in to judge as to which is the real one. The enormous crowds may be ploughed into by the onrush of as many as two
hundred steeds, with the fierce horsemen shouting, flailing, dedi-
cated unlike men I have ever seen elsewhere:

'One horseman, thrown from his mount, lay stunned. The am-
bulance surgeon followed by two stretcher-bearers rushed onto
the field to him. The goat had been dropped not twenty yards
away, and the rest of the horsemen were crowding after it, as
medical aid reached the fallen player. He was laid upon the
stretcher. As it was lifted he sat upright, realised he was no
longer on his horse, leaped off the stretcher, snatched a riderless
horse, mounted it, and was back in the mob, while the agents of
mercy, bewildered, ran for their lives with the pack bearing
down on them.'

Nobody knows with certainty the origin of this terrible, beautiful,
more-than-stunning event. Some say that it was developed by the
horsemen of Ghenghiz Khan, in the thirteenth century, as a training method for the Mongol hordes. But legend claims that it is far
older than that.

When Afghanistan was called Aryana, said to be as long ago as
4000 BC, the horsemen of these parts were so important that
several of the most ancient royal families added *Aspa* – horse – to
their names: and carried on the game.

The legend is that the Aryana people migrated Westwards and
to the South. These may have been the Scythians and the Sakas in
the one directions, and the Aryas, later the Hindus, in the other. In

143

India, thousands of years after the Aryas are claimed to have settled the country, the same word – *Juhr* – is used for a shallow pit as is for the Afghan 'goal' in the far-off mountains of northern Aryana today.

Though Buzkashi means 'Pulling the Goat', the carcass is always that of a calf, which is more robust, has a thicker skin. The exchange must have taken place at some time out of memory.

The Northern teams most often win, with enormous prizes offered by local magnates, to attract the most famous names. Yet Buzkashi is democratic, too. This mixture of horse-racing, war and polo, with rugby football and gymnastics thrown in, can make an unknown newcomer a national hero and the local equivalent of a millionaire – in a single two-hour game.

An American once turned to me, after what seemed to veterans to be no more than an average day's play, and said, 'I've travelled the world to see the greatest thrills there are. But, after today, I'll never be the same again!'

ISTALIF THE BEAUTIFUL

Because of the unbelievable profusion of
grapes, and the long Greek cultural period,
some have found in the place-name Istalif, the
Afghan pronunciation of the Persian-Hellenic
word for grape: Istafil.

After the turmoil of eating dinners and receiving visitors had been
got over, and our business put in train, we all of us determined to
visit the far-famed mountain skirts of Koh-i-Daman and Kohistan,
which are situated north of Kabul.

The Amir very readily granted us permission to do so, and
appointed an individual of influence to conduct and protect us:
several parts of the neighbourhood, particularly north of the Ghorband River, or what is called Kohistan proper, having only of late
been brought under subjection.

We set out from Kabul on the morning of the 13th of October,
and halted at Karez-i-Mir, about fifteen miles from which we could
see, in the hazy distance, a vast vista of gardens extending for some
thirty or forty miles in length, and half as broad, terminated by the
Hindu Kush itself, white as snow.

Next day we reached Shakardara, where there is a royal garden,
but which is now in a state of decay. Our next march was to
Kahdara, and thence to Istalif, the great point of attraction.

No written description can do justice to this lovely and delightful
country. Throughout the whole of our route we had been lingering
amidst beautiful orchards, the banks of which were clustered over
with wild flowers and plants, many of them common to Europe,
and which were also in profuse abundance along the margins of the
innumerable brooks which intersect the valleys.

The roads were shaded by noble and lofty walnut trees, which excluded the sun's rays, never powerless in this climate. Every hill with a southern aspect had a vineyard on it, and the raisins were spread out on the ground, and imparted a purple tinge to the hills. There were very few songsters, however, to enliven the scene, most of the feathered tribe having flown to a warmer climate.

The coldness of the air, which had driven them away, was to us bracing and delightful, and only served to increase our enjoyment. I must not, however, speak in detail of this charming country, nor do the far-famed gardens of Istalif require any aid from me to establish their supremacy.

We pitched our camp on one side of the valley, and directly opposite to us, at a distance of about a thousand yards, rose the town of Istalif in the form of a pyramid, terrace on terrace, the whole crowned with a shrine embosomed among wide-spreading plane-trees.

Between us lay a deep and narrow valley, at the bottom of which was a clear, rapid and musically-sounding brook, on both sides of which the valley was covered with the richest orchards and vineyards.

Looking down this stream, the dell gradually opens out, and presents to the eye a vast plain, rich in trees and verdure and dotted over with innumerable turreted forts: beyond all this, rocky mountains are seen with the fresh snow of yesterday upon them; and over these again tower the eternal snow-clad summits of the Hindu Kush.

The scene was as sublimely grand as it was beautiful and enchanting. The yellow autumnal leaves rustled in the breeze, and the crystal waters rushed in their rapid course over craggy rocks with a noise which reached the summit of the valley. Thessalian Tempe could never have more delighted the eyes of an Ionian, than did Istalif please Boetian Britons.

The people illuminated their town in the evening, in honour of their visitors. It had a pretty effect, but the beauties of art could not in our opinion compete with those of nature.

Not so with our escort; they declared that Istalif had at all times been the abode of pleasure and that, without wine, not only would the illumination lose its value, but Nature herself would be worth nothing.

We accordingly sent a few bottles of wine, to which they did the

146

amplest justice, although the *Muhtasib*, a chief constable of Kabul, was of the party.

On the following day I taxed him with this departure from the rules of his sect. He bore my bantering with great equanimity, and replied with mock heroic dignity, 'Who, my lord, suspects me – me, the Muhtasib – of indulging in wine? My duty is to reform the morals of others.'

An English traveller

PART FOUR

HEARD IN THE
TEAHOUSE...

It might not be true to say that one can get a
complete education in the Afghan tea-house:
but there are not many places left with such a
repertoire of stories.

GENEROSITY OF SPIRIT

A merchant of Kandahar used to import goods from India, to the south, and trade them with a Herat trader who specialised in things from Iran in the west. The two men were fast friends, though they had never met; carrying on their transactions by correspondence and caravan.

The Kandahar man decided to visit his friend in Herat, and made the journey: being received with delight and hospitality, the two cementing their social and commercial ties even further.

After a few days in Herat, the visitor glimpsed a veiled but enchanting figure in the street, and instantly fell hopelessly in love with her. He confided this passion to his friend; saying that he 'must marry her or die!' The Herati made enquiries and said:

'Never let it be said that anything can dissolve the bonds of friendship or the generosity of a man of Herat! I shall discover whether the lady returns your feelings. If she does, I shall make all the necessary arrangements for your wedding.'

He did not tell his friend that the woman was the one to whom he was himself engaged to be married. And, the lady consenting, the marriage was effected.

The couple returned to Kandahar and, some months later, the man of Herat, through a commercial calamity, lost all his money. Literally begging from door to door and caravan to caravan, he made his way to Kandahar, hoping that his friend might help him in his misery and deprivation.

When, however, he arrived at the door of the Kandahar merchant, he saw that he was being taken away in chains. 'This man is a suspected murderer,' the police told him.

The Herat man, having nothing to offer but his life to aid his friend, called out, 'Take me instead! For it is I, not this man, who committed the crime!'

So he was thrown into a dungeon.

The Kandahar man, released, stood, day after day, outside the jail and – though he was innocent – constantly claimed that it was he who had done the murder.

When the case was heard, however, the Kandahar man was treated as a madman, and the merchant of Herat was sentenced to death by hanging.

The time for the public execution came and, as the condemned man was being taken to the scaffold, the real murderer was present. He saw an innocent man about to be killed, and his friend, also innocent, trying to offer his life in exchange.

The true murderer leapt forward, crying:

'I am a man of Mazar! If a Herati and a Kandahari can show generosity, so can I! I am the real culprit: hang me!'

The judge supervising the execution ordered that the three men, each clamouring to be hanged, should be taken to the court of Shah Shujah.

The King, receiving each in private audience, and applying the ultimate oath upon them, discovered the truth.

He then ordered the heralds to tell the story to the people, to test their reaction. Immediately the relatives of the murdered man petitioned for clemency for the killer. They were from the city of Jalalabad, and jealous of their honour. 'We shall not be outdone in generosity, either!' they cried in unison.

So Shah Shuja pardoned the murderer and gave rich presents to the man of Herat, who fell in love again and married; the murderer reformed, the Kandahari merchant flourished more than ever, with many beautiful children – and everyone lived happily ever after.

IMPOSSIBLE

In Afghanistan, as in many other Eastern lands, it was customary for the King to set challenges for the people, which were taken up in open *darbar*.

One day King Abdur-Rahman announced that he would give a

hundred silver pieces to anyone who could make him say the word 'impossible'.

When the day of the contest arrived, and everyone was assembled at Court, a rascal stepped forward and said, impudently, 'You are descended from a bandit!' He knew that, on competition days, anything could be said without penalty.

The King hesitated, and his brow grew dark. Then he remembered himself, and said, 'That is possible, for it all depends upon what you mean by a bandit.'

Then a philosopher rose and said, 'The world does not exist!'

'Quite possibly it is all an illusion,' said the King. 'Though if you believe that, I wonder why you are competing for material things like silver coins.' A wandering dervish strode in and shouted, 'Kings are useless and should be abolished!'

'That is also quite possible', said the King; 'though I doubt whether there is much point in the argument.'

Finally, Mulla Nasrudin held up his hand. 'Your father,' he said, 'borrowed a hundred gold pieces from my father, and the date on which the loan must be returned to me is today.'

'That,' said the King, smiling, '*is* impossible! For your father, whom I remember well, was ragged and penniless like you. But you have won. You'd better have the hundred silver coins instead of the gold.'

FATE

The King of Bokhara, on his way back to his capital from a pilgrimage, was caught in a terrible storm in the mountains, and had to take refuge in the guest-room of a small village.

As he tossed and turned on the hard bed, he heard a voice saying, 'A child has been born in this village. It will not survive.'

Another voice now said, 'A child will live for some years, and will be killed by its father.'

Yet a third voice declared, 'A child will grow up, will kill the King of Bokhara, marry his daughter, and reign in his stead.'

In the morning the King had his attendants, who were camped all around, to search the village and bring him any child which had been born recently.

Most of the people there were old: and there was only one child, which had been born some weeks before.

The King had the family brought before him. 'You will give me this child,' he announced, 'and I will give you a thousand dinars. Unless you agree, I shall kill all three of you.'

The terrified parents agreed, and the King took the baby with him on his horse, until the cavalcade was crossing a bridge over a deep ravine.

Then he threw the child into the valley.

It so happened that a poor peasant woman was collecting sticks on the mountainside when she heard the baby's cries, found him and took him back to her hut. Another woman, who had a child of her own, suckled the baby, whom they called Saughat – the gift.

Saughat grew up a strong and handsome youth. He was apprenticed to a confectioner in the nearest town, and related the story of his strange appearance in the valley and his rescue, to all and sundry. The tale eventually arrived at the ears of the Bokharan King.

The King, under an assumed name, sent Saughat some poisoned preserved fruits. With them was a letter, asking him to prepare a similar confection, which should taste exactly similar to this sample.

Saughat was starting to taste the fruit when his master said, '*I* am the master-confectioner here! It is for me to taste and to prepare.' So saying, he took a spoonful and fell dead.

After a time, the King again heard that Saughat was still alive. Accompanied by his groom, a trained instant killer, he set off in disguise for the town where Saughat lived.

Putting up at the caravanserai, the King sent a message asking the youth to come to the stables urgently. 'As soon as anyone appears at the stables in the middle of the night, kill him,' he ordered the groom.

But, alas for his plans, the King heard a commotion among the horses and, thinking it meant the end of Saughat, ran out onto the dagger of his groom. The young man had ignored the message.

And this is the beginning of the story, to make you understand that things may happen, and may not happen; and you will have to know a lot before you can trust prophecy.

In the meantime, you can practise, yourself, storytelling by adding to our tale how it was that the confectioner's assistant eventually married the King of Bokhara's daughter and took his place on the throne.

TWELVE WORDS OF WISDOM

A man named Dehkan, from the wilds of Badakhshan, realised that he could only scrape a bare living in his home territory: collecting pine-kernel nuts and selling dried white mulberries for flour to his neighbours.

He decided to journey to the city of Khanabad, in Afghan Turkestan, to find work. 'I shall labour for some years at whatever I can,' he told himself, 'and then I will be able to return home, perhaps with wisdom, to end my days in peace and contentment.'

In Khanabad, having crossed mountains and deserts and after plodding through deep forests, Dehkan went from one job to another, living frugally and saving every penny he could towards the realisation of his ambition.

Throughout his working career, Dehkan remained a simple soul. When many years had passed, and he was on his way home-wards with three hundred silver pieces, he was attracted by the serene manner of a wizened sage whom he saw sitting at the wayside.

'Give me some wisdom, for I would like to learn,' he asked the sage, bowing with appropriate humility.

'Five words of wisdom for one hundred silver pieces,' said the sage.

Dehkan handed over the money, and the man said:

'A boulder is not safe. Now be on your way!'

Dehkan continued along the road, trying to ponder the meaning of the words of wisdom. After some days he came upon a second sage, sitting by the wayside.

'Wisdom for sale,' said the sage. 'Only a hundred silver pieces for four priceless words.'

Dehkan paid the money and the sage said:

'A bridge is safe. Now go on your way'.

Dehkan went on his way, thinking over the words.

Some days later, Dehkan joined some other travellers, journey-ing in the same direction: merchants heading for Wakhan and the ancient Silk Route to China. They were plodding along by a stream when they saw a third sage.

'I am going to buy some wisdom,' said Dehkan, taking out his last hundred coins.

Now, during the journey, Dehkan had told his companions about the first two sages and their advice, and he had come in for a great deal of derision. 'After all your sufferings, after a lifetime's work and saving, you want to give it all away to an old fool who is not wise except in the ways of charming money out of people!' shouted the other travellers.

But Dehkan, taking no notice, approached the Third Sage and, holding out his money, asked for wisdom.

'That will rate three words,' said the sage, putting the money away. 'Climb a tree. Now be on your way.'

His fellows mocked him even more when Dehkan repeated the phrase. 'Twelve words for three hundred silver pieces! Why, we'd give you a thousand words for even one. But you haven't got even one left, have you?' they jeered.

Presently, the party, hungry and thirsty, espied a beautiful teahouse nestling in the shade of an immense boulder. 'Let's stop and rest here,' they cried.

'This may be the dangerous boulder,' Dehkan told them: but the others scoffed. 'That boulder has been here for a thousand years. Come on, let's get some tea.'

But, if the boulder had indeed been there so long, it was at last starting to move. It rolled and crushed the teahouse, and with it half of Dehkan's companions.

Rather shaken, the company started off when they had buried their dead. They forded rivers and climbed mountains, and made steady progress; and soon their sprits were quite restored. It was then that they came to a rope bridge over a yawning chasm. It looked terrifyingly frail. They were all hesitating, though Dehkan said, '*A bridge is safe*! That is what the second Sage said. Let us be on our way.'

He crossed safely, and was on the other side when he saw that his companions had been ambushed by fierce and heavily-armed bandits. There was nothing he could do as he saw the others led away, roped together; so Dehkan continued towards Badakhshan, just as poor as his merchant companions but – as he reflected – at least he was free.

When, finally, Dehkan limped towards the outskirts of his home village, he saw that a pride of lions was attacking the terrified villagers. They were dragging them out of the houses and bearing them away. Lions cannot climb trees, and there was a reason why none of the villagers had done so to escape the lions. The large number of trees in that district, from time immemorial, had been considered sacred. To climb one would mean sacrilege.

But, just in time, the advice of the Third Sage came into Dehkan's mind: *'Three Words – Climb a Tree!'*

In a moment, Dehkan was in the upper branches of a tall tree. He stayed there until the lions went away. While he was in the tree, however, he found, tied to the inner side of three branches, three large clay pots. Each one of them contained a hundred gold pieces.

When Dehkan went to sell his coins he was amazed to see something familiar about the goldsmith. In some strange way, his face was the same as the faces of each of the three wise men.

REPENTANCE

In Jalalabad city, in our southland towards the Pakistan border, there is an ancient saying, 'As repentant as Zabardast': and this is the story on which the comparison is based.

Zabardast was commander of the garrison, a swashbuckling oppressor who went about saying whatever he liked, doing whatever he wished, and taking whatever he wanted.

The Afghans are fond of keeping pigeons as pets, and Zabardast was no exception. Strolling in the market one day, he saw a small boy with three tame pigeons and asked their price.

'They're mine. I don't want to sell them,' said the boy, whose name was Intikam.

'If you were offered one golden *ashrafi* for each, would you sell them then?'

Intikam's father did not earn as much as that in a year, and he could easily get some more pigeons, he thought.

'Yes, I'd sell them for that.'

'Follow me home then, Boy, with the birds.'

Zabardast continued his walk, with the boy following behind. Eventually they arrived at the great house where the commander had his headquarters. Zabardast took the birds from Intikam and stepped inside. When the boy tried to follow, he was stopped by the doorkeeper.

Intikam had been robbed. Try as he might, nobody would take any notice of him. The doorkeeper kept him out; then the soldiers on guard drove him away; and even the local magistrate nervously advised him not to press his case.

Intikam watched the house, and followed Zabardast whenever he left the house for a walk. After some days he had a plan. There was a well which Zabardast often visited, to admire the young women who went there every day to draw water, and the lad disguised himself as a girl and waited there.

When the soldier swaggered up, the lad, with a veil drawn across his face, began to shout and wail:

'I have dropped my family's priceless water-vessel, chased in gold and silver, into the depths! Now I shall be beaten! Can nobody help me?'

Zabardast, hoping for some advantage, advanced, saying 'I, the great Zabardast, shall reach in and get it for you, fair damsel.'

'It's caught on a ledge not far below the surface,' panted Intikam, 'just stand there and lean forward a little, and your arm will reach it. Such a manly arm . . .' he giggled.

Bit by bit, praising and exhorting the villain, Intikam got him to assume such a posture that a slight push made him unbalanced, and he toppled in.

Intikam was not a Pashtun, and a frontier one at that, for nothing. To such people, the desire for vengeance is equalled only by their admiration of generosity. 'Curses upon you, Zabardast Khan!' he called down the well; 'I am Intikam, whose pigeons you stole last week!'

There was now such a howling and roaring from the furious Zabardast that the women drawing water fled in alarm: for he was promising to kill every human being he met for the next ten days after he was rescued.

Zabardast stayed in the well for hours, until word of his whereabouts and situation reached the garrison, who sent a party of men to rescue him.

Back in his house, Zabardast was in a terrible state. He was not only bruised and battered and half-drowned, but he was raving like a madman, unable to control himself.

Convinced that he had caught some terrible and intractable

disease in the well, and that it was haunted by demons, Zabardast devoured any pill or potion he could obtain, and called in doctors from far and wide: but these only made him feel much worse.

This went on for some weeks. Then Intikam, disguised as a wandering physician, with a hunched back and a dragging leg, arrived at the door. He was immediately admitted: for maimed physicians are regarded as the best.

Shown into the commander's presence, Intikam asked him how many servants and attendants he had. Then he sent each one away on a pretext, to obtain some complicated preparation or product, towards the cure.

As soon as they were alone, the boy threw off his disguise and said:

'Know, O Zabardast, I am Intikam, whose pigeons you stole. Now, your ailment is partly due to your vanity and excitability. Say that you will pay me, and will also forgive me for pushing you into the well, and you will be restored to health!'

'Never!' screamed the villain. 'I'll curse you until the day I die.'

'If you are incapable of honesty and generosity of spirit,' Intikam told him, 'as a Pashtun it is my duty to dispose of you, as a stain upon our people.'

He drew a knife and stabbed the commander to death.

GOOD REASON

They tell of one of the Afghan kings of long ago who used to spend three days on affairs of State, then could not be found for another three days, then took up his duties again for a further three days, and so on, for many years.

Nobody dared to ask him the reason for his strange behaviour; though there were plenty of guesses. Some said that he was a pious recluse part of the time, others that he had some illicit activity, yet others that he was given to fits of madness . . .

Then came the invasion, as so often before, of the barbarians from the North. The King, his commanders and Court fled to the high mountains to carry on the struggle.

Conditions were very hard and the grandees, and even the warriors, unaccustomed to this life, often became disheartened and were only rallied by the King, who showed a remarkable resilience and flexibility.

When the enemy had been expelled, and the Court resumed its usual routine, the Prime Minister praised the King for the way in which he had adjusted to privations and thus kept up the spirits of the others.

'It was no hardship,' explained the King. 'Because for many years, when I was absent for almost half my time from Court, I was living the life of the ordinary people, full of poverty and problems. How, after all, can a king rule if he does not know the way of life of the majority of his subjects, through personal experience?'

TIME FOR THE FOX TO COME...

There are people who feel that ancient folktales and wisdom anecdotes are archaic curiosities, of no current applicability.

Yet, one day in an Afghan teahouse I heard a traditional tale, current in books during the Middle Ages, applied to modern conditions.

A story-teller was tackled by another man, who said: 'Times have changed. Things which were once forbidden are now permitted, and the other way about. This is, of course, progress; but it is hard to become accustomed to such an era. Do your tales help us? I don't think so.'

'They help you to the extent to which you can see their relevance to today,' answered the sage. He continued:

'There was once a man who was on a journey through wooded country. In a clearing he came upon a snake, which someone had tied up: he thought unfairly. So he untied it.

'No sooner had he done so, feeling a sense of merit, than the Snake wound itself around his body, and began to crush him. He cried out, "Why do you do this to me, your saviour?"

'The Snake replied, "It is my nature. Besides, *I* say that it is good for you!"

'The Man, who had felt that he had done the right thing, now saw its consequences, and called for help.

'At that moment a fox appeared, and asked what was happening. Each told his side of the story.

'The Fox said, "Let me adjudicate," and the two agreed.

'Then the Fox said, "I cannot form a judgment from mere hearsay. Let the Snake be tied up again, so that the evaluation may proceed from that point."

'The Man tied the Snake as he had been before.

'Now the Fox said to the Man, "Leave the Snake where it is; for, however good it may seem to change things without understanding the consequences, your lack of wisdom as distinct from emotion disbars you from having the right to interfere with existing conditions. Arrogating to yourself the role of action ahead of perception, using imagination instead of common sense, led you into mortal danger."

'So the Man on that journey is still alive, and the Snake safely under restraint.

'But for *us*, the Fox has not yet arrived.'

THE HERO AND THE MYSTERY QUEEN

Once upon a time there was a poor lad, with no inheritance, who decided to improve his lot in life. Taking up a stone from the road of his native land, to remind himself of it, he set off with a stout staff and a bow and arrows, for a land where, according to what he had heard, worth and work were both rewarded.

When he got there, he worked so hard and so well that, at an early age, he became Prime Minister to a powerful and ambitious King.

Spending a great deal of time with this monarch, the young Minister heard him repeat, again and again, the tale of the mysterious Queen who lived in an adjoining country.

'From the time I was your age,' said the King, 'I have deeply desired to win and to marry this amazing woman. There were, and still are, several advantages. First, she is beautiful; second, I could add her throne to mine; third, she never ages, and anyone who marries her remains at (or returns to) the prime of life; fourth, to win this lady, one has to overcome certain barriers and perhaps enchantments, whose surmounting proves that he is really worthy of being a king and, indeed, a knight.'

This caused the youthful Minister to develop a strong desire to try to marry the lady himself. He decided not to tell the King, however, for the old gentleman now wanted the Queen even more than when he had been young: not least for the rejuvenation which the legend promised. But the Minister had sworn an oath to serve the King for every day of his life . . .

When he realised that 'every day' did not include the nights, he set off on his quest.

Thus, one night, he found himself at the first of the three great obstacles placed by the lady in the way of any would-be suitor. It was a wide moat, illuminated by lamps. Beside it was a notice, which read:

'Know, those of you who would win the Queen of Earth and Skies! You must cross this moat without a boat and without swimming; without building a bridge, and without using magical arts.'

The young man tried to urge his horse into the water, but it took one look at the prospect and refused. He dismounted, tethered his mount and walked to the water's edge. When he poked his staff onto the shimmering surface he found, surprise of surprises, the rod struck upon hard crystal, just a palm's breadth below the surface. He was able to walk, almost dryshod, right up to a strip of land which surrounded the castle walls.

There another notice caught his eye. It said:

'Many have failed to cross the moat, and a few have got this far. But beware! You are surrounded by a thousand slashing swords! Whoever would win the Queen must show both bravery and cunning. Only such a man should win the fair one and share the responsibilities of the governance of the Realm.'

He looked, and saw row upon row of luminous scimitars, poised on swivels, ready to slash anyone if they were disturbed; and he could not see the mechanism by which they were activated.

The youth absent-mindedly reached into his pocket, and his hand found the stone. He threw it at one of the swords. Instead of the sound of stone on metal, he heard only a dull thud. The sword was in fact only made of wood: and the swivel failed to work.

Moving rapidly through the forest of false swords, the young Minister froze in terror as he saw, ranged in front of him, lit by a myriad lamps, what seemed to be a limitless army of crouching tigers, with glittering eyes, their lips curled back in a snarl.

Hardly daring to draw a breath, he read the third notice, which proclaimed:

'Some have passed across the moat and beyond the swords and lived to read these words. But none, so far, has dared to brave the fury of a thousand tigers, however eager his desire to win the Great Queen!'

The youth reached for his bow and shot an arrow into a tree, a hair's beadth from the nose of one of the beasts. The animal took no notice. Moving forward, the Minister saw that it – and all the other tigers – were carved from stone, so cleverly decorated with paint and fabrics that he gasped with surprise at the skill of the deception.

Finally, he entered the castle, where he found that the Queen was as beautiful as the legend had promised; and, of course, they were married.

Now, this adventure happened in the course of one night. True to his oath and in fear of the King, the Minister thereafter used to return to his duties every day, and crept out in the evening to be with his bride.

Not long after the nuptials, the King had an important guest, and the discussions and feasting went on late into the night. The Minister was unable to leave his master until it was almost dawn. Hurrying to his castle, he entered the Queen's chamber only to see, in the first rays of the Sun, that she was lying in bed with a figure beside her.

In shock and horror, the Minister dropped his staff onto the floor and fled.

When the Queen awoke and found the stick, she realised what had happened. Instead of the dummy which she had placed in her bed to annoy and reproach her bridegroom, he had seen – another man. Would he ever return? Would he believe her if he did?

For several days she waited, but there was no sign of her consort. Dressing herself in travelling clothes, she left her castle and wandered over the face of the earth, seeking the fugitive, for he was not to be found in the King's country.

At length, after crossing mountains and deserts, searching forests and traversing oceans, the Queen found that her husband had become a recluse, sitting in a cave half-way up a mountain. She started to make her way to him.

But the climb was too much for her and, losing her footing, she fell over a precipice and died. The Minister never even knew that she had been looking for him, and he ended his days even more miserably than he had begun them; for the life of an anchorite who is trying to escape sadness is always without value.

So, too, it is said, end the lives of those who jump to conclusions, who attach themselves to commitments which prevent them fulfilling their potential; who may have skill and bravery and cunning but who seek to serve two ends. They also say that the ultimate fate of those whose desire is for power and adulation, and those who act precipitately or from jealousy, is to end their lives unfulfilled.

THE MAGICAL POWDER

There was once a handsome and talented youth who was just starting out in life when, by her evil arts, he was captured by a witch. Using dark enchantments, she made him forget who he was and where he belonged. All he could think was that he was the Witch's servant, and therefore had to obey her in everything.

One day, when she felt that he was sufficiently prepared for her purposes, the Witch said:

'My lad, you must now go and find, for me, the water pitcher which never runs dry. This is what you were created for. It is necessary to your service for me: and it is what you were created for. If you do not do it, you will drop dead.'

In his state of bewilderment, this seemed perfectly natural to the young man. He set off along the road from the Witch's cottage, travelling for miles and miles, for days on end. Sometimes people gave him food; sometimes he earned something to keep him alive.

He asked whomever he met about the pitcher, and, of course, there were all sorts of contradictory answers. The Witch had warned him that life would be like that, so he always recovered his optimism, however sad he temporarily became.

One day he met an old man sitting at the wayside. 'Where can I find the inexhaustible jug?' the youth asked. At first the ancient tried to talk him out of his quest. Finding that he could not, he took a clay jug from his pack and gave it to him, saying, 'Take this to your mistress. But it will not end your search.'

Finding that the pot poured water without ceasing, the young man thanked the oldster gratefully and made haste back to the Witch. No sooner had she grabbed the pitcher than she seized her captive's arm and said:

'Hasten, now, for you know that it is your destiny to seek and

164

find the purse which always has a gold coin in it, no matter how many are taken out.'

This seemed a reasonable objective to the youth, who set off at once to do the Witch's bidding. Again he travelled, this times from one country to another, always asking about the purse, and always getting contradictory answers.

Finally, when he had almost made a full circle of the world, the youth came upon the ancient sage once again. They sat down together; and the youth described his travels and spoke of his quest. 'The purpose of my life' he added, 'is to serve the old lady, and to bring her back the purse.'

'Do you remember nothing of the time when you were seeking the jug?' asked the sage.

This sounded like nonsense to the traveller. 'That means nothing to me, father,' he answered.

The sage now reached into his pack and brought out a purse. 'This,' he said, 'is the inexhaustible purse. Take it to your mistress. But remember, something may make you act otherwise than you are now doing, one day.'

For a moment, but no longer, the youth felt that there was something important in what the old man had said: but the feeling soon went away. More from politeness than for any other reason, he said: 'I am grateful for the purse. Do counsel me.'

'I'll do better than that,' said the ancient one. He took a tiny, cotton-wrapped package from his bag and handed it to the wayfarer. 'Remember this:' he said, 'if you throw the herbal powder I now give you into a fire, anyone sitting beside it will vanish forever.'

The young man thanked him again, and put the packet into his pocket. He soon forgot about them, as he hurried back to the Witch and presented her with the magical purse.

'Good!' she cackled, when she had tested it by drawing out coins, one after the other. 'Now you must hasten away, to find for me the girl called Hikma. She lives in such-and-such a land, and she is very beautiful. As soon as you have found her, bring her here, for she is to become my property, as you already are. It is her fate.'

This, of course, seemed reasonable to the youth, and he left forthwith on his quest. When he arrived at the far country where the girl Hikma lived, and found her house, he was entranced by her beauty. Although he had fallen in love with her, the Witch's spells were still working powerfully upon him; so he seized the maiden and carried her off.

When they arrived at the Witch's cottage, they saw that it was filled with gold coins, which she was frantically drawing from the magical purse as she sat by the fireplace.

'Mistress!' the young man called, 'I have brought you the maiden Hikma, to be your property, as I am already.'

But the maiden, who had come willingly because of the youth but was not yet under any spell, cried out, 'Save me, kind youth, for I love you!'

As soon as he heard these words, the memory of everything which had happened to him came flooding back into the young man's mind. He opened the packet which the sage had given him, even as the Witch was making her first magical passes to draw the girl into her power. Then he threw the contents into the fire beside which the hag was sitting.

In less time than it takes to tell, the old woman had disappeared.

Hikma and the youth were married, and they lived happily ever after, in a palace which they built from the fortune in gold which came from the magical purse.

And they always had fresh water, too, from the magical jug.

THE WAYWARD PRINCESS

A certain King of the Afghans believed that whatever he had been taught, and whatever he himself believed, was absolutely true. In many ways he was a just man; it was only that his ideas were very limited.

One day he said to his three daughters:

'All that I have is yours, or will be yours. Through me you obtained life. It is *my* will which determines your future, and hence it is my will which determines *your* fate.'

Dutifully, and quite convinced of the truth of these words, two of the girls agreed.

The third daughter, however, said:

'Father, although my position demands that I be obedient to the laws, I cannot believe that my fate must always be determined by your opinions, or by those of anyone else.'

'We shall see about that!' said the King.

He ordered the girl to be imprisoned in a small cell, where she languished for a year. Meanwhile, the King and his two obedient daughters spent freely of the wealth which would otherwise have been lavished upon the third girl.

The King, during this time, said to himself:

'The girl lies in prison: not by her own will, but by mine. This proves, sufficiently for any reasonable mind, that it is *my* will, not hers, which is determining her fate.'

The people of the country, hearing of their princess's imprisonment, said to one another:

'She must have done or said something very wrong for a monarch, with whom we find no fault, to treat his own flesh and blood like that.' It never occurred to them to dispute the right of the King to act in this way.

From time to time the King visited the captive girl. Although she was pale and weakened from her ordeal, she always refused to change her attitude.

Finally, the King's patience came to an end. 'Your continued defiance,' he told her, 'will only annoy me further. It may even seem, to others, to weaken my power; but I am merciful. I shall therefore banish you into the territory adjoining this domain. It is a wilderness, inhabited only by wild beasts and such eccentric outcasts as cannot survive in our ordered society. There you will soon discover whether you have any real existence apart from that of your family. When you have learnt sense, you may return.'

His decree was immediately obeyed, and the Princess was conveyed to the borders of the kingdom. She found herself set loose in a wild land which bore little resemblance to the sheltered surroundings of her upbringing.

Little by little, the Princess learned that a cave would serve for a shelter, that nuts and fruit could be found on trees as well as upon golden platters; that warmth came from the Sun. The wilderness had an existence of its own.

Soon she had water from springs, vegetables from the earth, fire from smouldering trees which had been struck by lightning.

'Here,' the Princess said to herself, 'is a life whose elements belong together, form a whole: yet neither individually nor collectively do they obey the commands, or adopt the attitudes, of my father the King.'

167

One day a wanderer, a man of great riches and ingenuity – as it happened – came upon the exiled Princess in the forest. They fell in love; he took her back to his own land, and they were married.

After a space of time, the two decided to return to the wilderness, where they built a large and prosperous city. In it, wisdom, resources and faith were expressed to their fullest extent, and everyone was happy. The eccentrics and other outcasts of the region, many of them once thought to be madmen, harmonised completely and usefully with this many-sided life.

The city, and the newly-prosperous land which surrounded it, became renowned throughout the entire world. It was not long before its power, beauty and wisdom far outshone the realm of the Afghan King.

By the unanimous choice of the inhabitants, the Princess and her husband were elected to the joint monarchy of this new and ideal kingdom.

At length the Princess's father decided to visit the strange and mysterious place which had sprung up out of a wilderness: and which, he was told, was peopled by those whom he and his like despised.

As he slowly approached the foot of the throne upon which the young couple sat, with bowed head, and then raised his eyes to meet those whose repute for justice, tolerance and understanding now far exceeded his own, the King heard the murmured words of his daughter:

'You see, Father, everyone has a personal fate and choice.'

From that day on, the Afghan King reformed: and transformed his own realm into what we subsequently always called *Mamlikat-i-Khudadad* – The God-Granted Kingdom.

PART FIVE

PEOPLE . . .

HOW TO DISCERN SECRETS FROM THE FACE

Sir Alexander Burnes, Head of the British Mission to the Kabul Court, collected much information on Afghanistan and its people and customs. He was interested enough in physiognomy as studied by the Afghans to include in his book *Cabool* a translation of a long dissertation on the meaning of various human facial features. The Envoy, sadly, was killed in the uprising against the British occupation on 2 November 1841. *Cabool* was published in England after his death. Under the circumstances, his knowledge of the Afghan form of protective Man-Watching, condensed below, was, most likely, of little avail.

This is a science which shows the secret dispositions and hidden qualities of mankind by a sight of the face and limbs. For instance, you see a man and immediately learn from his countenance whether he possesses good or evil habits, and what is suitable for him . . .

They who train the horse, camel, hawk, falcon, etc., can find from their appearance their good and bad qualities, and thus tame them immediately. If this is advantageous for beasts, it must be extremely useful to mankind.

THE FOREHEAD

If a man has a small forehead, it shows that he is rude and foolish. If it is neither small nor large, and has a frown, it shows the strength of anger; because when a person is in a passion, he looks so. If the forehead is large, it shows the man is overpowered by passion, or is lazy. If the forehead has successive lines, it teaches that the man is a boaster. If it has no lines, we should learn that the person is full of enmity.

THE HAIR

Abundance of hair is the proof of the existence of grief and worthless words. It is also possible that those having it have a mad temper.

THE EYEBROWS

If the eyebrows are long, and descend towards the ear, it shows that the man is selfish and boasting. If the eyebrows bend towards the nose, it shows foolishness.

THE EYES

If the eyes are large, it is a proof of his being lazy. Eyes large and projecting show ignorance and foolishness. Eyes deep-seated hide the darkness of the heart and an evil disposition. If the eyes be small and black, they show malice in the heart. If the eye be red, like wine, it is a proof of wrathfulness and boldness. Blue or light-coloured eyes bespeak a cold heart. Eyes that are open or staring give reason to believe that the possessor is quarrelsome. If yellow and quick in movement, it shows a man easily alarmed. If there are moles inside the eyes, it indicates the heart is not pure. If there is a black line all round the eye, we should believe that the man always thinks ill of others. If the eyelids are warped, the man is fond of cheating and fighting.

THE NOSE

If the nose is thin, it shows the man to be no stranger to disgrace, enmity and fighting. If the tip of the nose is thick and full of flesh, it is a proof of being destitute of understanding. If the orifices of the nose are open, it shows anger. The length of a nose, if thick, shows a want of generosity. If the nose is like an arch where it meets with the eyebrows, the individual is quarrelsome and bad.

172

People . . .

THE MOUTH

If the mouth is open or broad, the man is avaricious and full of gluttony. If the lips are thick, the man is a fool, but bold.

THE TEETH

If the teeth are thin and weak, and separated from each other, we should say that the man is feeble and lazy. If the teeth are numerous, the man is powerful: he is also avaricious and a vagabond.

THE FACE

If the flesh is in abundance on the face, we should think the man destitute of wisdom. If there is not much flesh on the face, we should think that the person is always deliberating, because deliberation causes madness, and madness makes the flesh scant. If the face is hard and covered over with lines, it shows sadness and a broken heart. If it is hard, broad and long, the man is considered of mean disposition, miserable . . .

THE EARS

If the ears are long, the man is destined to live long and have little sense.

THE NECK

A thick and strong neck shows rage. If thin, the man is of low heart. If the neck is hard and small, we should know that the person is given to fraud and pretended civility.

There are very few persons who are free from such defects, and have good features.

The portrait of Sir Alexander Burnes, CB, etc. which appears in his book shows a man with a large and broad unlined forehead and large eyes. The nose seems to arch where it meets the eyebrows. The black line running around the eyes may have been inserted by the artist.

173

THE WOOD-SELLER OF KABUL

Every morning by six, all the little booths in the bazaar are open, but the wood-seller, the *Chobe Farosh*, is always first. Before five o'clock he is already swinging the great axe which looks mismatched beside his tiny frame.

He hastens to get the wood chopped, because he knows the ways of his lazy customers – mostly servants from the nearby houses – who delay until the last moment and then come all in a crowd, expecting to be waited on immediately. He is a man of decision, of a certain dignity and status, and of method. A man in business on his own account.

His shop is no bigger than a smallish garage. In it are the stacked wood and a low seat for himself: a seat he has little time to use. There are no 'fittings' in the minute shop, unless we count a little tin kettle, a small charcoal burner, a teapot and a tiny tin of tea.

The floor is earthen; the walls are the same. There is no light, but then the summer is nearly seven months long, and in the winter all he needs is a modest oil lamp.

The Chobe Farosh is a grey little gnome of a man. He seems to be very old, and even older than that, until he begins to wield his axe, then there is no denying he is a master of the art of chopping wood. It is indeed an art, because the logs are big and tough, and the heavy axe does not look too sharp. I have never, in years, seen it sharpened.

The deft, even strokes, with determination and power, eventually reduce the huge logs to quite small pieces which will fit into the cooking stoves of Kabul.

If one feels impelled to say to him that he has the right knack, he

174

will quietly put down his axe, head on the ground, straighten himself taut, and say, '*Khanum* Lady: I am one of the old ones.' He will then smile a little, as though he would like to add that the young ones have not inherited the same degree of skill.

Undoubtedly he is poor, but he is always clean, both in person and dress. His wide cotton trousers, of blue, or green or white, are meagre, but they are spotless, and he has no cause to be ashamed of the patches, although they do not see eye-to-eye with the main colour. His waistcoat, patched too, is more the container of the inner pocket in which he keeps the day's takings than an article of apparel. It is securely buttoned, however hot the day. His jacket might once have been blue, or perhaps green. Now it is faded beyond fading any more. It, too, is patched. His shirt is fastened up to the neck, although sometimes, lacking a button, he has to invoke the services of a safety pin. He is not much of a hand at tying a turban; it seems unlikely that he wears one to add anything to his appearance. Whether grey, or blue or white, varying by the day, this headgear is tied rather lower upon the brow than is correct. The ends appear to get in his way during working hours, and he disposes of them by tying them either on the top of the turban or at the back of his neck. If he needs to wipe his nose, he releases them for the purpose, and reties them as before.

He makes a penny, or two, on the side, by selling country-grown tobacco. He places the wide shallow basket which contains it at an angle in the front of the shop; the tobacco, the wood, and the basket are all much of a colour.

As soon as the wood for the morning rush is prepared, the pile neatly stacked, and all the small untidy chips gathered, the little grey man takes the chips and makes up the fire in the charcoal brazier. Over this he boils his kettle for his tea. If there are few early customers, he is able to finish it more or less in peace. But, quite often, no sooner has he filled his little handle-less blue bowl than customers appear. Often there are as many as a dozen, all clamouring to be served at once.

The wood-seller takes no notice of their anxiety. Neither does he hurry. His calling is not one to hurry over. Merchants have dignity; it is only servants, with someone breathing down their necks, who hurry.

Abdul-Alim, is a man in business on his own account, has been

175

here, in this little shop, for nearly forty years. Customers may bring him money, but they are still of a lesser rank:

'*As Salamu alaikum*: Peace on you, Mr Wood-Seller.'
'*Wa'leik as Salam*: And on thee peace.'
'Permission to state: my master told me to hurry, I have to get the fire going.'
'Haste, my child, is from the Devil . . .'

The weighing is a methodical affair, and the customers must wait. The weighing apparatus might be called somewhat unusual, even unique, anywhere else. It is quite ordinary and correct in our bazaars. It consists of two large flat tins, one for the wood, the other for the weights. The tin pans are attached, by much-knotted ropes, to a horizontal stick. A loop of cord from this is held in the hand, to balance while the weighing is accomplished.

It is, above all, the weights which make for the peculiarity of the apparatus. These consist of bolts of all sizes, and round stones. Each represents a certain weight, which has been officially guaranteed at the Office of Weights. When, say, twelve pounds are required, two bolts of half that weight will be held together by an immense nail, which is screwed in to ensure the holding together of the bolts. The weight of the nail is taken into consideration. The stones represent as little as a quarter of a kilo while larger ones may weigh anything up to ten times as much.

I have often bought wood from him, weighed out with this contraption, taken it home and put it on my perfectly accurate scales: and found the amount always true.

The weighing out of the wood is of never-ending interest to idle passers-by. Heads are thrust forward and mouths stay agape as a piece of wood is added or removed, or a particular weight added or subtracted, just as though the onlookers were seeing all this for the very first time.

The little man does not enter into easy conversation. Sometimes he is moved to interfere when disagreements arise among his customers. He is usually a pacifist, but at such times his voice assumes the tone of an insulted dictator. He seldom has to repeat his disapproval.

Having served the early customers, he has a good look at the money they have handed over. When he is sure it is correct, after much mental addition – though he has always counted it just as carefully when he has made each sale – he puts it away, deep in the inner pocket. Again he tidies up the wood left on the pile, and only then does he return to the low seat beside the kettle.

The tea in his bowl is cold: he pours it back into the teapot, which he sets over the remains of the fire, fanning the charcoal into life. His mind never seems far away from his work. Except for the times when he quells rising trouble, his whole life is taken up with his own affairs. As he fills and refills the tea bowl, his eyes keep wandering to the wood ranged around the walls, and his bright eyes seem to be measuring the quantity needed for the day.

Sometimes, when there is a noisy, stand-up fight near his booth, even with the glint of raised knives, he will emerge, stand for a few moments taking in the scene, like a general contemplating attack, and then cross the road, into the middle of the fray.

From the shouting he learns that the quarrel is about the division of a sum of money which the head man of their group was given for porterage work done. Most often the wood-seller manages to settle the argument. At times, when tempers are beyond pacification, he quickly realises his mediation is useless, and just as quickly returns to his chopping. The contestants do not exist for him any more.

On the days when the countrymen bring the wood they supply to him – four days a week – they arrive at 4 a.m. Those mornings he is waiting for them by the time the donkeys draw up in front of the booth.

He will examine the wood carefully, looking more particularly at that which is more hidden. If he is satisfied with the quality, the logs are unloaded, weighed in his ramshackle scales, and paid for, slowly, with all due gravity.

The weighing is a long job, and the donkeys, tied up under a nearby tree, have time to eat the grass their owner has brought for them, and have a rest. That is, if the wood is up to specification, and that has only one meaning to the wood-seller. It must be right, because he sells only the thick, solid, good-burning variety. If the man has brought the thin, dry-as-paper kind, which fills the room with a pleasant fragrance (but is no good for cooking) he will have none of it.

The Chobe Farosh neither wrangles nor vituperates. He will shoot one sentence at the man who brought it, and turn his back

177

resolutely upon him. It will be no use for the other to plead his cause by saying the wood is 'this good and that good!' The wood-seller is not listening, and the man soon hastens anxiously away elsewhere.

The wood-seller does not encourage idle conversations attempted by passers-by. He will curtly exchange greetings with them. There is no chair for the convenience of gossipers placed outside his booth, as at most other shops. There is always a shortage of kindling in Kabul. Commerce, in the wood-selling business, takes precedence over chit-chat, social life, the superficialities prized elsewhere.

Very, very occasionally, a countryman calls upon him, some old friend whom he is genuinely pleased to see. Then the secret is revealed: he is addressed as Abdul-Alim, Slave of the All-Wise, with surprising intimacy. We may now know his name, but he must, for us, remain, with proper formality, Agha-i Chobe Farosh: Mister Wood-Seller.

The two will sit upon the wooden frame criss-crossed with rope outside the booth, and the water-pipe will be passed between them.

One cannot easily visualise him anywhere else when he is not in his little shop. One does not even like to imagine him in some other small dwelling, grey like himself, with the rather terrible little old wife who comes, now and again, to the shop for money. Like himself, she is old; one can see that even although she is enveloped in a veil. She does not seem to have either his desire or the ability to keep herself clean and tidy; nor has she his dignity and longing for peace.

From the moment of her coming, it is evident that he is not pleased at the intrusion. His voice, usually quiet, is not subdued when he replies to her. Hers is far from low when she speaks to him. There is a quality about it which irritates the husband. For a time he listens to her, as the pitch rises to the highest notes she can command, which is high indeed. He tries several times, unsuccessfully, to stop the flow of her abuse.

Where, he yells, between her threats, is he to get all the money she demands? She shouts back that he is a wood-seller, isn't he, and is that not a means of getting money? She says, with a nasty laugh, that perhaps he sits in the bazaar to watch the water in the *jui*, the drain, flow past. This she voices with surprisingly powerful lungs. Is not the selling of wood the means by which she is entitled to the insufficiency he so grudgingly gives her? Has she not a stomach like himself? That she would like to know! Do stomachs not demand food, irrespective of the kind of husbands their owners have? That, too, she would be glad to know. Irrespective, she repeats, of unprintable husbands with unprintably greedy habits! Can he deny that she needs food, even as those passing donkeys need it?

He replies, with blazing eyes, that the donkeys are of use, and deserve to eat. Upon this deprecating reference, the old woman appeals to the now-numerous onlookers, who have laughed loudly and encouragingly at her sallies. 'Have a look,' she invites them, 'at the meanest man that Allah ever set upon two feet. There is no need to look too hard,' she adds, 'because he is so old and ugly he would be recognised in the black of midnight.'

This causes much laughter, and the old man, whose wrath has been rising, thrusts a shaking finger in front of her veiled face, and asks the audience to listen, just listen, that is all he asks, to the daughter of lies, deceit and every kind of extravagance! His agate eyes blaze and his ragged grey goat's beard wags in keeping with the finger.

'Treat women gently, for they are of a gentler make,' intones a passing Mulla, trying to make peace.

The Chobe Farosh, now calm as any saint, turns innocent eyes upon him, 'Sir, I tried that for thirty years. The remedy is not that written in books, but the one which cures the patient.' The Mulla strides away, angry at the lack of respect for his own vain dignity – amid some laughter from the crowd. They know who has the upper hand in this frequent contest, for they have seen it all before.

As the old woman shrieks on, her hand, covered by the folds of her grubby robe, looks like the wing of some bedraggled bird darting about within a measured distance.

The wood-seller has evidently lost the argument. He turns his back on the old wife, and carefully and slowly extracts some money from the secret security of the pocket. He bends his head over the coins, as though taking a sorrowful farewell of them. 'There is no need to be so slow,' jibes the old woman, 'because in forty years you have never given me even the smallest coin too much.' Again the onlookers chuckle with delight. As the husband hands over the money, he drops it into the hand which looks like a claw. She

179

grasps it and counts it twice. She raises her voice to complain at the smallness of the sum.

He warns her, with head and beard and finger aquiver, turban bobbing up and down, that one day, before long, she will be responsible for his ruin, daughter of impossibility that she is. Then there will be no more money from anywhere, and what is she going to do then? He will be dead, cold and inert, unable to chop or to sell, she will stand in this very place, hand outstretched, begging from the Believers, may Allah make them more generous to her than she, in speech and action, has ever been to him . . .

She is quieter now, but one feels it is only because she has the money clutched in her hand, and her silence has nothing to do with a problematic future. As she arranges her veil in preparation for going, he warns her to spend the cash carefully, remembering all the time it is the sweat of his brow, and that the law of life is that that which we do not appreciate is taken from us. With this profound remark he retreats into the shop, and the old woman cackles a laugh in his direction, bending her steps towards the food shops of the bazaar.

Some of the onlookers, men and women alike, gaze admiringly after her, others purse their lips and give their heads a half shake, as though thankful that they have no such problems.

When Abdul-Alim thinks she is safely on her way, he emerges from his shop, walks into the middle of the road, and looks carefully into the distance, as though only the assurance of his own eyes is sufficient proof that she has really gone. 'There is no god but God,' he says piously, 'and Mohammad, upon whom be peace and blessings, is his Slave and his Messenger.'

He says his prayers the prescribed five times daily, washing himself before he spreads the clean piece of sacking on the ground in front of his shop. There, as he faces Holy Mecca, he no doubt thanks Allah for vouchsafing him bread and tea and the privilege of the strength to earn the same.

In the afternoons, when it is hot, he lies down for an hour as the echo of the Tope, the gun which signals midday, dies away. His string-bed could not be called comfortable, but it must be a solace, a real rest – after the rigours of swinging an axe for those seven hours. There is no mattress of any kind or any covering except the turban ends which he places over his face, to deter the attentions of the flies.

There will be, most likely, no customers during the hours of summer heat; and even if there are, he is on the spot, therefore he feels justified in resting until Kabul wakes for the late afternoon rush.

After his work is finished for the day, punctually at seven – he has no clock or watch, but he 'reads the sun', he closes the double door of his booth, making sure, with a long look up and down the road, that no straggling customer is approaching.

When he has turned the key in its massive, rusty padlock, he gives a final look around to make sure there is no untidiness in front for which he might be held responsible. The market's Superintendant is strict. Only then does he set off for the home over which his wife has all control.

One hopes, as the erect little figure disappears, that the lady has relented. That it was rhetorical, affectionate, stylised and acceptable grumbling, not unknown in some circles, when she threatened to send him supperless to bed, and that there is something nice for his supper. He has earnt it.

Morag Murray

181

TO WAR ON A STRETCHER: GENERAL NADIR KHAN

Afghan patriotism resides in the belief of an Afghan in the destiny of other Afghans. Our feeling, strong in each one of us, is that an Afghan is a unit whose being is bound up with that of his country and all his fellows.

This comes out most strongly, as I have myself witnessed, under stress.

A true example is that of Marshal Nadir Khan and his family. In the bitter Winter of 1929, the brigand Habibullah (the Son of a Water-Carrier: Bacha-i-Saqao) had, with his bandit band, seized the throne of Kabul. Marshal Nadir, from his sick bed in France, was carried aboard a P. & O. ship at Marseilles on a stretcher: determined to drive out the usurper. In February he was in Peshawar, near the Indo-Afghan border.

Amid tremendous difficulties, the Marshal and his brothers fought battle after battle with the supporters of the brigand, amid rising fears that, sooner or later, either Britain or the Soviet Union – or both – might step in and claim Afghanistan as their own.

During this time the women and children of the Marshal's family were held hostage in the Arg, the great palace-fortress of Kabul.

As the liberation forces approached the capital, one Moulavi Abdul-Latif, a man of many hues, arrived at the Marshal's camp with a message from the tyrant. All the prestige of Nadir Khan would be restored, it said, his family released and his lands and property given back to him – and he could rule the kingdom jointly with the usurper.

He wrote, in reply:

O Tyrant! Son of a Water-Carrier!
I have received thy message, from which I conclude that your advisers have not informed you of my precise motives. The single reason for moving against you is to remove the unhappy discord that prevails among our people and which is caused by you. My greatest desire is to establish peace and contentment in the Realm.
In this objective I would consider everyone among our people as my co-worker – even you . . .
I desire you to work for the betterment of the country. First, however, you must renounce your claim to rulership: for neither are you competent, nor is the nation agreeable to it . . . I shall struggle against you to the last . . . I have no more to say to you about this . . .
With regard to my family, all that I have to add is that each one of them has been entrusted to the safe-keeping of God, the All-Powerful . . .

When the liberators arrived at Kabul and prepared to bombard the fortress, the insurgents sent Nadir Khan a message. For every shell which was fired at the Water-Carrier's men, one member of Nadir's family would be killed.
The Lady Samarut-Siraj, wife of Sardar Shah-Wali Khan, brother of Nadir Khan, smuggled out this message to her husband:

In the name of God, fire! Attack, rid the country of this demon. We are not afraid.

The warrior brothers, saying a prayer, stormed the castle and released the prisoners unhurt. The bandit escaped, delaying the pursuit by scattering gold coins as he fled, but was soon captured.
Marshal Nadir Khan entered the city in triumph, and was at once elected king. Thereafter he ruled as Mohammed Nadir, Shah.

STATECRAFT AS BLUFF

Queen Victoria's envoys to the Court of Kabul, stiff with starch and tightly-cut uniforms, had come to Kabul to treat with the Amir: Abdur-Rahman Khan, reputedly a savage and suspected of having too much interest in the Russians.

The ruler, primed by his spies in India, had worked out his tactics well in advance.

Ushered into the Durbar Hall of the Arg, the Palace-Fortress, the delegation sat at the Amir's right hand, while he attended to the business of the day.

The courtiers, servants, guards, sat or stood, according to rank, observing the customary stillness, silence and decorum traditional in the presence of an Eastern king.

The Amir chatted amiably to his guests, pointing out notables, alluding to the price of grain, hoping that they had had a good journey through the Khyber and across the hair-raising Lataband Pass.

Suddenly, the monarch stiffened. 'Did you hear that?' he asked the Prime Minister.

'Yes, High Presence.' The man had heard nothing, but nobody says 'no' to a king . . .

'Captain of the Guard, forward!' roared the Amir.

'Captain: you see that group of grandees over there, against the wall? I distinctly heard a rustling from them, as if somone had moved.'

'Yes, Majesty.' Everyone looked at the gorgeously-dressed figures, with jewelled daggers and egrets in their turbans; surely the most favoured aristocrats of the Realm. Indeed, the British delegation had been trying to memorise their faces, thinking that they must be Khans at least, and possibly royal princes.

184

'There must be no such indiscipline in this Court. Shoot them!'

The Guard Captain gave the order without turning a hair; his men aimed and fired. The dozen figures buckled at the knees and fell to the ground.

Suspecting a trick to impress them, the British rushed over to the figures on the floor. No, the shots had not been blanks: the men were dead.

While the bodies were being removed, the Amir, all smiles, turned to the guests. 'Please continue, and pardon the interruption...'

The purpose of the visit had been to inform the Afghans of the immense power of the British Raj in India, just across the border. The delegation, however, as one man, realised that a tyrant such as this would hardly be impressed by anything. The British chief of delegation said, 'Your Highness is a cruel man...' but the Amir, with benign grin, only answered, 'I rule, alas, a strong nation.' The next day the visitors withdrew to safer territory.

They were not much pleased, either, when word came that the Amir had emptied the jails of men who were under capital sentence, dressed them as courtiers, and staged the scene to avoid enquiries as to whether he really was master of his own country.

Although all Afghans share a common feeling, which they call *Afghaniyyat* – Afghanness, they come from almost every ethnic stock. Successive civilisations, wave after wave of conquerors – or home-grown empires – have peopled the country with Greeks, Turks, Mongols, Arabs – and a lot more besides.

The various peoples have their own leaders, sometimes religious figures, sometimes landed aristocrats, sometimes tribal chiefs, sometimes all three. Like a microcosm of medieval Europe (some say the Saxons, *Saka-sun* and even the Angles, settled here in their early wanderings) the chiefs have had to use their wits as well as their muscles to stay on top.

Afghan kings, claiming suzerainty (usually disputed) over the whole country, have needed tremendous ingenuity. They had to deal with the Persians, the Russians, the British as well as with their own people.

From the time of the Great Game, with Britain and Russia vieing for hegemony in Central Asia, come some of the best tales of Afghan lifemanship. They didn't invent the term, but, like the fish who has no name for water, they lived in it.

Fighting and negotiating with their own people and also with their powerful neighbours, king after king in Afghanistan practised guile in much the same way as Abdur-Rahman Khan.

When, early this century, Amir Habibullah Khan was invited to India, he heard that the British were determined to impress him: so he decided not to be impressed by anything. The British account of the trip shows some irritation. Lord Kitchener thought that a trip in the basket of a balloon would really give the savage something to think about. When he came down, however, and was asked what he thought of this marvel, he only said, 'As a matter of fact, what I really wanted to do was to see the sea.'

He was rushed to Bombay and there, on the beach, the expectant officials asked, 'Is it not remarkable?'

'It certainly is *big*, I grant you that,' said the Amir.

King Amanullah Khan, just after the First World War, was still maintaining the tradition, according to Afghan legend. He had a well-trained and versatile army, and planned to invade India if the British did not concede that the Afghans could have embassies abroad. In North India the British were having manoeuvres and – supposedly as a courtesy, but more likely to impress – Amanullah was asked to send military observers. The message came back from the Ministry of War: 'Three civilian colonels (an Afghan rank) will attend.'

The Afghans have always relied, in fact and in propaganda, upon their irregular, partisan, forces. Amanullah sent suitable representatives.

The Afghans were invited to the Mess of a famous British fighting regiment, for dinner. When they arrived, they were seen to be well over six foot six inches tall, and large in proportion. Over their impeccable black uniforms, faintly reminiscent of the Cossacks, they wore huge sheepskin coats, fur inside and golden embroidery outside. Each man carried a rifle of the latest type and wore crossed bandoliers of cartridges. Hand-grenades were hung from waists, shoulders and even their arms.

Once they had been seated, the chief of the party said to the British Colonel: 'You will realise that we are not accustomed to your kind of food. I therefore ask permission for my own servants to bring in some of ours. It is only a small quantity: we have all been unwell – your water does not suit us – and so, for appearance's sake, we shall just have a bite or two.'

Naturally, the Colonel agreed and, at a signal, a file of Afghan cooks, all six-footers armed to the teeth, entered bearing huge platters of rice with chickens buried in them. Meatballs, several kinds of vegetables, bread, fruit, flasks of juices, jugs of yoghurt, the stuff kept coming in. Finally, apologising for their poor appetites, all of them – delegates and cooks – tucked into a meal which seemed never-ending.

Finally, the chief Afghan turned to the Colonel and said, 'You see, we are abstemious people; but of course, our appetite for war is far greater than our taste for food.'

Amazingly, this trick was played again and again by Afghan delegations to the British in India. Perhaps stiff upper lips prevented the stories being passed down in detail from one generation of administrators to the next. They probably only said, 'These fellows are bounders and savages.'

On one occasion, the Afghan King, due to attend a Durbar held in Delhi, had been given a timetable of the order of events which did not exactly meet with his approval. As with royal protocol, the Indian princes were to arrive first and be seated; then the British officers and high officials, followed by the Afghan King. As each appeared, those who had been seated would have to rise, thus demonstrating the order of precedence. Naturally, when the King of Afghanistan had been seated, the Viceroy would appear, and all – including the Monarch of the God-Given Kingdom – would have to stand.

Now, in Afghan eyes, though the English Viceroy represented the King in London, the real live monarch of Kabul, being himself a king, outranked him. But the Rajite protocol department of Delhi would have none of this. The Afghan would arrive *before* the Viceroy, and would stand as the National Anthem was played.

The Afghan, however, was looking over his shoulder towards Kabul. If word got back – and it would – that he had stood for the Viceroy of India, he would have a revolution on his hands. The Afghans had ruled India time out of mind: and they had viceroys of their own . . .

When the great day dawned, everything went, at first, like clockwork. Civilians and military arrived in due order of rank and took their places, followed by the Indian princelings. The carriage of the Afghan King was awaiting him, with a feverish aide de camp

187

brandishing his stop-watch, as in any London pageant of royalty. He had heard rumours that the Afghan might try to delay the ceremonial drive: and he had spare horses and coaches standing by. Even the Afghan outriders and servants had been liberally dosed with rupees, with more promised if all went well.

At the precise moment called for in the programme, the Afghan King stepped into his carriage. At the exact second laid down, it arrived at the Durbar. The King stepped down.

Suddenly, with a cry of pain, he stood stock still. 'I can't move: there's a stone or something in my boot,' he explained. 'You must, your Majesty,' gabbled the equerry, 'you have to be seated before the Viceroy arrives: and he will have set off from his residence by now.'

'Can't be helped, my child,' beamed the King. Assisted by a crowd of soldiers, secretaries, and the rest, he struggled to get the royal boot off as the Viceroy's carriage was heard approaching.

It was unthinkable that the Viceregal cavalcade should stop; and so it clattered to its destination. The Viceroy strode in, to the strains of *God Save the King*, as all rose. The Afghan King, by then, was sitting in the forecourt, trying to get his boot off and unable to rise.

Miraculously, as the last strains of the tune died away and all sat, the trouble cleared. The Afghan stood up and walked, with his escort, into the Durbar hall. The Afghan national anthem was struck up – and the Viceroy had to rise to his feet.

My grandfather was there at the time, and he told me the story. Reminiscing about such matters, he recalled being presented to King George the Fifth:

'The chief of protocol told me that I would have to remove my hat in the King's presence,' he said; 'but of course such an action is, in the East, a sign of disrespect. So I made a plan. I arrived at Buckingham Palace and my top hat was taken from me by a lackey. When I approached King George, I said, 'I seek your Majesty's gracious permission to do you honour in our own traditional manner.' He smiled and nodded, and I took out, from my inner pocket, a flat-folded karakul cap, and put it on my head. He obviously knew our ways, for he smiled and thanked me for treating him like one of our own.'

Times change; no doubt information percolates down. When

my father went to sign the Visitor's Book at Buckingham Palace, he was wearing an Afghan hat and did not remove it. Nobody tried to take it away.

Safia Shah

THE JAN FISHAN KHAN

In the West there are few parallels to the Eastern tradition that a leader combines the military and spiritual roles, supreme leadership and religious self-effacement. This emphasis is rooted in the Islamic ideal instituted by the Prophet: the ruler is expected to be the first in piety, in directing education and faith – and also an administrator and war-chief.

A century and a half ago, my great-great grandfather – Jan Fishan Khan – was famous for combining all these functions, as well as being a Sufi mystic of importance.

His title of Jan Fishan, interestingly, combined the two concepts: the spiritual and the temporal. Jan Fishan means *Soul-Scatterer*, and in its military sense it conveys the idea of a great war leader to the uninitiated. In Sufi devotional poetry, however, the origin of the term is found in these Sufi lines:

> *Gar dast dihad hazar Janam*
> *Dar pai mubarakat Fishanam!*

The whole five-lined Ode reads:

> O my adored one! I am so in love with you
> That I doubt my own existence:
> Although weak and powerless am I,
> If I were given a thousand lives –
> I'd scatter them at your blessed feet!

Jan Fishan, the Soul-Scattering Lord, was named Sayed Mohammed Khan, son of Sayed Qutubuddin Khan of Paghman.

He was also known as Shah-Saz, the Kingmaker, because of his role as a statesman.

190

He had a tremendous personality; and yet one of his sayings was, 'I am so often treated better than I deserve without demurring. Why should I invariably protest when treated worse than I deserve?'

Although, in the East, people are expected to live up to their ancestry, Jan Fishan would, in Sufi style, modify this; as when he said, at his Court one day:

Those who come, as we do, from a long line of celebrated nobles, should always remember those who have no such lineage.

Also recall that it is not uncommon for the members of several generations to remain in deliberate obscurity, in order to nurture the greatness which appears in their descendants, and to work unobserved.

Trivial people cry: 'How could he be anything, since we never heard of his father and grandfather?'

But many a precious gem remains, for generations, in the soil.

Some of the Khan's sayings are repeated, from memory or from diaries kept by his disciples. On ancestry, too, he had this to say:

Take no pride in your ancestry until you have achieved something to justify it. When that happens, you may find that you cannot take any pride in the achievements, because you will believe that they were due to your ancestry.

After the First Anglo-Afghan War, Jan Fishan became Nawab of Sardhana, in India; a State which tradition said had been the most ancient religious centre of the country. This is a legend very similar to that which surrounds Paghman itself.

Jan Fishan Khan not only had an enormous retinue of the greatest riders in Afghanistan, but he was himself one of the best judges of horseflesh. He called himself 'a slave of horses'. When someone asked him how an owner could be a slave, he said, 'If you want to be owned by a tyrant, become the owner of a horse.'

Once he was visiting the domain of a neighbouring prince. He was taken to the stables to look at the Arabs. Stopping at one of the stalls, he said:

'How could a man like this Nawab have a poor animal like this?'

191

The Nawab, who had been standing at some distance but had moved up unnoticed, to within earshot of the Nawab Jan Fishan, said:

'Is it worthy of a mighty Prince to speak thus when he is in a condition of guesthood?'

Jan Fishan turned to his Chief Minister and said:

'Inform his Highness why I spoke as I did.'

The Minister explained: 'The Sayed, aware that anything praised by a guest must be given him as a present, in accordance with the custom between rulers, criticised the horse in order to safeguard your ownership of it.'

In a country like Afghanistan, his disclaimer notwithstanding, ancestry has great importance. The reports sent to such people as the Amir of Bukhara, the Sultan of Turkey or the Emperor of Persia by their informants all dwell upon the hereditary factors. Thus the Divan Begi, a courtier of Samarkand, to his master:

After obeisances, I report only what is attested and confirmed by the highest authorities.

The Jan Fishan Khan is Lord of Paghman, but the family have multitudes of supporters and adherents throughout the East. The land is also known as Paghwan and Pamghan. His descent is from the Holy Imam Musa Al Kazim in the Prophet's blessed line, and from the Imperial House of Iran...

A secret dispatch to Constantinople says:

Since the Imam Hussain, grandson of the Prophet, salutations and prayers upon him!, married the daughter of the Emperor of Persia, the Apostolic Line thereafter combined with the Imperial Ajami one. Consequently, the Jan Fishan Khan's descent is the authentic, irrevocable Apostolic and Imperial one. A tree, showing the unsullied descent of this Sufi saint and war-leader, is attached, attested by the Naqib al Ashraf, the Leader of the Nobility...

And, reporting to the Amir of Bukhara, a dispatch says, in the early 1830s:

The Khan has all the genealogical and military, as well as administrative powers of a king. His name is Sayed Mohammed Shah, son of Sayed Qutubuddin Khan. He wears diamond-encrusted armour when on campaign; but, like all the men of this descent, he spends much time in humble garb, attending to his spiritual welfare, so that many braggarts are discountenanced by his humility. He walked, one and a half years, to Holy Mecca, barefoot...

A hundred and fifty years later, a high official of the Afghan Government in the USA was asked to give me a reference. It ran as follows:

I, Sardar Faiz Mohammed Zikria, former Minister of Foreign Affairs, Minister of Education, Ambassador and Emissary of the Royal Afghan Government, make the following notarised Statement:

ONE: The Musavi Saiyids of Afghanistan and Khans of Paghman are recognised as the descendants of the Prophet – May peace be upon him.

TWO: They are recognised to be of the most noble descent of Islam and are respected as Sufi teachers and erudite scholars.

THREE: Saiyid Idries Shah, son of the late Saiyid Ikbal Ali Shah, is personally known to me as an honourable man whose rank, titles and descent are attested and known by repute.

October 7, 1970, New York, N.Y.

I came across an original, notarised copy of this reference in some papers relating to a trip I made to the USA. What did the American to whom it was sent, in the first place, make of it all?

As Jan Fishan Khan once said:

'To imagine that you are not troubling others without understanding the many ways in which you can be a nuisance is as bad as imagining yourself to be a constant source of inconvenience to all.'

Half-way to America, though, historical statements do seem to have some effect. In England I had been proposed for membership of a scientific society: though I had no qualifications in the field. One of my sponsors (it was his idea) was Professor K. de B. Codrington, who had done important archaeological work in Afghanistan. He had been doing some research, too, on our family background.

When I was elected, I expressed surprise to Codrington. He said, 'They didn't want to have you at first, but I sent them some data that I'd collected.'

I said, 'I don't know what data it could have been – I'm no scientist.'

The Professor told me, 'I found a notarised Statement from Sardar Faiz M. Zikria, from New York. It said that you were all right. That did the trick.'

Idries Shah

GENERAL ARNOLD'S CAMEL TRAIN

From a chronicle of the First Afghan War:

Brigadier General Arnold of the Army of the Indus, having been long suffering under a liver complaint, breathed his last at Kabul shortly after our arrival there.

This officer was distinguished for his qualities as a *bon vivant*; and, having laid in a good store of necessaries for the campaign, was almost the only one who fared well amidst the general privations.

He kept an excellent table along the route, and an invitation to it was always regarded as amongst the lucky chances by which fortune signified her favour.

Good living could not, however, protect the General against disease, and he fell ill at Kandahar of a malady which is often said to be the result of it.

He was carried from Kandahar to Kabul in a palanquin, and took no part whatever in the events [the march and storming of Ghazni, major events of the First Anglo-Afghan War] which occurred between those places.

His remains were interred in the Armenian burial ground outside the walls of the city, and his effects were publicly sold by auction a few days after.

The General had left Bengal with about eighty camels laden with baggage and necessaries, of which about five and twenty remained at the time of the sale.

His trunks were filled with quantities of plate, a goodly provision of snuff and cigars, and such an immense stock of linen that it occupied two days of the sale.

195

His cooking apparatus was most elaborate and ingenious, and we could not help wondering at the uses to which the infinite varieties of small and curious articles of which it was composed were devoted.

The prices at which these effects were sold will appear incredible to the European reader, but it must be remembered that it was the scarcity, in fact the almost total impossibility of getting them, that enhanced their value.

The cigars sold at the rate of about two shillings and six pence each, the snuff at ten shillings an ounce, a few bottles of beer, a liquor of which no other officer in the army possessed a drop, at thirty shillings each; and some choice wines at from three to four pounds a bottle.

The other things brought proportionate prices: the shirts fetching from thirty to forty shillings each. The amount realised at this sale must have been enormous.

PART SIX

HUMOUR...

ADVENTURES OF THE AMAZING MULLA NASRUDIN

Nasrudin tales are told by Sufis and dervishes to illustrate aspects of human behaviour and workings of the mind. The one about the donkey who became a judge reflects – however exaggeratedly – the stubbornness with which unsupported ideas can warp a person's thinking:

WHOM TO BELIEVE

Mulla Nasrudin had an insatiable craving for knowledge, but did not seem to know what knowledge was. As a result he asked a local wise man the stupidest questions, always based upon random assumptions.

One day the Mulla noticed that his donkey was missing. He ran to the wise man's house.

'Well, Mulla, what is it this time?'

'My donkey is gone! Where can I find it?'

The wise man was quite fed up with the Mulla. 'Nasrudin,' he said, 'the donkey has run off, turned into a man and been appointed the magistrate in the next town.'

Thanking the wise man for his information, the Mulla trudged to the court. There sat the magistrate, and Nasrudin shook his fist at him:

'Come home at once, you foolish animal!'

The magistrate was furious. 'Who are you and how dare you talk to me like that? I'll have you sent to the cells!'

'I'm the well-known Mulla Nasrudin, and I have it on the best authority that you are my donkey.'

199

'That's ridiculous. Nobody in his right senses would credit such a thing!'

Nasrudin drew himself up to his full height. 'Say what you like,' he said, 'I prefer to believe the statement of a wise man rather than that of a donkey.'

Wisdom, according to the Sufis, can only be acquired when one is ready for it: though people insist on seeking enlightenment as and when they want it. The Sufi's task, however, includes trying to impart knowledge in the right way, at the right time, to the people who are able to receive it:

SAYING ISN'T TELLING . . .

Mulla Nasrudin and a party of his friends went to listen to an address by a Sufi who was visiting his town to talk to a group of the Sufi's own disciples.

The visitor gave a long speech, and everyone listened respectfully; though Nasrudin's friends could make neither head nor tail of it.

Walking home, one of his companions said, 'Mulla, what was he talking about?'

'Ah,' said Nasrudin, 'if *he* wouldn't tell, neither shall I!'

One of the tasks of a spiritual disciple is that he should overcome the deceitfulness in his mind, which constantly betrays him. This is an aspect of the 'commanding self', the accumulation of instinct and experience which clouds the perceptive faculty:

I DID REMEMBER

Mulla Nasrudin, when on a visit to Damascus, received a letter from a merchant in his town, asking him to bring back some silk and perfume.

He forgot all about it.

Arrived home, he saw the merchant in the street and cried out, 'I could not bring back the things you wanted: your letter did not arrive . . .'

THE REMEDY

Some say that Nasrudin lived in the time of the great conqueror Tamerlane, and was one of his advisers.

One day, so goes the tale, Timur the Lame called the Mulla and said:

'Nasrudin, the Empire is full of slanderers. How can we stop their evil work?'

'You can never stop crime unless you punish all the criminals,' said Nasrudin.

'You mean the slanderers?'

'And their accomplices – those who listen to them,' the Mulla reminded him.

SCISSORS AND HONEY

The King wanted a large number of gorgeous robes made for a special ceremony, and the Royal Tailor had to take on several assistants to cope with the work. Mulla Nasrudin was one of them. He was not very useful as a tailor, so the Master Tailor sent him out on some errand.

While the Mulla was out, the Palace sent a load of sweetmeats to be given to the workers to encourage them.

'Never mind about Nasrudin,' said the Master Tailor, when the confections were being distributed; 'he doesn't like halwa anyway.'

When the Mulla came back and his fellow-workers told him this, he decided to pay the boss back.

A representative of the Court had been sent to oversee the work, to make sure that none of the valuable fabric was stolen, and to ensure that the robes were finished on time.

Nasrudin took him aside. 'It would be a tragedy,' he said, 'if my master's infirmity were to affect the completion of the work.'

'Infirmity? What do you mean?'

'Well, he is given to fits of madness. When one of these comes over him, he destroys everything in the place.'

'But that is terrible! This silk was brought from China, and specially woven . . .'

'Then let me advise you, Intensively Glorious Ornament of the Court,' said Nasrudin, 'the Master Tailor must be seized and given a beating, as shock treatment, the moment he begins to show signs that the seizure is about to start.'

'What signs?'

'Well, he begins turning things over as if looking for something, and runs his hands over the material, as if seeking bumps.'

The courtier thanked the Mulla, and kept a close eye on the Tailor.

Nasrudin then took his master's scissors and hid them. Soon the Tailor was looking everywhere for them, running his hands up and down the cloth to seek a bump, lifting things up and looking underneath . . .

'Seize that man, tie him up and beat him, quickly!' shouted the supervising Courtier.

After this treatment, and when the reason had been explained to him, the Tailor rushed over to the Mulla, shouting, 'Since when was I insane?'

'Since I ceased to like halwa,' said Nasrudin.

OPINION AND FACT

The confusion of opinion and fact is one of the most common and most bewildering of human tendencies. We all know that otherwise perfectly rational people, from time to time, will show that they not only prefer opinion to fact: they will be unaware that they are making the preference.

Some Nasrudin stories attempt to improve this situation. By giving us a joke which can anchor the absurdity of this opinion-fact conflict in the memory, they make us think twice before saying absurd things.

One day Mulla Nasrudin said to his wife, 'Bring me a piece of cheese. Cheese is nutritious, pleasing to the taste, and easy to eat.'

'Mulla!' she cried, 'there's no cheese in the house.'

Nasrudin continued, 'Cheese can go bad and smell. It can give you nightmares – and it costs too much.'

'Now,' said Mrs Nasrudin, 'which statement is the right one?'

'It all depends,' said the Mulla, 'on whether you have any cheese or not.'

HANDS FULL

One day Nasrudin went on a journey, his steps taking him across a dangerous, bandit-infested valley.

He carried, for protection, a gun in one hand and a sword in the other.

Half-way across the valley, a robber stopped him, went through his pockets and ran off with his valuables.

'Ah,' said Mulla Nasrudin, 'If I hadn't had my hands full, the fellow would never have got away with it.'

LATEEF THE THIEF

It is related in the books of the wise that a man
of faith was seen bowing before the corpse of a
hanged man swinging from a gibbet. A
passer-by asked him why he should pay homage to a convicted felon. 'Because,' said the
man of faith, 'that is a man who died for his
beliefs.'

Saadi of Shiraz, in his *Orchard*, reports that someone once said to
him, 'Theft is better than slander.' Saadi exclaimed: 'How strange!
What good do you see in thieving, that you can call it better than
calumny?' The other said, 'Thieves live by their daring: the slanderer does evil and gains nothing.' Thieves, quite rightly, have a
bad name in all communities. But if a slanderer is worse than a
thief, do not speak against anyone. As the Wise have truly said, 'If
someone who says anything against anyone becomes a thief, he is
already making progress!'

Like all other human groups, thieves have their own rationale
for their trade. The greatest thief of all time, known as Lateef the
Thief, is reputed to have told a tale which he said explained the
usefulness – indeed, the necessity – of his craft. Some say that it
shows that many – perhaps too many – things in this world can be
put in far too many ways.

INDISPENSIBLE

'Know, O Fortunate Ones,' Lateef said, as he sat in his retirement
under a tree instructing novices, 'that without thieves there would
be occasions on this Earth of ours when justice is not done, and
when the innocent suffer.

'In our very ancient thieves' lore there is a moral tale which has fortified the spirit and nourished the acquisitiveness of many a laggard in the ranks of thiefdom: helping to maintain our numbers and preventing the development of backsliding.

'This is the tale of the pious man and the thief. One day a thief, feeling that he should keep his hand in, as it were, and not finding anything much worth stealing, came upon a simple man of piety astride a donkey, carrying a lamp in his hand and with a chicken at his side for rations.

'The thief watched him until the ancient had settled down for the night under a bush. Then he crept up and took the donkey, the lamp and the bird.

'When the philosopher woke, he lamented the loss of his goods, and cursed whoever had taken them. Though pious and a philosopher, this man was no enlightened being. First, he was attached to the material things of this world; second, he did not even suspect that there might be some advantage for him in his loss.

'Even when he reached the nearby town, and found that the Mongols had slaughtered every man, woman and child in it during the night, he did not perceive what the thief, lurking nearby, came to understand:

'In the night the donkey might have brayed, and attracted the attention of the murderers. The lamp, if the ancient had woken and lit it, would have given his position away. And the chicken might have crowed, and therefore been an instrument of the old man's death.'

THE MAGIC SACK

'Lying,' continued the veteran robber to this open-mouthed audience, 'is often said to be a bad habit. But to us it is less than important, because it is derivative. Lying, O Sons of Good Fortune, is only a form of thieving. Why, I well recall an instance when lying brought me one of my most interesting exploits, though there was a smaller profit than from a really spectacular theft.

'I was hidden in the roof of a house one evening, waiting for an opportunity to slip in and steal something. I had seen the man of the house ride away at sunset, and I expected that his wife would soon go to bed, when I would be able to ransack most of the rooms.

'Suddenly, there was a gentle knock on the door. The woman

205

admitted her lover, and sat him at a table on which she soon arranged all manner of luscious dishes.

'They were about to partake of this elegant meal, when they heard the trumpet of the husband's outrider announce his unexpected return. The woman, in a panic, pushed her lover into a large closet, and piled the viands onto shelves beside him, motioning him to stay silent until she could effect his safe release.

'As I continued to watch, fascinated, the husband came into the room and informed his wife that the man whom he had gone to meet had been called away and had sent a messenger to tell him this. "The courier intercepted our cavalcade and saved us a profitless journey," he said, settling down to smoke a pipe. Then he asked for food and his wife, after darting a guilty look towards the cupboard, said that there was none in the house.

'Immediately – such is the agility of mind of the master-thief – I had an inspiration. I climbed quickly down from the roof and knocked boldly at the front door. When admitted by the servant, I strode purposefully to the Divan, where the master of the house sat, looking askance at me.

' "Have no fear, Honourable Sir," I said, in my most mellifluous voice, "for I am a noted seer and magician. As I was passing this house I had a supernatural prompting that I should place my thaumaturgic powers at the owner's disposal. Am I to assume that I have the pleasure of addressing him, in the person of your distinguished self?"

'Of course, the man muttered confusedly that he was, indeed, the master there. "In that case," I continued, "my perceptions tell me that you are hungry and should be provided with a banquet which befits your high rank and enormous piety."

'I said to the wife, who had been standing there with her mouth open, "Madam, if you open the door of that closet, you will find a magical meal, just cooked, which should suffice his Excellency here: he upon whom the benign Huma bird has cast the shadow of its illustrious and miracle-working wings." She hesitated, and her husband, overcome with curiosity – and perhaps hunger – stood up, walked to the door and opened it himself. There, of course, he saw tray upon tray of the choicest delicacies, prepared for his wife's lover.

'He made as if to withdraw a tray of kabobs, when I raised my arm imperiously. "Stay!" I cried; "it ill befits one of your

Eminence's pedigree, attainments and high potential that he should serve himself. Look deeper into the cupboard and you should find there a spirit in human form, whom I designate your servant. He will do all the work."

'He peered inside and, sure enough, there was the wife's lover who clambered out and began to carry the food from the shelves to the table. Now the husband and wife, attended by the servant, ate and drank, and thanked me for my generosity.

'"It is nothing," I said modestly; "it is my duty to obey my promptings. And that reminds me that another supernatural whisper tells me that the lady here owes seven gold coins to a poor man in the town. I am to be the messenger who restores the money to him. You do owe it, do you not, dear madam? I asked, turning to her and giving her a covert wink."

'"Yes, yes, of course I do. It had quite slipped my mind," she muttered, and gave me the gold.'

The disciples twittered with excitement at this wonderful tale, heard from the lips of the Master thief himself. But Lateef silenced them with a baleful glare. 'It is not proper, in the presence of the illuminati of thiefdom,' he growled, 'that novices should observe anything other than silence. For this infraction of decorum I am tempted not to continue the tale.'

Chastened, the audience begged him to forgive them and to continue. Lateef said:

'You may think that I had been well enough paid for my evening's work. But something told me that, if I were to tarry but a short space of time longer, even more golden metal moon-faces would jingle in my purse that night. So I waited, applying the spur of silence to the withers of my host's curiosity.

'At length the husband said, "Tell me, O great and redoubtable magician: do these supernatural promptings come to you without any long and arduous training? Or do you have to work hard and ceaselessly to acquire your remarkable powers of perception?"

'I said, carelessly, "It would be churlish if any detail of even such recondite knowledge were to be withheld from an illustrious magnate such as has just deigned to address me! I shall therefore tell all, omitting no detail."

'I then took out from my sleeve the close-woven, silken robber's sack which I always carried rolled up there, and displayed it to him. "This," I said, "O One whose intellect would descry the mark of an ant's foot upon a black rock at midnight, this is the sole apparatus which is employed in the miracle which you have witnessed this evening."

'I could almost feel his greed as he handled it. Then he said, "I would give anything to possess an object such as this."

'"Know, O Sandalwood-Scented Patrician," I at once responded, "that in magical circles it would be regarded as a solecism beyond redemption were I so to fail in courtesy as not to offer the magical sack to you as a present, viewing your condescending to accept it a signal mark of distinction towards my miserable and unworthy self."

'He was absolutely delighted, and pressed into my resisting hand a bag containing five hundred gold pieces. After warning him that all the magic would depart from the sack if it were used more than once in twenty-four hours, I took my leave. Nor did I forget to say that the servitor whom I had conjured up was a spiteful Jinn, who should be beaten regularly, and kept tied up as much as possible.'

THE GOLDEN HORSE

When the disciples assembled for the next session, Lateef smiled expansively and at once began to speak.

'Deception, dear friends, has been considered by the less well-informed to be something of tremendous power and evil. Yet, if you think on the matter more than superficially, you will soon see that it – like lying – is nothing more than an aid to theft. It is, in a word, a secondary form of thieving. Though not worthy of being regarded as an art, it is sometimes useful. It can even bring in showers of gold, sometimes without penalty.

'I will illustrate from one of my recollections. Another thief and I had arrived in a certain town where we put up in the caravanserai. I had hoped that I would find some rich pickings there, but was soon disabused of this. My friend, who had gone to the bazaar for food supplies, came back with the news that everyone there knew that the traveller at the inn was the great Lateef the Thief.

'I asked my friend how he knew this.

'"Easily", he said; "for no sooner did I enter a shop than the owner told me that I was consorting with the greatest thief in the world, and that I should be ashamed of myself."

'This gave me an idea. I said to my friend, "And who did these worthy merchants consider *you* to be? Evidently not a thief, at any rate."

'"No", he said, "they all seemed to think that I was your servant. You see, you are dressed in rich brocade, while I am only wearing my rough thief's garment."

'I told him to go to the shop of the very richest merchant in the city, and to engage him in conversation. Since we could not carry out any direct theft, I had made a plan based on stealing's little sister – deception.

'The following day my friend found the richest merchant, who proved to be interested in news from afar, and told him tales of his time in Kashmir, where the merchant had never been – any more than had my friend, but that is another subject.

'The merchant then started to speak about me, in much the same vein as the others had; wondering why such a simple and decent sort of fellow as the one before him could work for a notorious thief.

'"Ah," said my friend, "it is because I am fascinated by his horse."

'"Horse?" said the merchant, "what is so special about a horse?"

'"I am not supposed to say – it is a secret," said the thief. But the merchant cajoled him and flattered him, and finally my friend pretended to blurt out the story which we had arranged.

'"Lateef," he said, "is not troubling himself to do any more thieving. This is because he has stolen, by guile, an amazing horse. This is a horse which eats hay and drops gold coins. That's why Lateef is so splendidly dressed."

'Well, naturally the merchant became excited at the possibility of getting hold of the horse, but feared deception: and that is where the first part of my own deception came into play. He detained the thief while he crept round to the serai to watch me feed my horse.

'I had guessed that he might do exactly this. So, when I had given the horse its feed, I collected the dung and sieved it with water, pocketing ten gold ashrafis with a shout of glee.

'The next day I had a visit from the merchant. He offered me ten thousand gold pieces for my horse, and I refused. Finally he went as high as twenty thousand, and added the threat that he would denounce me to the authorities as the renegade, Lateef, if I did not sell the animal. With a show of reluctance I agreed. In order to clinch the matter, I asked that he hire me as the horse's groom, saying that I did not want to be parted from such a loving companion. When I made that stipulation, the merchant's eyes glistened with pleasure. I could almost read his mind, as he planned to discharge me as soon as he got possession of the horse. He led it away, and I agreed to take up my duties as groom the following day.

'In less time than it takes to tell, however,' ended Lateef, 'my fellow-thief and I were shaking the dust of that town from our feet.'

The disciples shook their heads in wonder at Lateef's tale; but one, who was a slow thinker, asked:

'Master Lateef: how did the gold get into the horse's dung when you sieved it?'

Lateef smiled. 'Just try feeding a few gold coins into one end of a horse and see what comes out of the other end . . .'

IMAGINATION

When Lateef reached the third specialised subject at the heart of thievery, his face, turned towards the attentive scholars, was stern.

'Know, O gallant warriors of illicit abstracting, tonight's address plunges into the very kernel of our trade.

'I speak of the subject of Imagination. Imagination, once you have the correct attitude towards it, will readily be perceived by all of you as nothing but a form of deception: which we have seen to be a form of lying, which we have asserted is a form of theft.

'A person imagines something. If he is a thief, he is half-way towards success. He may picture himself creeping over the roof-tops to steal a valuable vase. He may imagine his escape from the pursuit: not to mention visualising the moment of ecstasy when he holds the prize in his hand.

'Again, and equally as valuable, there is self-deception, in which someone actually steals – even if it is only common sense, time and prospects – from himself.

'And, as a masterstroke, there is the implanting of fanciful concepts into the minds of others, whereby a thief can pave the way to stealing or even save his life. I shall give you, now, an illustrative instance of the last-mentioned technique, drawn from my personal experience.'

210

THE GARLIC THEFT

Lateef paused, while the members of the audience held their breath, aware that they were in the presence of one who had made history, and was about to impart secrets.

'One day,' said Lateef, 'I was in the most terrible situation. I had been trapped – yes, even Lateef has been caught from time to time – and thrown into a dungeon. Through treachery and the skill of the Grand Vizier; but the details are not relevant to imagination, so they need not detain us now.

'The Vizier, cunning and overbearing as he was, kept me in his private cellar, hoping to extract a reward when he, triumphantly, announced to the King that he had caught and was holding none other than Lateef, the Thief.

'I sent a message, through a servant of the Vizier who sympathised with anyone unfortunate enough to fall into his master's hands, to my fellow-thieves. They sent one back: but it was depressing. Since our band was hidden some distance away and there were many problems, it would be two days before they could effect my escape so I had only my own resources of wit and imagination to rely on.

'Two days would have been too late. The Vizier, burning with the desire for a triumph, would announce my captivity to the King that very day. The King, for his part, would be sure to demand my presence, and would have me killed on the spot: for I had thrown doubt upon his omnipotence by evading his officers for so many years.

'In his imagination – and we are talking, remember, of this very thing – the Vizier saw me languishing in his dungeon. He saw, in the same way, himself reporting to the King, and his reward, perhaps a thousand pieces of gold. It was this imagination that I planned to use, to use against the evil Minister: and by the employment of my own imagination into the bargain.

'I guessed that the Vizier would come to see me, to crow and cackle, on his way to the royal audience. I also know that the Vizier was fond, above all things except money and power, of – garlic. I induced my jailer to get me a piece of the very freshest, very finest, garlic to be found in the city.

'Sure enough, the Vizier entered the dungeon, dressed in his gorgeous Court robes, beaming and rubbing his palms together.

As he did so, I rose, and pretended to be confused, hiding something behind my back. Naturally, he strode forward and demanded to know what it was. I handed him, as if reluctantly, my garlic.

'The moment he saw the bulb, he snatched it and started to chew, not stopping until he had eaten the lot. The first part of my plan had succeeded. Now for the second part. "My Lord," I said, after he had announced that he was about to inform the King of my capture, "I accept my fate with due submission. But, as your Elevatedness has eaten so much garlic, I humbly suggest that, when speaking to the King, you do not breathe into his face. As you know, a garlic breath is not exactly a zephyr from Paradise."

'"You are right, dog of a thief," mused the Vizier, and went on his way. The third part of my plan depended upon the fact that the King, like so many monarchs daily threatened with deceit, insurrection, plots and the rest, was a highly suspicious man. I counted on the likelihood that his imagination would misinterpret a probable action of his chief Minister.

'Sure enough, when the Vizier approached the King to whisper the news to him, he averted his face, so that the garlic fumes would not reach the monarchical face. This was his reason; but the King, as I had surmised, took this as a sign that the Vizier was looking away from him for a reason. That reason, in his overheated imagination, could only be that there were plotters present among the courtiers, that they planned a coup, and that the Vizier, knowing about this, did not want them to think that he was too intimate with the King. If he were not, of course, the plotters would spare his life.

'Giving no reason, the King dismissed the Vizier and declared the Court closed, to make the supposed conspirators afraid that they had been betrayed.

'So nobody knew that I was in the dungeon and, in due course of time, my friends rescued me.

'And so, my friends, lion-cubs of the profession of stealth and daring, always remember the power and function of imagination and its close relationship with theft.'

Lateef smiled, and gazed fondly at the upturned faces of the students who sat at his feet. The following tales of his exploits are taken from the books and memories of those who knew him, those who approved of his exploits and those who did not, during his long life as the master-thief of all time.

THE CORPSE

It was an hour before dawn and Lateef had spent all the money from his latest theft. He looked around his tiny room and found that he only had a thin, worn blanket, a sheet of paper and a piece of charcoal. 'I might as well be dead,' he thought.

The idea set his imagination to work. As the sun came up, people of the town saw a pathetic sight. Under a blanket by the side of the road was a human form, and on a notice beside it, scrawled in charcoal, were the words:

> HAVE PITY ON THIS CORPSE:
> THERE IS NO MONEY TO BURY HIM!
> PUT DONATIONS IN THE TIN CUP.

Lateef lay as still as death, while people, great and small, sad and sighing, compassionately dropped their coins, of copper, silver or gold, into the receptacle. All the while Lateef's hand, under a hole in the blanket – for the cup had no bottom – was stealthily transferring this bounty to his pocket.

When the sun had nearly reached the meridian, the King, on his weekly progress in state towards the Great Mosque for the midday prayer, saw the shrouded figure and halted the procession. He sent his Chief Minister to investigate. When the man had returned to the Royal palanquin and explained the matter, the King became wroth.

'It is intolerable to the honour and dignity of the Throne, let alone the decency of the Realm,' he thundered, 'that such conditions should exist!'

'Should exist, O Fountain of Wisdom!' intoned the courtiers.

'Let the local Mulla, allegedly a man of faith and decency, be called and reprimanded. Then let him take the body of this unfortunate wretch, wash it preparatory to burial and inter it decently, on pain of a whip-thrashing.'

'A whip-thrashing, O Imposer of True Justice!' cried the sycophants: obeying the customary Eastern custom of echoing the wise words of the ruler.

'And,' continued the King, 'when this is done, the Mulla may approach the Sublime Gateway to be given ten pieces of gold.'

'Ten pieces of gold, Elevated Scatterer of Generosity!' shouted the elated crowd, astonished and delighted at the combined sagacity, right-thinking and problem-solving abilities of their beloved ruler.

Amid the customary, indeed obligatory, roar of 'Long live our Amazing Monarch!' the King went on his way.

The Mulla was called and given his orders. He hired a handcart and took the supposed body to his own home, where he laid out the corpse and began to wash it. Presently he found that he had used up all his soap. Mumbling, 'I'll have to go to the market for soap, what a nuisance, this will take at least half an hour . . .', he went out of the house.

Lateef the Thief seized his chance. Finding the Mulla's ceremonial robe and biggest turban, he dressed himself in them, anointing himself with perfumed oils, and made his way to the Royal Palace. After being announced as the Mulla and getting his ten gold pieces from the hand of the King himself, Lateef bought new – and less conspicuous – clothes and hid in the city's maze of back-streets.

Meanwhile the Mulla at first thought that the corpse had revived, due to some miracle wrought by the Mulla's own sanctity. But then he reasoned that it would have been a strange kind of miracle that would reanimate a corpse which then stole his best clothes. Recalling that the King had threatened him with a whip-lashing, he made his way to the Palace.

After hearing the story, the King was furious. 'None may laugh at our beards in this disgraceful manner!' he roared.

'Laugh at our beards!' repeated the whole Court, dutifully.

The Police Chief undertook to track down Lateef with amazing rapidity . . .

THE KING'S JEWELS

The Heralds were sent from street to street, with the King's proclamation: 'By the King's command: The Thief must be found! Whoever is instrumental in effecting his arrest will have his or her mouth filled with jewels . . .'

214

Lateef, hearing this from a safe place of concealment, had an idea. 'If the King can threaten me, I can do the same to him . . .'
He wrote a letter, and threw it over the Palace wall. It said:

'Know, O King, that the camel-driver may have his plans, but the camel has his plans, too! Look after your jewels.
                    Signed: Lateef the (reanimated) Thief.'

The letter, which landed at his feet as he walked in his enclosed garden, worried the King. He collected his most precious jewels and put them in a bag. Then he confided to the Queen: 'Lateef may get into the treasury. I have, therefore, put your priceless pearls and my diamond collar in a leather bag, under the wardrobe. You can get it out by pulling at the fine string, thin as a hair, which is attached to it.'
'My hero, O all-wise King!' cried the Queen: (for even she was not excused the usual eulogy) 'you always know what to do.' But Lateef, who knew that the treasury was well guarded, had wanted the King to become nervous enough to move the jewels . . .
The very same night, Lateef captured a large lizard and tied a thin but very strong line to its tail. Then he threw it up the sheer wall beside the King's bedchamber. The lizard attached his powerful suckers of his feet to the wall, and Lateef climbed up by means of the dangling rope.
Entering the bedchamber, Lateef saw that the King and Queen were deeply asleep. He searched the room, but could find nothing. So he tiptoed to where the Queen was lying, and whispered into her ear:
'My love, where was it that I put those valuable jewels, do you remember?'
The Queen, still fast asleep, answered without thinking, and even omitting the customary plaudits: 'You really are the limit! I think you're going senile. Don't you remember, you told me that they were under the wardrobe, and you pull the bag out by the string attached to it?'
Suppressing a chuckle, Lateef moved silently across the room, retrieved the bag of jewels – and escaped in the same way that he had entered.
In the morning, the King went to find his collar of diamonds: but, of course, the jewels were gone. 'Lateef has been here!' he

roared, turning out the guard. They searched the entire palace, from top to bottom, and found the lizard and the rope still attached to its tail . . .

When the Chief of Police, shivering with apprehension, was brought before him, the King ordered him to find the thief within a week. 'Failing that, your head will be cut off!' he stormed.

'Box his ears, to speed him on his way!' he added, to the Chief of Protocol.

With these words echoing in his bruised ears, the policeman scrambled backwards from the Royal Presence.

The Chief of Police walked, day and night, through the streets of the Capital, looking for the miscreant, who, he realised, could be none other than the redoubtable Lateef the Thief, whom none had ever been able to catch.

THE EARRINGS

Looking through his loot, Lateef saw that he had an unexpected bonus: there was a valuable emerald earring caught on the string of the pearls. The other earring had fallen on the carpet during the theft. 'What a pity it's not a pair,' he thought. When he sold the jewels, he put the single earring aside.

Meanwhile, the King had come across the other earring: and a thought, then a plan, occurred to him. He sent a courtier to a jeweller in the town. The man said, 'Please place this item on prominent display in your shop-window. If anyone shows an interest in it, send your assistant with all speed to me, keep the man talking, and you will be well rewarded.'

A day or two later, while on one of his usual reconnaissance walks through the town, Lateef saw the duplicate of his earring.

He went home and brought the other one, and went into the shop. As soon as he asked to see the jewel in the window, the jeweller sent his boy rushing to the courtier's house.

Now Lateef, with the jeweller gabbling away to keep the transaction going, went to the shop door. Suddenly he started to shout:

'Come to my aid, O people! I am oppressed!'

A crowd swiftly gathered, and Latif showed them the two earrings:

'Know, O lovers of Justice, that this dishonourable man is trying

to sell me the pair to my own wife's earring – which I have here –
which he must have stolen, or bought from a thief!'

The jeweller tried to protest, but Lateef said, 'Do you or do you
not agree that this earring was in your window, and that I brought
the other one in myself?'

'Well, yes . . .' began the jeweller.

That was enough for the crowd. By the time the King's courtier
and the police arrived to arrest Lateef, he had walked away, and
they were just in time to rescue the jeweller from the mob, who
proposed to lynch him.

LATEEF AND AFEEF

Lateef now had plenty of money, but he could not keep out of
mischief. The very next day, walking in disguise through the town,
he saw a huge iron man-cage set out in the market-square. In it was
a notorious robber named Afeef. The Chief of Police had had him
brought there from a dungeon, as part of a deep and cunning plan.

Now Lateef hardly knew Afeef, but the policeman reasoned that
Lateef would not be able to resist trying to rescue him. 'If he steals
your Majesty's own jewels, he will certainly try to steal this man
from under our noses,' he told the King. 'My plan is to keep a
watch and foil him. I have set guards beside the cage, day and
night. If Lateef comes, we shall have him.'

The King was greatly cheered by the prospect, and his heart
softened somewhat towards the Police chief. 'Don't let him make
fools of us this time, that's all,' he said.

The chief bowed low. 'May I be the sacrifice for your Majesty's
life . . .' he intoned. 'I may well have your life if you fail,' shouted
the King, his peevishness reasserting itself.

Lateef loitered, unrecognised by the policeman, his spies and
the guards, near the cage, among the milling crowd of citizens, who
were baiting the unfortunate Afeef within. It was too dangerous,
Lateef realised, to attempt a rescue. There were too many people
about; whatever he thought of, even if he got Afeef out, they
would get in his way.

Suddenly an old woman, carrying a pitcher of milk, hearing
someone say, 'That's Afeef, I hear he's going to be hanged in the
morning', started to weep and wail. She was Afeef's mother,

bringing him some milk – and she had recognised Lateef, even through his disguise.

Grasping his sleeve, she cried, 'Lateef, save my son's life!'

'I'll not be able to do anything if you identify me like that!' hissed Lateef. At that moment he heard the crowd murmuring 'Lateef, Lateef': and the Chief of Police himself was striding towards the cage.

Quick as a flash, Lateef seized the pitcher of milk, smashed it on the ground, and fled.

The policeman grabbed the old woman and said, 'I'm going to take you in for questioning. Why are you crying – you must be connected with this case. And which of these people is Lateef, or which way did he go?'

Afeef, very quick on the uptake and anxious to save his mother from interrogation by the evil police, shouted, 'What do you mean, Lateef?'

The policeman turned towards him. 'That's what everyone is calling out, isn't it?'

Afeef laughed. 'They misheard, blockhead. The woman cried "Nazeef!"'

'And what would she shout "Nazeef" for, you son of a goat?' screamed the other man.

'Nazeef means "clean",' said Afeef.

'I know that, you ape's behind!' howled the Police chief. 'But why should anyone shout "clean!"?'

'Because, Father of Ignorance,' smirked Afeef, 'because she was selling milk, and calling out "clean!" describing it'.

'And why is she crying?' asked the policeman, suspiciously, 'if she has nothing to do with the case?'

'Because, toenail of a newt's uncle,' Afeef told him, 'because someone knocked the pitcher from her hand, and she has lost all her milk, that's why! Now let go of her.'

'Yes, let go of the poor woman!' howled the crowd, none of whom was especially fond of the police.

The policeman, baffled, beat a retreat with such dignity as he could muster. That evening, alarmed by the reports from the town, the King sent for him. 'I hear you almost started a riot today, trying to arrest a poor old woman after she had lost all her milk,' he said. 'Well, I have one thing to tell you: any further blunders from you, and I'll have your head sawn off, slowly, with a blunt knife . . .'

'It was a normal matter of routine human error, your Majesty, in the course of my enquiries . . .'

'I'll give you enquiries!' screamed the King. 'What about capturing Lateef the thief, instead of persecuting poor old women?'

'Majesty, I have a plan,' said the unfortunate policeman. 'It is to do with coins . . .' But the King was too annoyed to stand the sight of the man any more that day. 'Stop babbling about coins and come and tell me tomorrow, if you must, when I have composed myself a little,' he said grumpily, dismissing the miserable guardian of the peace.

By this time the whole town had heard how the quick-witted thieves had fooled the forces of law and order, and there was much chuckling in the teahouses and caravanserais. Lateef, now in another disguise, laughed as loudly as anyone. And, realising how cunning Afeef was, he decided to rescue him.

Late that night, when the moon was high and the market-square was deserted apart from the two guards, Lateef prepared himself. He smeared charcoal dust on his face, stuck two paper horns to his head, and stuck black feathers onto a tattered cloak. Then he approached the guards at the cage, slowly flapping his arms from side to side.

'Stop this foolery and get away. This is a royal prisoner!' said the first guard, as Lateef approached.

Lateef flapped his cloak faster and thrust his face into that of the other man. 'So, thou wouldst bandy words with me, who could take thee in a trice to the nether regions, for toasting over eternal fire . . .' he rasped.

The man goggled at him, and then the other said, hoarsely, 'Beware! This can be none other than the Angel of Death, on his nightly rounds. Please spare us, poor conscripts, O Great Angel! Be merciful.'

Lateef gave a horrible chuckle. 'That's better my lad! Now, just give me your keys.'

'Keys? I can't give up the keys to the cage . . .'

'If you don't give them to me, I shan't be able to take away the prisoner, shall I? And I have strict instructions that his time has come, and I must deliver him to Hades almost immediately. Of course, if your duty forbids it, I might just be able to take one of you two instead, and hope that the guardians of Hell will accept him. I might create a diversion. Yes, if you care to make it worth my while . . .'

The terrified guard thrust the keys into Lateef's outstretched hand and Lateef opened the cage door and beckoned Afeef out as the two now hysterical guards ran for their lives . . .

The following day, neither the King nor the Police chief dared to show his face in the Capital, for everyone knew the story of how Lateef had laughed at their beards. The King was, indeed, so downcast that he hardly raised his hand to lash the policeman, whom he had had brought before him, bound hand and foot, for a little sport. His heart, for once, just was not in it.

The next day, however, the demoralised policeman crawled into the Royal Presence and muttered his 'great gold coins plan', guaranteed to trap Lateef.

'I suppose I've got to give you another chance,' said the King, miserably, 'because there isn't anyone else to handle this affair. But, I warn you, there are only a few days left . . .'

'This time we'll do it, Majesty,' promised the policeman.

THE GOLD COINS

Knowing that Lateef could not resist a challenge, the Chief of Police had had twelve gold coins, borrowed from the King, placed on the parade-ground just beside the Royal Palace. 'You see,' he explained to the King, 'Lateef will know that they are there, and will come and pick them up. Nobody else would dare. As soon as he does, we've got him.'

'That sounds like a splendid idea,' – the King was quite cheered up. 'By tomorrow night he'll be in our hands.'

All the next day, the policeman and the King were strategically seated on a turret overlooking the parade-ground.

Soon after midday they saw, with mounting excitement, some-one start to cross the arena. 'My men,' the policeman excitedly explained to the King, 'have instructions not to approach anyone until he picks up a coin. When this man – who must be Lateef – actually steals one, they will pounce. They are everywhere, in concealment behind those carts you see drawn up here and there.'

But, though their eyes, and those of the watchers, never left the strolling figure, he showed no sign of seeing the coins, and certainly did not stoop to pick up anything at all. Finally he disappeared into the distance.

'That couldn't have been Lateef, after all,' they concluded.

But, all that day, nobody else appeared. As the sun began to set, the King sent the Chief of Police down to recover the coins. 'Someone might take them in the dark, and we don't want that, do we?' he said. 'Anyway, at least we've shown that Lateef can't steal in broad daylight, when people are watching.'

Lateef, however, had smeared his shoes with treacle, and picked up the coins as he strolled along. What the King had to say to the Police chief when he brought the news of the disappearance of the gold cannot be committed to paper without it bursting into flames . . .

The policeman was now in a piteous state, and Lateef judged it time to break him down a little more, by making another personal appearance. So, next time he saw the unfortunate man in the city square, Lateef ran up to him, and danced up and down in front of him, calling out, 'Catch me if you can!'

The policeman drew his sword, which only made Lateef caper all the more. Slashing wildly, the policeman cut off one half of Lateef's long moustache before Lateef ran away, easily outpacing him.

'This time I've got him!' cried the officer, in delight. 'All I have to do is to issue an order that anyone with half a moustache is to be arrested and brought before me.'

The next morning the police were out in force, combing the city for men with a half moustache. They arrested sixty of them before realising that half the men of the capital had half their moustaches cut off. Lateef had been the rounds, with a pair of scissors, in and out of their houses, snipping the adornments from their sleeping faces . . .

The Chief of Police was now having hysterical fits of shouting and weeping, and sometimes howling like a dog, sometimes laughing uncontrollably. He was very near breaking-point.

AT THE APOTHECARY'S SHOP . . .

Five days after the King's ultimatum, the Police chief was lucky enough to espy Lateef in the street. Lateef had wearied of staying in concealment; and besides, he felt that inspiration would come to his aid if the pursuit got too close.

Lateef saw the Police chief out of the corner of his eye, recognised him and started to walk faster, his mind working furiously. The man was a hundred yards behind when Lateef spotted an apothecary's shop just ahead. Rushing in, he threw down a gold piece and hastily told the druggist and his two assistants:

'My poor brother, whose guardian I am, has insane fits. He's following me now, and may become violent. Take this money, great men of wisdom. When he comes in, seize him, bind him to a chair and keep him quiet until he calms down!'

Then he rushed out of the shop through the back door.

The Chief of Police did not have a chance. The chemist and his men were all powerfully built, and they soon subdued their victim. The tied him hand and foot, forcing an opium potion down his throat into the bargain. When he regained consciousness, they gave him shock treatment, hitting him with bamboo staves.

The wretched policeman, at the end of his tether, ran to the Court, and begged the King to cut off his head without delay, raving, 'I can't stand any more, death would be better than this . . . Lateef The Thief is the cleverest man in the world . . .'

The King, now that the man's nerve was broken, assigned him to the royal stables as a labourer, and had the heralds announce, in every street and market place:

'Hear this, hear this, let nobody say that he has not heard! His Majesty commands the presence of Lateef the Thief, and guarantees him a free pardon in return for a recital of his adventures!'

His Majesty was as good as his word. When Lateef had presented himself and related his adventures, he was appointed – Chief of Police.

FOUR WORDS

As Chief of Police, Lateef still retained some compassion for his old associates. One of them, a dangerous bandit, was captured and, try as he might, Lateef could not get him released. The bandit had not only stolen from rich and poor, but he had sworn at the King himself, when taken before him in chains.

Humour

The bandit was sentenced to death by hanging.

On the day of execution, a heavily-armed squad of soldiers carried the condemned man to the scaffold. In his official capacity, Lateef stood by as a witness to the execution.

'Lateef, save me!' implored the miscreant. Lateef shook his head, and pointed sadly at the soldiers and police swarming around the market place. 'But, Lateef: what about your inspirations?' asked the unhappy man.

As the noose was being put around the bandit's neck, Lateef suddenly got his idea. 'The King is dead!' he roared at the top of his voice.

At these terrible words, the crowd started loud lamentations, the police and the soldiers ran for their barracks. The bandit escaped, of course.

When the tumult had died down, the King sent for Lateef, to be brought before him in chains.

'How dare you do such a thing?' The King was purple in the face with rage. 'To suggest that I might be dead is tantamount to *lèse majesté!*'

'Your Majesty,' said Lateef, 'if with four words I can save a human life, and do no harm to others, why should I not say them?'

'But pardoning convicts is my own prerogative,' complained the King.

'Commoners are allowed to do things which kings do,' said Lateef, 'except that kings are better at such work.'

'And what does that mean, pray?'

'It means that I could never approach anything like your Majesty's elegant simplicity of power,' Lateef told him; 'because what took me four words, you could have done in one – by simply saying "Pardoned!"'

'Lateef, I'll never be able to keep up with you,' said the King, and dismissed him with costly presents in appreciation of his flattery – but relieved him of his post as head of the Police force.

PARROTS

Talking parrots were all the rage in Lateef's home town: everyone wanted them. Nobody would so much as look at a dumb parrot, so Lateef was able to pick up a pair of them, guaranteed not to talk, no matter what the inducement might be.

223

He betook himself to a caravanserai.

Everyone knew Lateef's reputation and so, few were the people and hardy the soul, who would do any kind of business with him. Thus it was that, seeing him sitting there, with two great cages covered in cloth, nobody wanted to buy them.

But, as is the way in the East, almost everyone was prepared to talk about business.

'What have you there, Latif?' asked one rich merchant, indicating the cages, 'talking parrots, I suppose?'

'Yes, O great King of Merchants,' said Lateef, 'the talkingest parrots in the world.'

'I suppose they know more words than anyone else's?'

'Yes, at least a hundred words.'

The merchant thought that he would have some fun at Lateef's expense. No doubt the thief's birds knew one or two words, even half a dozen. He would be sure to be exaggerating. He said, 'What a pity! I was looking for two parrots who would not say a thing, no matter how hard you tried to make them talk.'

'Ah, they're very rare that kind,' said Lateef: 'would you pay much for two such unusual birds?'

To keep the joke going, the merchant said, 'Yes, I'd give this bag of gold for such a pair.'

'Thank you,' said Lateef, taking the gold, 'you can have double this back if you can get either of these to say a thing!'

THE TREASURY

Now, Lateef came from a very long line of thieves, stretching back, father to son, for many centuries. He had inherited an ancient parchment, written by an ancestor, which was only to be unrolled by a master-thief of his family who had successfully sold a non-talking parrot. Lateef opened it.

The words on the parchment told him that there was a secret entrance to the King's underground treasury. The builders had roofed the place with granite blocks which were so well fitted that a knife could not be inserted between any of them. But, in one place, they had installed a block on a swivel, which could be opened by anyone who knew its location.

Lateef found the secret entrance, and made several trips to the treasury, taking away bags of gold.

Presently the Royal Treasurer noticed that gold kept disappearing, and doubled the guard on the doors – without result. Then he went to the King, in fear and trembling, to report on the mystery.

'This can be nobody except Lateef,' said the monarch; and called in his wisest Vizier.

'There must be another way in,' reasoned the Minister. 'I shall find it for your Majesty.'

He ordered a large quantity of straw to be brought and burnt inside the underground chamber. Stationed outside, the Vizier watched, until he saw smoke rising from a certain spot, through the only crack between the granite blocks.

The Vizier was excited beyond measure, and planned to locate Lateef single-handed, so that he could get the huge reward offered by the King.

Positioning himself in concealment outside the entrance to the secret entrance, the Vizier waited until he heard Latif, in the dead of night, approach. Lateef entered the passage, and the Vizier still waited. When he emerged with a bag of gold, the Vizier followed him back to his hiding-place, dropping, at intervals, grains of corn from a bag which he carried, to mark the trail.

But Lateef was his equal in cunning. When day dawned, the thief looked out of his window and saw the grains, stretching along the street. Quick as a flash, Lateef went into his back-yard and brought out three chickens, which he set to eat the corn. By the time the Vizier, with the King in tow, arrived at the treasury to follow the trail, all they found was – a flock of chickens, scratching for worms.

THE HUNCHBACK

One night Lateef was prowling in a graveyard, for he had heard that a miser was in the habit of going there to hide money. As bad luck would have it, three soldiers had been posted there by the King, to strengthen their resolve, as he wanted them for a night attack on an enemy and they were nervous in the dark.

They saw Lateef and, as it was after curfew time, they seized him.

'I'll give you a reward if you let me go,' pleaded Lateef; 'I was only visiting the grave of my sainted ancestor . . .' But the soldiers, hoping for promotion, refused.

'We can't desert our post,' said one, 'so we'll tie you to a tree, and take you back to the guard-house in the morning.'

Binding him with a strong rope, the soldiers went into a small building nearby, where they fell asleep.

Now the miser who used the graveyard as his treasure-chest was making his way to the hiding-place of his money when, as dawn was breaking, he saw Lateef, tied to a tree.

Lateef saw him at the same moment, noted that he was a hunchback, and his never-failing inspiration came to his aid.

'Brother,' said Lateef, 'has it gone yet?'

'What do you mean, "gone"?' asked the miser.

'There is but one meaning to the word "gone",' hissed Lateef. 'I am talking about my hump. I'm tied to this magical tree, which as everyone surely knows, miraculously cures hunchbacks in just a few hours, if they are tied to it. Look and see if my hump is gone, there's a good fellow.'

The miser looked and, sure enough, Lateef's back was as straight as a die.

'You have no hump!' he exclaimed in amazement.

'Excellent!' said Lateef; 'now, untie me quickly, for I must be on my way.'

The hunchback released Lateef, with trembling fingers. Then he whined, 'Kind sir, you may have noticed that I, too, am a hunchback. Please tie me to the tree so that I may be cured; and come back for me later in the day. Do this kind service, and I will reward you well.'

'All right,' said Lateef, 'if you insist.'

When the soldiers woke up, they found that their captive had been changed into a hunchback and, thinking he must be a magician, let him loose after making him promise not to cast any spells upon them.

ENTER AREEF

One day a man named Areef approached Lateef and said, 'I am a master thief, and I would like to join you and Afeef. One man is only a thief, however good he may be at his craft. Two makes a partnership: but three – three, now, makes a band. And a band of thieves is altogether more intimidating, more traditional, than a single one or even a partnership.'

Lateef consulted Afeef, who thought it was a good idea; but the partners agreed that Areef should be tested before he could join their select company.

Areef produced his idea, and schooled the others in it.

Thus it was that, shortly afterwards, the three men visited a notorious miser and moneylender namd Bakhil, with their proposition.

'The three of us,' said Lateef, indicating Afeef and Areef, 'are merchants. We have a sum of money which we are taking to Bokhara. We'll be three days on the road. We need your advice how to safeguard it.'

Bakheel was curious. 'Why are you taking money to Bokhara?'

'Didn't you know?' asked Lateef; 'there's a rush on gold there. We plan to buy goods, bring them back here, and make a tremendous profit.'

'Maybe I could join you . . .'

'I don't know about that: after all, the more money we have with us, the more likely thieves are to get to hear about it . . .'

Finally, Lateef and his friends allowed themselves to be persuaded to take the miser along with them. He suggested that they hire a body of armed men to protect the party.

'First, it would cost a fortune. Second, how do we know the guards would not rob us themselves?' said Afeef.

'Anyway,' said Areef, 'I'm not sure that I trust you men. Supposing two or more of you gang up on me? After all, we don't know each other at all well.'

Eventually, it was decided that all the bags of gold would be placed on one mule, and everyone would watch everyone else. The moneylender's hoard was by far the largest. And the heavy bags belonging to the thieves contained only worthless iron bars . . .

The party set off on the long journey, with everyone watching everyone else, and keeping one eye on the heavily-laden mule.

After several hours' plodding along the road, the travellers came to an inn with a luxurious steam bath. After enjoying a meal, Lateef suggested that all should relax their weary limbs in the bath. 'But we'll all have to go in together,' said the miser, 'otherwise one of us might make off with the money.'

Afeef said, 'Better still, we'll also tell the woman bath-keeper to look after the mule, and not to give it up to any single one of us. The whole group must consent before she releases it.'

227

Thus agreed, they all entered the bath-house.

After the hot bath, then the cold, then the steam, and the massage with perfumed oils, Afeef said, 'I wish we had a comb, my hair and beard could do with some attention.'

'That's true,' said Lateef, 'but I'm too sleepy to bother.'

'Go and ask the woman to give us one,' said Afeef.

'Go and get me a comb,' Areef said to the Moneylender.

'Why don't you go, you lazy scoundrel?' said Bakheel, luxuriating in the warmth, and wanting to keep up his half-dream of all the profit he would make from the trip.

'Oh, all right, then,' grumbled the thief. Areef plodded out of the bath-house to where the woman keeper sat.

'I have to take the mule away,' he told her.

'Not until all your friends consent: that's the agreement,' frowned the woman, suspiciously.

'It's all right, we've changed the plan.'

'I can't give it to you unless everyone else agrees.'

'Well, then,' said Areef, 'hear for yourself.'

He shouted 'Friends, are you all agreed that she should let me have it?'

'Yes, of course!' they all called back.

So Areef dressed, took the mule, and was well on his way back to the thieves' den before anyone realised that he was missing.

And that is how Areef was pronounced a worthy member of the gang.

ELIXIR OF YOUTH

Lateef tried every way he could to get into the house of a rich old man, named Juki: but the place was too well secured. He had to have a different kind of plan to part the man from his money.

One day, Juki was walking home when he saw a bent figure, with long white hair, carrying a placard. On it was written: 'I know the secret of the Elixir of Life! For a hundred gold pieces I can reveal all. Learn my secret now!'

Now, Lateef had heard that Juki had been making enquiries about rejuvenation, for he feared death above all things.

Juki stopped in front of the disguised thief and read the message. Then, as he was moving away, he laughed. 'If you can make old people young, why don't you start with yourself?' he said, scornfully.

'Kind Master,' whined Lateef, 'I have only one packet of the wonder herbs which rejuvenate, enough for two doses, and so am not able to take advantage of this marvellous treatment myself. If, however, you would give me the chance of treating you, I could prove that my words are true.'

The miser was no fool, and he, too, had a plan.

'Very well,' he said, 'come into my house and tell me all about it.'

As soon as they were inside, Juki led the tottering Lateef into a cellar and locked him in. 'Now,' he said through a slit in the door; 'give me your potion or whatever it is, and I shall let you out when it works.'

'But how can I trust you to pay me, or even to let me go?' said Lateef.

'What do you propose?' asked the rich man.

'Fix a high shelf in this dungeon, and put the key to the door on it, together with a hundred gold pieces. It should be too high for a feeble wretch such as I have become to reach. I will take half the herbs, and you can have the other. If I am rejuvenated, so will you be: and I shall be able to reach the key and the money.' The miser agreed, and arranged the shelf, key and money.

Lateef passed him a packet of dried herbs. 'Make an infusion of this, and you will be thirty years younger by tomorrow morning,' he said.

As soon as the miser had gone and Lateef knew that he must be asleep, he threw off his disguise, took the key and the money, and was away.

CAMEL'S HEAD

Lateef was, of course, a master of disguise. One day a friend came to him saying that the merchants in the Street of the Silk Traders were a bunch of thieves or, at least, swindlers; so he decided to become one of them.

Disguising himself as a Kurdish silk merchant, his face heavily muffled, he took a bundle of rare silk to the Traders' Street and cried, 'Who'll buy this? Things of great excellence!'

The merchants gathered around. Like all crooks, they were

suspicious of everything, and asked Lateef if the bundle was silk all through.

'No, of course not!' shouted Lateef; 'there's a camel's head in the middle!' The man paid what Lateef asked, laughing . . .

He had unrolled the silk before Lateef was halfway down the street. Spitting and snarling at the deception, the silk merchants hauled the disguised Lateef – the 'Kurdish merchant' – before the court of summary justice.

'I only told the truth,' said Lateef.

Case dismissed.

Idries Shah

THE LAND OF FOOLS

The origins of Foolsland tales are too far back for anyone to find them; but the country and its people are with us still. Many of the Mulla Nasrudin or Wise Men of Gotham (and similar) tales are straight out of the Land of Fools. So are reports, often about bureaucrats, politicians or 'experts' which appear daily in the newspapers throughout our present-day world.

In the East it is often said that vanity, pomposity or greed are what cause otherwise sensible people to qualify for naturalisation, full citizenship, of the Land of Fools.

A recent anecdote about an academic who was rather full of himself seems to bear this out:

He received a letter one day from the British Broadcasting Corporation. It said, 'We would like you to give a talk on television on your subject, "Nothing Exists and Therefore There is Nothing to Say About It".'

The letter ended, 'The fee will be a hundred pounds.'

Delighted, the pedant wrote back accepting. His letter contained these words: 'I agree to talk for £100. Please let me know where to send the money.'

Citizens of the Land of Fools may be found almost everywhere. I was once asked by the editor of a magazine to write an article, with which I enclosed some photographs. On the back of each enlargement I had rubber-stamped 'REPRODUCTION FORBIDDEN WITHOUT WRITTEN PERMISSION'. The editor telephoned to ask me to get the written permission of the photographer. I said, 'That's me!' There was a long pause. Then the editor said, 'I hardly think that's possible. After all, you could have *told* me, you didn't need to have a rubber stamp made.'

You know, with so many wonderful civilisations of the past now extinct, and hardly a trace remaining, I take great comfort in the reflection that it seems less than likely that the people and ways of the Land of Fools will ever die out.

But they don't seem to keep their exploits in written records; so I have decided to do something towards this.

WHAT IT'S LIKE . . .

Three men of the Land of Fools came upon a deep well.

'You go down and see what it is like down there,' said their leader to the most junior Foolslander.

He jumped in, fell right to the bottom, and was killed by the impact.

The others waited two hours for him.

'Let's follow,' commanded the leader, 'after all, if he hadn't liked it there, he wouldn't have stayed so long.'

Assumptions based on superficialities are as alive and well today. Mr Ray Bull told a meeting of the British Psychological Society how this can work. People shown pictures of people with, for instance, scars, were likely to judge them as dishonest . . .

And the great Harry Houdini, master escapologist, used pure Foolsland thinking when faced by a challenge at a jail. Shut in a cell and invited to get out of it, records Harold Kellock, in *Houdini*, he could not get the door lock to open. He tried every trick he knew; and, in the end, leaning exhausted against the door, he found that it swung open at a touch. It had not been locked.

GAMBLING STONE

A wily merchant, having sold all kinds of useless goods to the people, was leaving the Land of Fools when a local citizen came up to him. 'Who are you?' asked the Fool.

'I'm a travelling merchant; you know, I sell things.'

'Go on then, sell me something.'

This was too good a chance to miss, the merchant thought. He picked up a stone and, improvising, said: 'This is only two dinars. It is a gambling stone.'

'What's that?'

'Well, you take that hammer you're carrying, and if you can crack the stone, it gives you ten to one in whatever money you've wagered that you'll split it.'

'I'll buy that, all right,' said the Foolsland man, 'for this is a pretty heavy hammer and that stone does not look too strong. It's money for old rope.'

The merchant took his two dinars, and sped away.

The Fool picked up his hammer and said, 'Ten to one in silver that I split you first time!' He hit the stone a mighty blow, but it did not crack.

'All right, then, you won that time. Now I'll bet you ten to one in GOLD that you can't stand this one!' He hit it even harder, still without success.

'Right. I owe you ten pieces of gold and ten of silver. I'll go double or quits with you!' And the Fool, using both hands and all his strength, brought his hammer down on the stone with a mighty blow which jarred his arms up to the shoulders.

Still the stone remained unbroken.

'You're just a thief and degenerate, tempting people with promises of money. For that I'm not going to pay you. Furthermore', continued the stalwart Fool, 'I'm going to throw you into these bushes, where nobody will see you, to fall for your blandishments . . .'

People will go to tremendous lengths to follow up a train of thought which has no reality whatever. In November 1981, hundreds of television viewers jammed the switchboards at ITV. They had just seen, in a fictional serial ('Crossroads') a motel burn down. They wanted to know whether one *imaginary* character, Meg, was safe or not.

YOU CHEAT!

One of the men of the Land of Fools met another on the road.

'Guess what I have in my hand,' he said.

'A camel.'

'You cheat – you saw me pick it up!'

And – while we are on irrelevancies – at Loughborough on 1 August 1969, a sales manager was charged with stealing Lord Lanesborough's walking-stick at a Young Conservatives' party. It was explained on behalf of the accused that he 'was chairman of his village cricket team and captain of hockey. He went to the party after playing cricket'.

EQUITY

One Foolslander brought a case against another. 'This man struck me and put out one of my eyes,' he complained.

The accused man pleaded guilty.

After long cogitation as to the appropriate compensation, the Judge gave his verdict:

'Take your other eye out and send it round until you find someone with one which matches it. Buy that one, and we'll fine the accused an equivalent amount of money.'

But we should not be too surprised at the difficulties of some Foolslanders in dealing with problems. A teacher at an Assistant Mistresses' Association Conference in London said that near-illiterate pupils taking the Certificate of Secondary Education 'usually gained a very low grade in CSE, but they were credited with having passed it'.

EATING DOG

Among the little-known customs in the Land of Fools is that they call sheep 'dogs' and dogs 'sheep'.

A trickster who hoped to sell a sheep for an enormous sum to the gullible folk of Foolsland entered their country, driving a scruffy ewe in front of him.

'Ho, Friend!' shouted the first fool whom he met, 'Where are you going with that dog?'

'Idiot!' said the trickster, 'this is a sheep, and a mighty fine one; not a dog . . .'

He went on his way and presently came upon a couple of other fools standing by the wayside. 'Nice dog you have there: or it would be, if you fattened it up a bit,' said the first Foolslander amiably. The Trickster frowned. The second Fool said, 'Dogs make good eating, sometimes . . .'

The Trickster was now becoming confused. He saw a policeman nearby and shouted, 'Some evil men are trying to make me believe that a sheep is a dog.'

234

'What sheep?' asked the policeman.

'Why, this one, here.'

'That, Sir, is a DOG, if you don't mind. It's my belief that someone has been trying to convince you that a dog is really a sheep . . .'

With a wild cry, the Trickster took to his heels, abandoning the animal.

'Unclaimed property,' said the policeman; and the Fools made a meal of it.

The British Foreign Office might take note of the perils of confusion due to language. The House of Commons Foreign Affairs Committee reported on 21 July, 1981 that only half the staff at the Embassy in Paris could speak French. Only a third of those in Bonn knew German. *The Times*, on the following day, noting that Sir Anthony Kershaw said that some diplomats' knowledge of languages was 'frankly rotten', recorded that Embassy staff were reduced to sign language.

LITIGATION

An ordinary man strayed into the Land of Fools while on a hunting expedition. Near a small village he shot a bird.

No sooner had he picked it up than he was surrounded by villagers. They took him to the local Court, where he was charged with murder, and assigned an advocate to help defend him.

When the case was called, the first Foolsland plaintiff said, 'The bird was my father's reincarnation. I am waiting for him to settle our family's debts. Now he's been killed, we'll have to wait for generations: for he'll now go back to the bottom of the list of reincarnees . . .'

The second Fool said, 'And, as the owner of the pond where the bird was, I claim the value of all the fish he has eaten.'

Other claimants added their own stories.

The accused was in despair. But his counsel drew him aside and told him how to plead.

When the Judge asked whether the Defendant had anything to say, he answered:

'I plead guilty, and will give all the compensation which the Court may decree. There is only one problem. My own father, who was very rich, has been reincarnated as a newt, and we shall all have to wait until it is his turn to become human again, so that he can tell us where he buried his hoard of golden treasure.'

'That's reasonable enough,' said the Judge; 'everyone will just have to wait.'

Of course, the law in England has its own, special, approach to human life. At the time of writing, it is possible to get drunk on a Sunday after buying alcohol; but one may have to do so with frozen feet, since, beer may be sold on the Sabbath, but it is forbidden to sell socks . . .

JUDGMENT

An Outsider (as other people are called) went into the Land of Fools with a confederate, determined to play a trick, and make a profit from the stupidity of the Foolslanders.

They dressed themselves in costly garments, the better to impress the Fools.

The two men soon came upon a simpleton with a sheep. 'Friend Foolslander,' said the first trickster, 'give us that animal.'

'Why should I?' asked the Fool.

'Why, haven't you heard?' said the second Outsider, 'The End of the World is coming in three hours' time. There won't be any need of meat or wool then.'

'In that case,' said the sheep's owner, 'we might as well eat it. I'll cook a meal now for the three of us.'

A feast of roast lamb seemed quite a good start to the day, so the two interlopers agreed. While the Fool was collecting wood for the fire, they espied a deliciously cool stream. Talking off their clothes, they plunged into the water for a swim.

Suddenly they realised that the fire, which had been blazing fiercely, was giving off great clouds of smoke, and they got out of the water to see what was amiss. They were just in time to see their robes, turbans and shoes burnt to cinders.

Dancing up and down with grief and fury, the desperate Outsiders shouted, 'Why did you do that?'

'Well,' said the Fool, calmly, 'if the End of the World is as close as you say, you'll not be needing clothes, will you? You did say there would be no call for wool . . .'

GOLD AND SACKS

The tricksters whose clothes had been burnt managed to fool some Fools out of new clothes, and continued on their way, determined to make up for their losses.

They got a gold piece out of one Fool, by telling him that it was missing from a library, having been out on loan too long. They showed the Fool the date on the coin, as proof, and promised to return it.

Arriving at the Capital, Foolstown, the pair beat two sticks together until a crowd collected.

'What are you doing?' one of the Fools asked.

'We are travellers, and it is dangerous to carry money, in case one is robbed. So we use these magic sticks.'

'How do they work?'

'You just beat them together, saying "Tilla-Tilla", and a gold coin falls to the ground.'

One trickster beat the sticks, while the other, unnoticed by the Fools, threw down the coin which they had promised to take back to the library.

The King of the Foolslanders happened to be in the crowd. 'I'll give you ten gold pieces for those sticks,' he offered.

'You can have them for that, since you are a king,' said the first trickster. 'But remember,' said the second, 'you can only get one gold coin every three hours, that's why we can't repeat the performance immediately.'

'Sounds logical,' said the King, and went off happily.

After three hours he tried the trick, and was enraged to find that no gold appeared. 'I've been swindled!' he roared, and gave orders for the swindlers to be found.

The crooks took the ten gold pieces and left the city in a hurry, eventually arriving at a prosperous village. One hid in the woods and the other went to the market place.

He went up to a potter and bought a cheap clay cooking-vessel. Then he started to recite strange words over it. 'What are you doing?' asked the potter.

'Making a self-cooking pot,' explained the trickster.

'What's that?'

'A pot that cooks by itself, so that you need no fire or fuel.'

The potter thought, 'I'd make a fortune selling pots like that.' He asked the Outsider, 'What would you take for your secret?'

'How much have you got?'

'I've saved about a hundred gold coins . . .'

'That'll do. Just buy some meat and herbs and I'll give you a demonstration.'

When the materials were bought, the potter sat down to see the magic wrought.

'We can't do it here. Magical cooking has to be done in the woods. Are there any woods near here?'

'There are some quite near,' said the potter; and together they went to a place near which the swindler's confederate was concealed.

The Outsider told the potter to sit down and memorise some magic words while he put the pot with the ingredients in it behind a bush with his eyes closed. 'Now count to a hundred,' he said.

The confederate emptied out the raw food and poured a newly-cooked stew into the new pot. Then he tiptoed away.

The potter could hardly wait to count out his gold and make his way, with the magical pot, back to his shop.

The crooks slept that night in another part of the forest, and were making their way home when, as ill-luck would have it, they came upon the potter, who had been trying all night to make the magical pot work.

'You have swindled me!' he shouted. 'Give me my money back.'

The first Outlander said, 'Why, wouldn't the pot cook for you?'

'No, it did not!'

'Then you must have put fat in the stew.'

'Of course I did!'

'That was foolish of you. Didn't you notice that I put no fat into ours?'

The Fool scratched his head, 'Yes, that's right.'

'Well, you idiot, you should have followed the instructions to the letter. There was fat enough in my stew, wasn't there? That's because the pot supplies its own fat. It's an added bonus! Get away, before I take it back.'

The potter, fearful of losing the magical vessel, beat a retreat.

But the altercation had taken so long that the Foolsland King's patrol, looking for the men with the 'magical stick', arrived and captured one Outsider, though the other got away.

THE KING'S DAUGHTER

Not taking any chances with such a dangerous swindler, the soldiers tied him up in a sack. Coming to a teahouse, they went in for refreshment, leaving the sack, well secured, outside.

A few minutes later, a Foolslander passing by, saw the sack and started to prod it.

'Who's that?' shouted the Outlander, from inside.

'Just a passer-by. What are you doing in that sack?'

'I am in terrible trouble,' the swindler said.

'I don't want anything to do with trouble . . .' began the Fool.

'I don't blame you, friend. Be on your way, thankful that you don't have to marry the King's daughter and have all the trouble of ruling half his kingdom.'

'Is that why you're in that sack?'

'That's right. The soldiers are in the inn. They were told by the wisest men in the land that the first man they came upon today would be destined for the Princess's hand. Oh, dreadful fate!'

'Look here,' said the Fool, 'I wouldn't mind marrying the lady. If I let you out and take your place, nobody will know. How about that?'

So they changed places, and the crafty Outsider got clean away.

Of course soldiers in general are not as foolish as those who left the captive outside the teahouse, as we all know. And that is in spite of this extract from a Court report in the *Leicester Mercury* in 1971:

'Mr D Barker, for Swaran Singh, said he had no education whatsoever. He had done well in the Army for many years.'

THE GOAT

Now the Land of Fools has a neck of land intruding into it, a part of the ordinary world, across which Fools often passed, taking advantage of the short cut between one part of their Kingdom and another.

The King Fool had bought a goat, the first one ever to be seen in the capital. No Foolslander for miles around knew how to milk it: so two courtiers were commanded to take it for milking to the only Foolslander who knew how to do it. They set off at once.

Crossing the territory of the Outsiders, the Fools came upon an inn. The day was hot, so they stopped for a cup of tea, tethering the goat outside.

The innkeeper recognised, from their strange clothes and foolish way of talking, that his visitors were Foolslanders, listened to the excited discussion of their important mission, and decided to have some fun with them. This, of course, is one of the hazards of being a Foolslander, and one cause of their sporadic wariness. The landlord slipped out of the inn, milked the she-goat and put a billy-goat in its place.

When the Fools got the animal to the milking-shed, the farmer pointed out that it was a he and not a she. 'Must be a mistake', they muttered, and set off back to the Palace.

Again they rested at the inn, and this time the innkeeper switched goats again.

When they reached the palace, the King inspected the nanny goat and, furious, sent them back with it, after giving them a tongue-lashing for being such fools.

Of course, the same thing happened again, and again, and again. Finally, the King himself took the goat to be milked: with just the same result as every other time.

That is how he was able to realise that the territory of Outside was a land of magic, where billy goats turned into nannies and vice-versa. It became not only the proof of the reality of sorcery, but also the cause of the law forbidding Foolslanders ever to stray outside their own country.

And, incidentally, some say that this tale is the origin of the proverb in our Dari language: 'If you have no troubles, buy a goat'.

Of course, one might think that the goat could have communicated something of its adventures with the innkeeper to the courtiers. On the other hand, in spite of what animal lovers insist, there are Foolslanders among them as well as among us. In July 1981, thieves broke into a farm near Barcelona, where a watch-dog, a Doberman Pinscher, had been left on guard. The dog itself was stolen.

THE PERSIAN TROOPER

Once upon a time a man from the Land of Fools married a woman from the Real World, who soon got fed up with him. He would not give her a divorce, so she laid her plans.

A young and handsome man lived in the house next door, and the two fell in love. She instructed him to dig a tunnel between their two houses, and to show no surprise, whatever happened.

When the secret passageway was complete, the lady said to her Foolsland husband, 'I am feeling somewhat fatigued today, and I hear that my twin sister, who lives next door, wants to see me. Please go there and tell her that I am well enough, but wish to be excused a visit.'

The fool got up, went to the next house and asked to see his sister-in-law.

When he was shown into the main room of the house he saw his neighbour sitting on a sofa and, beside him, the duplicate of his wife. Of course it *was* his wife, for she had changed her dress and run through the passage into the next house.

The Fool spoke to the lady, and when she answered, he could have sworn that it was his own wife. She smiled. 'We are identical twins,' she said. 'The only difference is that we dress slightly differently.'

The Fool, still not completely convinced, rushed back to his own house, to find his wife sitting there, relaxed and sighing, on their sofa. 'Did you give my message to my sister?' she asked.

After that, day after day, the Fool tried to work out what was happening, and tried little plans like giving his wife a necklace hoping that she would wear it in both places; as he thought that she might be a witch with powers of bilocation.

Finally, however, he came to the conclusion that he had been too much of a fool, and went to his neighbour to apologise. 'Not at all, my good man', said the neighbour, who had been waiting to carry out the next part of the plan.

He plied the Fool with cakes filled with hashish, until the idiot was in a deep sleep. Then he dressed him in the uniform of a Persian trooper, and put the appropriate papers in his pocket, shaved his head and thrust him into the street.

When the Fool recovered what wits he had, he had something of an identity crisis. Looking down at his uniform he wondered whether he was, indeed, a Persian trooper. He knocked at the door of his house and asked his wife.

'Well, who do you think you are?' she said, 'I don't know. Go and ask some of your friends.'

The Fool happened to be a leatherworker, and he made his way to their quarter of the town. When they saw this figure approaching, and having a dislike of the predatory habits of Persian troopers, the leatherworkers threw stones at him, driving the poor Fool away. 'Get away, Persian dog!' they shouted.

He sat down by the roadside and searched his pockets. In one of them he found an official order to the commanding officer of the Persian forces in Abadan, saying that Firoz Bakhtiari, a trooper, had special instructions to report, two days thence, to him. He was to be given rations of bread and meat, and paid a hundred silver pieces a month. The neighbour, unknown to him, worked in the military headquarters, and had had no difficulty in obtaining the orders.

The Foolslander, scratching his shaven head even more urgently, went back to his house and spoke to his wife. 'Wife,' he said, 'I seem to have become a Persian trooper, and these orders say that I must be in Abadan very soon or I shall be punished.'

'According to the terms of our marriage settlement,' she told him, 'if you leave me for more than a few days, we are divorced.'

She called the local judge, who accepted and registered the details of the divorce – and the Fool and his wife went their separate ways. He did well in the Army, and she was happy with her new husband.

If there was such a thing in Persia at the time, the Fool when he came to his senses might perhaps have applied for legal aid. Even then, he'd have had to be careful. There was a case in 1972 in England where the High Court was asked to give compensation to a man who had received legal aid for seven years against his former employers. The case had been before a lower court. It was only when the matter arrived at the higher seat of judgment that it was discovered that the man had never been in an accident at all.

NUTS AND APRICOTS

A man from the Land of Fools had strayed out of his own country, and found himself wandering along a highway. As it happened, a courtier on an urgent mission was coming along. He had just remembered that it was his King's birthday, and he had not sent him a present.

The other man, who seemed to have nothing to do, looked like a godsend.

'Would you like to earn some money?'

'Yes, indeed, your honour.'

'Very well. Go into the nearest town and buy a load of coconuts with these gold pieces. Take them to the King, who loves them, and say that they are from me for his birthday. Do you understand?'

'Yes, my lord, I can do that easily enough.'

The Foolslander found a fruit stall and showed his gold, asking for the best coconuts available. 'Why don't you buy apricots?' asked the fruit merchant. 'They are much more delicious.' He wanted to get rid of his soft fruit first.

That seemed like a good idea, and the Fool loaded himself up with apricots.

Arrived at the palace, the Fool explained his mission and was shown into the King's presence.

'Majesty, I have been sent by such-and-such a courtier with these for you . . .' he began.

Now the King had been looking forward to receiving coconuts, and the sight of the apricots only infuriated him.

The poor Fool was seized and held, while the King squashed the ripe apricots all over him. Then he was thrown out.

'Thank goodness,' reflected the Foolslander as he limped away, 'if I *had* bought coconuts, he'd have broken my head with them . . .'

The Fool would have done better, it might be thought, if he had gone into art rather than fruit. In 1978 a picture painted by William Turnbull won a major prize – £3000 – in a contest.

Entitled 'Untitled No. 9', it consisted of plain white paint on plain canvas.

There is, however, a blue ground under the white, which may make a difference.

INFORMATION

The great problem for Fools, as for the rest of us, is whether information is accurate. A Foolsland man once went into a neighbouring country and had to spend the night in a caravanserai full of strangers.

Shown into the dormitory, he naturally began to worry. 'If I fall asleep, as I must,' he reasoned, 'how shall I know which of these people I am when I wake up?'

Someone asked him why he looked so perplexed, and he explained.

'That's simple, Foolslander,' said the other man, 'simply tie this balloon to your ankle. Then, when you wake, the person with the balloon on his foot will be you.'

'Thank you, friend,' said the Fool, and he tied on the balloon and immediately fell into a deep sleep. Then the other man untied the balloon and attached it to his own ankle.

In the morning the Fool awoke, saw the balloon on the foot of his neighbour in the dormitory, and couldn't work it out.

'I can see that you are me,' he said to the sleeping form, 'but then, who, if you are me, am *I*?'

The accuracy of information can cause problems in our own world. In *The Times* during February 1974, Mr Michael Mason reported that in an important reference book – *Whitaker's Almanac*:

'The 1973 edition gives the telephone number 01 639 9239 for the National Industrial Relations Court. Phone this number and you will find yourself talking to the manager of a Chinese takeaway restaurant.'

When I telephoned the number twelve years later (on 24 June 1986) I did indeed get the Chinese takeaway, against a considerable background noise of the clattering of dishes... The same person answered the telephone on 1st May 1990 – after 16 years.

THE REASON

The Fools, you will not be surprised to learn, have their own wise men, just as we have. As I have noted, their sagacity is not recorded in dusty tomes: it is passed down in the oral tradition, the result of full-blooded individual experience, not of sterile theory like that of philosophers.

One renowned Foolslander, famous in Middle Eastern history, was called Maimun, whose name was honoured in poem, joke and song from Spain to Afghanistan. We are fortunate that wandering story-tellers – like one from the High Pamirs on the Afghan-Chinese border who related to me the following fragment – have preserved accounts of his sagacity for at least a thousand years:

The hidden teaching of the Land of Fools, according to the bard who sang this anecdote, is that what we call the normal world is really upside down. It is, in fact, the majority of the people of the world who are fools, not the Foolslanders. In order to experience this truth, and to bring its reality back to his compatriots, Maimun once travelled into our land, disguised as an ordinary person, a native.

He took a job as a servant to a wise man, who said: 'I shall take you on for a trial period. Above all, you must remember that I expect you to anticipate my every wish.'

Maimun bowed, and the master dismissed him. The following morning the master called him, saying 'The day is half gone, you lazy wretch! Get up and start the house-cleaning.'

'Not until I've had a good meal,' said the Foolsland sage.

'Good meal?' roared the master. 'Why, it's only five in the morning!'

'You just said that the day was half gone, and my contract, if you recall, guarantees me a good meal at midday,' Maimum told him.

'Anyway,' blustered his employer, 'get up and unbolt the front door, immediately.'

'That's quite impossible,' said Maimum.

'Impossible? How can it be impossible?'

'Because it's already open. You told me to anticipate your every wish. Well, late last night I realised that you would ask me to unbolt the door, so I did it then, anticipating you . . .'

Such was the irrationality of the 'normal' man that, Maimum explained, he was chased out of the house. The wise man from the Land of Fools didn't care: he had enough information and experience, acquired in less than a day, to prove that the rest of us are crazy.

OFF WITH HIS HEAD!

The Land of Fools, as we have just seen, produces people with an admirable sense of logic; though there has to be an ongoing teaching system, a sort of perpetual seminar, to preserve and maintain this valuable capacity. One may have to pay a heavy penalty for forgetting logic – or even if one hasn't forgotten it:

The King of the Land of Fools once ordered a man, who had sat down in his presence without being ordered to do so, to stand up immediately.

'Cut off his head!' commanded the King.

'But, your Majesty,' stammered the man, 'I did what you told me, didn't I?'

'Oh, yes, you did that all right,' said the King, 'but I gave you no assurance that you would be safe just because you obeyed me.'

This rueful Afghan tale is paralleled, in a sense, by a discovery I made in England.

In Britain, the law says, farmers who find the Creeping Thistle on their land must notify the authorities and destroy the weed – or be punished.

The law also lays down that anyone harming another plant, the Thistle Broomrape, will be punished.

But the Broomrape lives off the Creeping Thistle. If you obey the first law, escaping punishment by your obedient action, you may kill the Broomrape's host. If you do, you have committed a punishable offence.*

Idries Shah

* The Wildlife and Countryside Act protects the Thistle Broomrape; the Weeds Act (1959) insists that the Creeping Thistle be destroyed. (*The Times*, London, 1 November 1982, p 10, col. 1.)

PART SEVEN

WISDOM . . .

A GOLDEN DAGGER

Pashtun sayings, proverbs and similes

A pure gold dagger cannot stab.
If you can't give me a halfpenny, at least call off your dogs!
Cats don't catch mice to please God.
Even the Judge was drunk when the wine was free.
He reckons his importance by the elephant-load.
There is no currant without a stalk.
A frog hopped onto a wall and cried, 'I can see Kashmir!'
The wood is burnt, but the ashes are a nuisance.
While the butchers were arguing, the cow dropped dead.
A sandal is not a shoe; a cap is not a turban.
When the shopkeeper has no work, he weighs his mud.
He is sinking in too little water.
Heed the troubadour, burn the dinner.
The yellow dog is brother to the wolf.
A lame crab walks straight.
It's your donkey, but you still have to pull it out of the ditch.
Storing milk in a sieve, you complain of bad luck?
You can beat anyone – if you have a golden slipper.
He saved his ears, but lost his head.
An intelligent enemy rather than a foolish friend.
When an ant says 'ocean', he's talking about a puddle.
Five of them would run from the bang of one empty gun.
He learnt the language of pigeons, and forgot his own.

When the hen gets fat, she stops laying.
The blind man asks God for two eyes.
Annoy the tailor, but you may go shirtless.
Not cheap without reason, nor dear without value.
If you are a rose, leave it to the nightingale to praise you.
His stomach is full, so he thinks he speaks Persian.
Try to get action by soft words: but don't complain to me.
It may smell like a melon, but is it going to make you sick?
If you want to keep camels, have a big enough door.
Don't show me the palm-tree, show me the dates.
Learning makes some Mullas and some into devils.
Go out from your village: don't let your village go out from you.
If the master gnaws bones, what will he give the dog?
In the shop of the sightless jeweller, ruby and pebble are one.
A mother and daughter fought, and a fool thought they meant it.
The crow is clever – but look at what it eats!
Hot milk burned him – so he's afraid of yoghurt.
A duel of hawks – and a pigeon wanted to join in.
Grumbling and carping are the muscles of the weak.
The night may be dark, but the apples have been counted.
Yes, the nephew is a thief: but the uncle is a magistrate!
Your aspirations are in heaven, but your brains are in your feet.
The mud of one country is the medicine of another.
A stick for the nobody, a hint for the nobleman.
No deceit, no merchant.
Same donkey, different saddle.
The rose is beautiful, yet its feet are in the mud.

SCHOLARS AND AFGHANS

People often wonder why it is that scholars attack one another so bitterly. It seems to me that it is not because they are scholars but because they are *people:* so people should not be so mystified. My friend Sufi Abdul-Hamid Khan once told me an old Kabuli story about this very question.

There were once five Afghans sitting arguing about something. The first said to the second:

'You have no right to an opinion, you are not an Afghan at all, you don't speak Pushtu, only Dari.'

The second said:

'Then neither are you, if it comes to that – you were born in Turkestan.'

The third said to the second:

'And you are not, either; you're a Shiah heretic!'

The fourth said to the third:

'And you are not a true Afghan, for you were abroad during the War of Independence!'

And the fifth said to the fourth:

'But you are not an Afghan either – your father was born in India!'

The first then said to the fifth:

'And I don't think that *you* are an Afghan, for you were educated and worked abroad for years, in the West!'

In a lull in the fighting they agreed to go to a respected Sayid (descendant of the Prophet) and ask him to adjudicate. He said:

'You are *all* Afghans – it is this diversity which characterises the Afghan nation.'

'Don't listen to him,' said the first Afghan, 'these Sayids are

251

really Arabs by blood, and what can they know about what an Afghan is?' There was uproar again.

The second Afghan said:

'There were Afghans here before there were Sayids.'

The third Afghan agreed, and said:

'Lots of them are born abroad, all over the place – you wouldn't call that an Afghan family!'

The fourth shook his hand and said:

'Some of them are heretics.'

The fifth patted him on the back and said:

'And they are always talking about "Peace", and you can't be sure that they want to go to war!'

And they left the Sayid's house in the very best of moods. A guest who was there said:

'But you haven't settled the problem for them: who *is* an Afghan?'

'I have settled their main trouble,' said the Sayid, 'which was that they could not get on together. As you see, they are now as harmonised as anything. And as for what an Afghan is – there goes a bunch of Afghans: a lot of people who feel as good as each other; and who may start to feel at any moment that each is better than the next: but woe betide anyone who annoys them: for they will combine against him, agreeing like one man, and rediscovering their unity.'

'But what about their saying that a Sayid is not an Afghan?' asked the puzzled visitor.

'A Sayid,' his friend said, 'is a human being. If an Afghan is less than a human being, a Sayid cannot be one. An Afghan is a human being. If he is more than a human being, he cannot be a Sayid.'

I had quite a wild time myself, once, with a scholar or two, who made assumptions about me and tried to act on them. In the end, they were the ones to come unstuck; and I, fortunately, had to do nothing about it. Though this kind of thing is widespread among scholars, it gets other kinds of Afghans very hot and bothered. Luckily for them, scholars tend to have short memories, so they don't get too traumatised by what they, themselves, call 'in-fighting'.

There is an ancient Afghan story on this very pattern, which I can't resist telling you.

There was once a scholar who strayed into a bazaar, peopled by all kinds of individuals of the ordinary sort. They were, on the whole, unable to tell that you don't joke with men of the mind, but should always treat them with respect. The scholar was learned, but knew nothing about fruit.

Now this scholar came upon a fruit-stall where a number of large melons were on sale. He had never seen a melon before, so he addressed himself to the proprietor.

'Tell me, with all despatch and succinctly, the nature of this item which you have exposed for sale.'

The fruiterer, not knowing that he should be polite to the educated, saw the other as an idiot.

'That, Reverend Sir, is an elephant's egg.'

'Indeed. What an extraordinary fact. I shall take one home and have it hatched. Then I shall have an elephant of my own. It would seem to follow that this could be of utilitarian value.'

The scholar bought the melon, and started to carry it towards his house. On the way, however, he tripped and the melon fell from his arms, rolling down a hillside.

The scholar ran after it. He had nearly caught up when the ripe melon struck against a boulder and broke open.

A hare, which had been sleeping nearby, woke up and, alarmed by the noise, ran frenziedly away.

The scholar, seeing the hare seemingly leap out of the elephant's egg, concluded, logically enough, that it was a baby elephant. It was his property, and he hurried in pursuit.

The hare, of course, quite soon outran him.

When he arrived home, the scholar's wife asked him what kind of a day he had had.

'Less successful than I would have wished,' he said; 'I learnt some new facts, but my elephant's egg broke and the baby one which it contained unfortunately outpaced me . . .'

Of course, it's not only scholars or Afghans who act like this. Making assumptions from too little information can do it for anyone.

Idries Shah

WISDOM OF THE ELEPHANT

There is an ancient Eastern fable which I have tried to help make known extensively in the West, often known as the *Tale of the Elephant in the Dark*.

In this story a number of people creep into a circus tent at night, anxious to find out what is in it. They have heard that the circus has come to town, and also that it has brought something known as an elephant. But they do not know what an elephant actually is.

These people now try to identify the elephant by feeling it. One feels the tail, and thinks that it is a snake. One contradicts him: he has felt one of the legs: 'No, it is a pillar,' he says. A third, touching the elephant's trunk, concludes that the beast must be something with a hosepipe on it. And so they fail to understand, even after being in close contact with an elephant, whatever it can be.

Now this story is often used to introduce people to our own type of philosophy; and a very good introduction it is, too. Masses of books have been written by otherwise learned men, claiming that we are mystics, or resemble Greek or Hindu or Buddhist thinkers; or that we are a reaction against Islam, or even a form of exaggerated Islam. Do you note the resemblance to the men crawling around the elephant in the dark tent?

So, the first thing that we teach, quite obviously, is that you may have to look at – or feel – the 'Elephant' in parts, but you must not make rash assumptions about it. You will eventually add up the parts: but if you do, you will not come up with a mass of unrelated ideas: the snake, pillar, etc., but with something you did not know existed – the 'Elephant'.

In order to prepare people to view and otherwise experience the 'Elephant' which is our philosophy WHOLE, we have to deal with parts, as a sort of introduction, just as you would if you were describing an elephant to people in the dark. These parts, corresponding to the individual elements of the elephant, are the talks, lectures, books, experiences and ideas put forth in them by the teachers of this system down the centuries.

In order to understand enough to progress, however, we have first of all to make sure that the audience is capable of understanding. We have to go a step at a time. If, for example, we had a number of people in a dark tent containing an elephant, and they did not even know what a hosepipe or pillar were, we would not even have analogy. We would have a number of people who could not even get to the stage of the adventurous townspeople who stole out at night to find out something about the strange thing called *An Elephant*. Sufi teaching, therefore, initially provides the spoken and written materials which provide this essential basis. Such materials, since they can be written down and thus given out in a handy form, have to be read and considered before anything else can be done.

This process we call familiarisation. In order to familiarise people with what they need to know, we have first to know a lot about such people. Then we script written materials to provide what they need. It is for this reason that Sufi materials are, in every generation and in each cultural area, re-projected by the teachers of the philosophy.

Most people, quite naturally, assume that because they can ask a question, they can as easily understand an answer to it. This is because they have experienced the fact that one learns by asking questions. But such people have, of course, made the mistake of imagining that, because one kind of question can be asked and answered easily, ALL questions follow this pattern. But, if you look at it, this cannot be true at all. If I ask you 'What is a chair?', you can point to one, and we can all see what you mean. This is an example of a simple question and answer. But if I ask you 'What is the taste of strawberry jam?', what would you answer?

This means, of course, that there are different kinds of experience: one, the experience of a chair, which is easy for most people and not confined to special circumstances; the other, the taste of strawberry jam (or whatever) which requires the presence of jam and taste-buds.

How do we provide the jam and educate the taste-buds?

In Sufi teaching, this is done by what are called *impacts*. An impact may be a story, an event, or a statement. The Elephant in the Dark tale gives you an impact. This impact is designed either to illustrate something (the nature of the problem with the elephant) or else to fix it in your mind, as the story does. There is also another dimension in the tale or impact, which for the moment we can only call 'educating the taste-buds', since there is no commonly accepted term for it.

The nearest we can come to referring to this element of experience is to say that it is like a skill or art, and once you have it, you are able to use it.

What has just been said is quite enough for an introduction to our subject. It should now be studied. The way to study it is to look through books of stories such as we have published, and see where people are shown as jumping to conclusions, asking questions that they lack the basis to ask usefully, or imagining that our subject can be described in terms taken from other subjects.

Above all, at the early stage, familiarisation with the kind of story and the way in which it is used is important. We receive, every year, literally thousands of letters from people, from all over the world, asking questions that are already answered in the books. Or else, quite frequently, sending in stories which do not at all fulfil the requirements of the teaching-story which we use. Get to know the characteristic 'flavour' of the teaching-story, for that will be of enormous value to you.

Remember our saying, 'You can't pour anything out of the jug until you have put something in'. That something is contained in the thirty or more books which have been designed to prepare people for this knowledge. It would be unfair of us to expect you to understand the answers to random questions posed by you without this background. It would be equally useless for you to start asking questions until you have the necessary information on the basis of which to ask the questions.

Remember, too, that in addition to analysis and discussion of written materials, there has to be perceptivity. The tales are not mechanical or preaching a belief. They are there to develop capacities in you. Let them seep into your mind.

Remember, too, that Sufi study is not *all* in stories, or by means of tales. Since Sufi anecdotes have been published in greater numbers than formerly, self-appointed experts have taken to saying, airily (even in reference books) that, 'Sufism is taught by

means of tales alone'. Shun such superficialists for your information. But know that the story is of very great importance.

THE TALE OF THE CURRY AND RICE

Let us look at a traditional story, in some of its usages – the Tale of
the Curry and Rice:

In this Indian tale, a hungry man went into an eating-house and
ordered curry and rice.

'I am in a hurry,' he told the waiter.

The waiter went off and was soon back. 'Here's some curry,' he
said, 'but the rice will take a few minutes more.'

The customer, smelling the curry, was now even hungrier.
Tempted, he devoured the curry on its own.

Some minutes later the waiter arrived with the rice.

'Plain boiled rice?' said the diner; 'I need some curry to go with
this.'

The waiter went to fetch it; but the hungry man, smelling the
aroma of the rice, polished it off.

He had just finished when the waiter returned with the curry.

'Your curry. Finished the rice, then?' he said.

'Bring me a little more rice to eat with this curry,' said the
diner . . .

And so it went on.

This is told as a sort of running joke by those who only want the
joke-content of a tale. Many people get a great deal of fun out of it.
And why should they not?

And, of course, there is the only too familiar reaction of the
pedant: who will say that the man should have brought the curry
and rice together . . . But then we would have no story to use as an
illustration.

An illustration of what? Of the fact that people choose things
which attract them, and 'devour them piecemeal'.

They try to do this with Sufi materials. Sufis, who are certainly as
intelligent and often as learned as scholars, are on record as
assailing the latter quite energetically for the assumption that the
pedantic method is the one and only one to yield results. What it
does yield is – one kind of result.

Narrow academics, or those with a similar mind, also love to criticise the tale as an example of the 'faults' of Sufi learning. 'If Sufi thought,' they crow, 'comes as erratically as the curry and rice in the story, it must be just as unsatisfactory.' If you think like that, too, please stop interesting yourself in Sufi matters at once: because you will, anyway, in the long run. What the academic has failed to remember is that many generations of scholars have spent their whole lives in studying the works of the great Sufis (such as Rumi or Ghazzali) – people whose work would not have existed if they had not learnt through such analogies as that of the curry and the rice!

It is not that narrow scholars prefer pedantry to learning. It is that they very often imagine that pedantry *is* learning. Most unfortunate of all, large numbers of them, over the centuries, have tried to apply this technique to Sufi affairs. Their books are everywhere, even today.

Pedantry is a learnt posture, not a normal one. If you are tempted to adopt it, think about it first.

CONTRACT AND ASSUMPTIONS

There is an ancient Eastern fable which is designed to illustrate many things, and we can use it to examine one or two of these in this study-piece.

Called *The Tale of the Sands*, it goes like this:

There was once a stream, starting out from a tiny spring of water, which moved along, joined by other streams, until it became a mighty river. It was eventually so long, so deep, so strong, that it eventually regarded itself as mighty and invincible.

After passing through forests and plains, for hundreds of miles, the river found itself pouring into a huge expanse of desert, so vast and so deep in sand that the water first produced quicksands and then began to disappear. In the distance it saw a high mountain, and it thought, 'If only I could get to that mountain, and pile myself up against it, I would be able to rush over to the other side, and find my fulfilment in the ocean beyond.'

But not only could the river not move any further forward, but it came to realise that, even if it reached the mountain, it would never be able to get across the towering peaks.

What was it to do? So far, all had gone well, with people praising the cooling waters, fishes living in it, the land tasting of it and taking up some water to provide abundant crops. Then had come the bogging down, the barrier of the sand, and the inaccessible mountain beyond.

The river tried, again and again, to surge forward across the sand, but, again and again, its waters merely sank into the ground.

Then, first gently, then with increasing power, the river heard the rushing of the wind. And the wind spoke to it:

'If you stay here, you will perish,' said the wind; 'but if you allow me to carry you high into the sky and over the mountain, I can drop you down on the other side in the form of rain, when the drops can collect again, become a stream and then a river, and finally you will be able to join the ocean. This is the pattern of all winds and all rivers, and unless you accept it, you will get no further.'

But the river said, 'All throughout my existence, as far as I can remember, I have been running water. How, then, am I to change to the role of passenger? Not only that, but how do I know that you will honour your bargain, and deposit me safely on the other side?'

The wind just rustled, said nothing, and went on its way.

Now, left to itself, the river found that it was losing more and more water, draining its life out into the illimitable depths of the sand, and it began to think. 'I can't go forward on my own,' it reflected, 'and I can't stay here, because I am disappearing into the earth. I must, therefore, accept the proposal of the wind.'

Presently, the wind came back, and started blowing across the water on its way to the mountain. 'Stop!' cried the river, 'and take me up, for I see now that I have nothing to lose . . .'

So the wind lifted the stream, little by little, onto its wings, and carried it safely to the mountain, where it released it as gentle rain. Finally, collecting together, the droplets formed pools, then rivulets, then streams and a mighty river, which gushed into the mighty ocean beyond.

Now the human being, from time to time, is just like that river which became a stream. He makes assumptions, like the river assuming that his life will always go on in the same way. He tries to make contracts with people or with life, like demanding explanations before he can understand the answers.

The purpose of Sufi study is, initially, not to give guidance or to make people rely upon others or on dogmas. It is to give the sort of information and experience which will enable people to understand things which they do not, and to make contracts, if these are necessary, which really do work.

TO BE, TO DO

A famous Sufi was asked what he did.

'I do nothing at all,' said the Sufi.

This sentiment was deplored by worldlings ('idleness is sinful') and applauded by dervishes ('a man whose "I" is inactive is wholly activated by God').

This shows what worldlings are like, and also what dervishes really are. In contrast, Sufis (*ahl-i-rasida*, the Arrived Ones) deplore the saying, but for a different reason. Because someone whose personality has really been replaced by Truth will not say 'I do nothing' in the ordinary sense. He will say, 'I am'.

A Sufi said, 'If someone asks you what you are or what you do, you answer according to what he does or what he is. This is the exercise of sense and due courtesy, since, if a young child asked you what you were, you would not answer, "I am a philosopher". To do so would be to be guilty of neglecting to take account of the child's needs. Your reply, in this case, would be "I am the father of your friend Zaid"; or "I am your uncle," according to circumstances.'

THE IGLOO

A member of a United Nations mission to Afghanistan used to argue with a certain scholar about Sufi ideas. The scholar was convinced that he knew all about the Sufis; had he not read their books and lectured on them? He bitterly resented the foreigner's knowing anything about the subject. 'You are a Canadian,' he said, 'and Sufism is a part of *my* cultural heritage, not yours. Therefore my opinions about it are better than yours, and I do not choose to instruct you or to dispute with you.'

But the Canadian was looking for a Sufi teacher, and could not believe that this man really was one. The word went around the bazaars that this strange infidel was challenging the Afghan savant, and felt that he had a right to study the Sufi Way whether or not he accepted the cultural background. People in general thought he must be mad.

And he did seem to them to be mad, when he was found one day living in an igloo which he had constructed from ice-blocks, in the very garden of the eminent scholar, in the city of Kabul.

The scholar was enraged; the people crowded around; the police were sent for.

In the middle of the hullabaloo a real Sufi teacher came past and listened for a few minutes. Then he took the Canadian and said: 'I shall teach you, for they do not understand anything.'

They went on their way, and the matter was discussed for months and years. Finally, when the scholar was describing the 'mad Canadian's' actions and those of the 'false Sufi' who took him away, at a public gathering, another real Sufi was present. He stood up and said:

'The Canadian knew more of the *Ilm-i-Isharat* (science of allusion) than any one of you; so let that be the verdict on your ignorant ravings about false Sufis and mad Canadians.

'The Canadian was an Eskimo. The scholar had claimed that all the Sufism belonged to him, as his patrimony. The Canadian's answer, in object-lesson form, was "If Sufism is yours, because it is found here, and not the property of all – I claim that snow, on which I have built my igloo, and ice, of which it is made, is mine wherever it is found, since I first saw them in the frozen north of Canada."'

THE MENTALITY OF THE PHILOSOPHER

People often ask about the difference in thought and mentality between a Sufi and a philosopher. This story underlines one of the differences:

There was once a scholastic philosopher who spent much of his time advising a Sufi, whether he needed the counsel or not, to keep away from women at all costs. 'They can be the ruin of you!' he insisted.

One day the Sufi noticed that the man of learning had not come to see him, and he enquired what had befallen him.

'He has fallen in love,' reported one of the Sufi's disciples, returning from the thinker's house.

261

The Sufi immediately rose and, accompanied by his pupils, went to the home of the sage.

When they arrived, everyone was surprised to see the philosopher being ridden, with a bit in his mouth and reins tied to his ears, by a beautiful young lady, up and down the street. The philosopher was besotted with her; she, for her part, made him do whatever she felt like.

The Sufi called out:

'I thought that you warned me against women, saying that they can be the ruin of a man!'

'Exactly,' panted the philosopher, as he trotted down the street with the fair damsel spurring him, 'and you see how right I was!'

As the proverb has it: 'Put an eye-patch on a one-eyed man, and he will call out: "Goodnight!"'

THE PRIEST, THE SUFI AND THE DISCIPLE

A priest went to the assembly of a Sufi, and found that he discussed all his affairs very freely with a young disciple.

'You should surely keep that youth in awe of you,' he said to the Sufi; 'Certainly my experience shows that when you trust too much to people's free choice they respect you less, and this does nothing for their devotion to you or to your cause.'

The Sufi answered:

'Come with us on a journey and I shall show you something of what this means.'

The three started on a journey. Presently the Sufi said to the Priest:

'What a magnificent flock of sheep there is over there.'

The priest said: 'Those are not sheep, they are goats.'

The Sufi insisted that the animals were sheep, and finally the priest said testily to the disciple: 'Now you tell me – are they sheep or goats?'

'Undoubtedly sheep,' said the youth, without a moment's hesitation.

Not long afterwards, the three passed an orchard of apple trees. 'Delightful pears,' said the Sufi.

'They are apples!' shouted the priest.

'What do you think?' the Sufi asked his disciple.

'I think they are pears,' answered the disciple instantly.

The priest got more and more angry.

'What are those men doing, over there?' the Sufi then asked, 'I believe they are soldiers.'

'Yes, they are soldiers,' said the disciple.

'They are not soldiers, they are women, and they are clearly so!' shouted the priest.

And so it went on, and on, and on.

The journey lasted for several days, and each day the Sufi saw something that the priest did not; or did not see something that the priest did. And always the disciple agreed with the Sufi and not with the priest.

Finally, when they had returned to their starting-point, the Sufi said to the Priest:

'You think that I confide in my disciple too much, and that he is likely to develop lack of respect. Now you have seen with your own eyes, that he will support me even when I am wrong.'

'But,' said the priest, 'how did you manage to produce such a condition in the young man? As a priest I have to be above reproach. If I were to tell one of my flock that blue was green or hens were sparrows, they would lose faith in me. . . .'

'It is a long story,' said the Sufi, 'but I will abbreviate it for you. You see, priests try to make people accord with everything in this world as reality. They swear that this is this and that is that, and that no deviation is possible. The result is that when people realise that things are not consistent in this world, they lose faith in the priests. Priests themselves, as you have yourself said, must be above reproach. This means that, although he is a man like other men, if he says or does something that people do not approve of, they lose faith in the priest and also in what he represents.'

'It is far from thus with my own flock. We believe that this world is defective and that things are *not* what they seem. Further, when I first met this young man, I told him: "I am defective and human. Do you want to follow me? I can lead you only if you want to be led, because none can demand obedience, only lead it when it is already there. If you follow me, you may get nothing for your pains: are you willing to take that risk, for we can offer no guarantees. . . . ?"'

At this point the priest, imagining himself to be in the presence of the devil, withdrew from the discussion. No doubt he is still carrying on, somewhere, in the way which he thinks is true. It is to be hoped that his judgement on that matter is better than his evaluation of the Sufi as the devil. . . .

PEACHES

There were once three families whose diet was dried peaches, in different forms.

One family boiled the peaches with sugar and drank the syrup. The second family put the fruit in the sun and ate them when they were as hard as stone. The third family cracked the stones and ate the kernels, throwing away the peach itself.

Now, although they all started with the same fruit, none of them ever ate peaches in their original state; and yet, oddly enough, many members of the families hankered after something which they often called, when speaking to one another, 'the real thing'. And the members of each family believed that their part of the peach was nearer to the true peach, to peachiness.

A traveller from another country passed through their land one day and heard them discussing their problems. He said: 'You're all wrong. Peach is something complete and fresh, something more original, something nearer the source.' They drove him out in short order.

A second traveller, some time later, said: 'You're all partly right.' But they drove him out, too, saying: 'How can he know anything? And anyway what's his motivation?'

Yet a third traveller arrived, and he said:

'Stop all this drinking and dried-fruit eating and stone-cracking for a time, and then I'll show you something.' But they had become too attached to their activities and their diet; even more than that, they were obsessed by the search for 'the real thing', which was addictive, and they were addicted to the habit of argument. So they drove him out as well.

Now everyone started experiments. Syrup was boiled for longer and shorter periods, dried peaches were minced and even fried; stones were cracked by all kinds of methods. Nobody could say that the three families relaxed in their efforts to find the real thing. And, of course, everyone also talked about the three travellers. One of the most frequent remarks about them was: 'They all said

different things, therefore only one of them could have been right.'
Some tried to systematise the 'ideas' of the travellers; and they
only produced hopeless solutions. And the wrangling, except for a
relatively insignificant and unheeded few, goes on still in the Land
of the Three Families Who All Ate Peaches.

Now, those people can't be like us, can they? And we, of course,
can't be anything like them. How do we know? We know, because
we can see that the difficulty of the three families was that they
always approached everything with prior assumptions. Not only
the individual assumptions of the clan – that fried or boiled peaches
or peach stones were the way to the real thing, but also the
all-important negative assumption, that fresh peaches could never
be the real thing. That was what was at the back of their minds.

Idries Shah

THE GOURD

Khushhal Khan, (1613–1689) of the Khattak clan, is the greatest Afghan poet of the Pashtun people. A great warrior and leader of the resistance against the Moguls, he was captured and imprisoned by the Indian Emperor Aurangzeb, and wrote some of the finest of his people's national poetry while in jail.

In his poem, *The Gourd*, he contrasts the apparent power of the rapidly-growing vine – the Mogul Empire – with the permanent strength of the plane-tree, symbolic of the Pashtu-speaking tribes:

> A Gourd vine climbed up the trunk of a Plane
> And he began by saying to the Tree:
> 'O Plane, how long have you been growing?'
> The Plane Tree said, 'Two hundred years I am,
> As I reckon it, within six months or so.'
> The Gourd plant said, 'What a long time it has taken you -
> In a single week I have equalled your height!'
> The Plane said: 'Just wait, for the Winter's hard:
> And then let us speak of growth and state.'

His words have encouraged Afghan patriots for almost three hundred years. Today, these lines are recited, as relevant now as then, by the frontier fighting men:

Honour

> The word Pashtun itself means honour, glory:
> Without honour, what does *Afghan* mean?
> Freedom comes only from the sword -
> With that we ruled even Hindustan.
> But we have lost our unity: that is our sin.

266

God! Grant us honour and unity again!
So old Khushhal may rise, youthful once more!

THE AIR-MERCHANT

Sultan Mahmud of Ghazna, the Idol-Breaker, was a great Afghan conqueror; but many aspects of the government of the Empire baffled him, as it became more and more complex and extensive.

His wise slave, the famous Ayaz about whom there are many stories, refused high office, but stood at Mahmud's elbow, giving advice when the King asked for it.

Sultan Mahmud was perplexed, one day, when he realised that one of three important ministers must be embezzling vast sums of money – but it was so cleverly done that nobody could narrow down the list of suspects any further.

'Ayaz,' said the monarch, 'the culprit must be caught, or the Empire will fall. On the other hand, I cannot afford to alienate the support of two of the ministers by interrogating them all: for each has great support in our domains. We need to determine which is the miscreant, and we must be right first time.'

'Mahmud,' said Ayaz, 'give me full powers, and I shall undertake the task.'

'You have complete authority to investigate.'

Ayaz called the three ministers and said:

'It is the King's desire that you three shall each attempt to bring the wind into due subservience to him. As a great king, he surely owns the air above the land as well as everything else. Only administrative dereliction of duty or lack of ingenuity can explain the continuance of this abuse.'

The grandees bowed and took their leave.

After some months, Ayaz summoned the three men to the Court and, in the King's presence, asked each how he had approached his task.

The first Minister said:

'I have made cooling chambers through which the air circulates at various angles, providing relief in the Summer for our lord the King. And the system may be used by the people if they so wish.'

The second Minister approached the Throne and said:

'I have built windmills which grind flour and provide revenue for our lord the king and employment and food for the people.'

The third Minister said:

'I have established a tax. Everyone must pay a fee for the daily use of air for breathing.'

Ayaz bowed to the King and said:

'The first two Ministers have provided, respectively, solace and revenue, working constructively, for the King and for the people.

'The third Minister has not only provided nothing, and has even taken away a right from the people. This is the act of a tyrant, of a deceiver and an embezzler.'

The third Minister was so astonished at this conclusion that he immediately confessed his guilt.

CHANGING THE FUTURE

It is related among the wise that Sabir Shah, who crowned Afghanistan's first monarch, King Ahmad, was visited by the ruler at his retreat near Kandahar.

'I wish to know the future, Great Sage,' he said.

'I have made you a king,' said the Sufi, 'is that not enough? And could you endure the burden of foreknowledge?'

'It should, indeed, be enough,' replied the King; 'but I have the burning desire to know what will befall. And I am prepared to bear the burden. I cannot rest until I know what my future is to be.'

'Absolve me from responsibility,' said Sabir Shah, 'and you shall have your wish.'

'I do absolve you,' said the King, delighted.

'Now go,' said Sabir Shah, 'and the future will be made known to you.'

Some days later, the King was resting in the shade of a tree when he heard two birds twittering. As he listened, he suddenly found that he could understand the meaning of their speech.

'The King's horse may go lame,' said the first bird.

'In that case it would throw him,' said the second.

'So he would miss a meeting with Emir Yusuf's army...'

'And the Emir, angry, would refuse to become an ally.'

The birds flew away, and the King called for a fresh horse every day, with several more always kept in reserve.

He met Emir Yusuf and they formed an alliance. This pact strengthened the Emir, who attracted more and more supporters and competed for the throne. This forced the King to campaign almost continuously for sixteen years.

Worn out with fighting, the King one day found himself listening to two other birds, chirruping on a rock:

'If the King's horse had gone lame, he'd have been thrown, would have missed Emir Yusuf, and the Emir would have had no power to challenge him,' said the first bird.

'Yes, indeed. And the King would have been safe, and the Kingdom secure, prosperous and tranquil,' answered the second bird.

The first bird said, 'But the King wished to change his future . . .'

After that, King Ahmad found that he could no longer understand the speech of birds.

THE BAG OF GOLD

The Emperor Babur, as a matter of prudence, placed a bag of gold in a hollow tree near his fortress-palace. One day, he thought, he might have to flee, for the lives of sovereigns were always at risk.

A dishonest courtier came across the gold, and stole it. Babur thought that the culprit might be this man, but was not quite sure.

He invited the man to dine and, among other subjects, spoke of hidden gold. 'I have hidden some money – I shall not tell you where – and I am wondering if it is enough, in case of an uprising.'

'How much is it, your Majesty?' the courtier asked.

'Only five hundred gold pieces. I think I'll put another three or four thousand there; don't you think I should?'

'Yes, indeed,' said the man, thinking greedily of what he might now steal, if he put the stolen gold back, and the King added three or four thousand gold pieces more.

When he went back to replace the gold, the Emperor was waiting for him . . .

'Your greed gave you gold, but it has destroyed you as well,' he said.

269

SPEAK FIRST AND LOSE

A newly-married couple moved into their new house and started to quarrel almost at once.

The husband said, 'Close the door, there is a draught.'

The wife answered, 'I am not a slave – shut it yourself.'

'I tell you what,' said the husband, 'let's see who can keep silent the longer. The first person to speak shuts the door.' She nodded her agreement, and they sat down, with the wind whistling around them.

The day wore on, and neither of them moved. Some thieves, passing by, saw the open door and walked in. They examined everything in the house, including the silent pair, whom they took for statues. Then they stripped the house, and even took the bride's jewellery.

Still neither had moved, or said a word. Darkness fell, and the Watch, finding the door open, came into the room. 'Shut this door,' said the Captain of the Watch. Neither partner moved.

'You must obey the orders of the Watch,' shouted the Captain.

Unable to elicit any response, the men of the Watch dragged the couple to jail.

In the morning they were taken before the magistrate at the court of summary justice.

'If you don't speak, it's contempt of court,' he told the husband. Getting no answer, the judge said, 'I'll have you whipped if you're not careful . . .'

Suddenly, the woman cried out, 'Don't hit my husband!'

'You've lost the bet,' shouted her spouse. 'Now *you* have to shut the door.'

THE AMIR WHO WAS A BEGGAR

This remarkable allegory of how one may change one's way of thinking and acting is a Sufi story from *Tales of Afghanistan*, by Sayeda Amina Shah:

Once upon a time there was a great and noble Amir who became so proud and haughty that he forgot how to rule his people wisely. Instead of ruling them with care and understanding, he grew more and more interested in the riches which poured into the state coffers from taxes and fines.

His courtiers were so occupied in flattering the ruler that no-one spoke the truth to him, or advised him about the true position. Therefore he thought only of money, jewels, and fine clothes, forgetting the simple things of life.

There were a thousand slaves in the royal palace, black and white, young and old, and daily they prayed to Allah to save them from the tyranny of the Amir.

Now, one night, when the moon was full in the sky, and the stars shone with a frosty light, the Amir had a dream. It seemed to him that he was in a strange place, where there was inexpressible peace and serenity. An angel, writing in a book with a golden pen, appeared and said:

'O unfaithful Amir, Servant of Allah, why do you oppress your people and forget the teachings of the Koran?'

And the Amir answered, 'I cannot understand the meaning of these words! How can I be an oppressor . . . ? I have the loyalty of a thousand slaves, black and white, old and young, and everyone in the kingdom bows to me when I pass by.'

271

The Vision spoke again. 'Change everything about yourself, or you will regret it. Thinking, doing, living, all must change.'

Then the Amir saw the angel write again in the golden book, and vanish.

Next day, early, the Amir was determined to enjoy himself. He ordered the finest horses in his stables to be saddled, so that he and the entire Court could go hawking. The nobles and huntsmen were dressed in magnificent robes of honour, and their hawks had jewelled hoods. The hunting cheetahs were brought as well, and soon they began to chase the game.

One cheetah went off so fast after a gazelle that none but the Amir could follow it on his Arabian stallion. Further and further ran the gazelle, with the cheetah behind it, and the Amir following behind, so that soon all the courtiers and huntsmen were left far behind. The Amir spurred on his horse, and suddenly the cheetah stopped, puzzled. The gazelle had vanished.

The Amir dismounted, and looked about him. Where could the animal have gone? It seemed to have disappeared into thin air.

All at once a great wind blew up, and it blew and blew, until the Amir was nearly blinded. He hung on to the horse's bridle, but it seemed as if the wind was about to blow them off the face of the earth. His cloak and turban were whipped off, his body was stung as if by a thousand whips. He shaded his eyes with his hands to protect them, and the horse, neighing with fright, galloped away.

The Amir was in a terrible state, his eyes were burning with the stinging sand, his clothes were tattered and torn, and his hair tangled like that of a dancing dervish. He was utterly lost, and alone, without money or servants.

'What am I to do?' he groaned, sinking to his feet; and his senses left him.

For a time he knew no more, until he opened his eyes to find that a Nomad was bending over him, giving him a drink from a water-skin.

'How did I get here? My head seems possessed by a thousand demons,' faltered the Amir, trying to get up. He was lying on a pile of skins, in a Nomad encampment.

'Rest, brother, rest,' said the Nomad. 'You were found not far from this place by one of our children, after yesterday's sandstorm. You will be all right now, you can come with us when we move our flocks to follow the grazing.'

'But I am the *Amir*, the sovereign of this land! I insist that you take me back to my Palace.' He tried to rise.

'What? *You* the Amir? In that torn and dirty shirt and one sandal? Surely you must be affected by the sun-madness. We are miles away from the Amir's city, and as for his Palace, none of us has ever seen it, for there is a high wall around it guarded by soldiers. It is as much as our lives are worth to go to the Palace, let alone take you with us and tell them that you are the Amir!' And the Nomad roared with laughter.

In two days' time the Amir recovered his strength, and he was given a brown sheepskin coat by his host. He could not believe what had happened to him, but hoped that in time he might be able to find his way back to his own kingdom. When the tribe of Nomads moved on, they took him with them, promising to show him where the nearest town lay. He trudged along, with hope in his heart, and arrived at last at the huge iron gate of his own Palace.

'Stop, you tattered rascal!' shouted the guard. 'This is the residence of our most noble and worthy ruler. Get back to the steps of the mosque, where you belong.'

'But I am the Amir! Let me in, for I have been lost in the wilderness since I went hunting, and after being rescued by a Nomad, I have now returned. Open the gate this instant, or I shall have you whipped!'

'What an impudent beggar you are! I swear by my beard that you shall be whipped yourself if the Captain of the Guard comes out to you!' roared the soldier, and pushed the wretched Amir away.

'I tell you, I *am* the Amir. Send for the Captain of the Guard, and I will identify myself,' shouted the unfortunate potentate.

'Our noble Amir is at this very moment on his knees in the Palace courtyard, for it is the time of the noonday prayer,' said the soldier. 'See for yourself, look through the gates at the right and watch the Lord of the Faithful place his forehead to the ground in obeisance to Allah.'

Sure enough, the Amir squinted through the gate and looked to the right as the soldier bade him, and there he saw a figure, dressed in *his* clothes, and wearing his ruby ring, kneeling upon a prayer-rug. He knew at once that this must be an angel, for around the figure there seemed to be a golden light.

Thunderstruck, he wandered from the Palace, and went through the streets, like a man in a trance. Since it was so long since he had been seen by his people, no-one recognised their Amir and evidently they accepted the angel as their ruler without question.

So the Amir who was now a beggar travelled from mosque to mosque, asking for alms, for he had never learned how to do anything but hunt or ride. Day by day he grew stronger, until he was able to carry bundles for women shopping in the market, or hold horses for merchants, earning a few coppers a day. At nights he slept against the outside ovens of the houses of the rich, and eventually he gave up all hope of ever being known as the Amir again.

Each Friday the new Amir distributed food and money to the poor, and with the needy of the city the unhappy Amir lined up for his portion. He looked upon the face of the angel who had taken his place, and the visage was so dazzling he had to look away. Daily the people began to respect the new Amir more for his kind actions, and the lessening of taxes, and his wisdom in adjudicating cases between those who brought lawsuits before him.

One night, the house where the beggar Amir was watching, waiting to go to sleep beside the oven when all the people were in bed, caught fire. He raised the alarm, and brought out two children who had been trapped in their room at the top of the house. He disappeared as soon as they were safe, and hid himself in a corner of the yard, where animals were being saddled for the dawn start of the caravan.

In the night he had a dream, and thought himself to be the Amir again, but in the morning, with the beasts were snorting and stamping all around him, he found himself a beggar indeed.

That Friday, when he went with all the other needy ones to the Palace for his dole, he received it from the hand of the angel Amir, who smiled at him and said, 'Well done, servant of Allah, soon you shall recover what has been lost'. And then there was such a dazzling light from his countenance that the Amir had to look away.

Next day, when a runaway horse came stumbling through the streets, with its eyes wild and its mouth flecked with foam, the Amir who was a beggar stepped forward into the horse's path and stopped it, calming it with soothing words. Then the owner's servant came running up, praising his courage and calling blessings down upon his head.

The people of the market flooded around him: the fruit-vendor gave him oranges, and the sweetmeat-seller a pound of succulent halwa, while from the upper windows of houses harem ladies showered coins around his feet. The sandal-maker made him accept a new pair of fine leather sandals, saying, 'Wear these, my friend, they are good enough for the Amir himself!' Everybody laughed and slapped him on the back, calling him a brave fellow.

Now, the former Amir was beginning to feel more human than he had for many years, and he bitterly regretted all the injustices he had done when he was ruler in that place. He said aloud to himself, 'What fine people these are in my city. Would that I were their leader once more, for now that I know them and their trials, as I never did before, I would be considerate to all men, and respect them.'

No sooner were these words out of his mouth than the angel dressed as the Amir appeared before him and said:

'O servant of Allah, everything about you has now changed, and for the better. It is time that you returned to your rightful place. Go in Peace.'

Then the angel vanished, leaving a pile of fine clothes and the ruby ring behind him. These the real Amir put on, and became once more his old self. He went to the gate of his Palace and ordered the guard to open it. This time the soldier bowed low and threw the gate open in a trice.

So the Amir returned a wiser man, and ruled his people justly for the rest of his days.

PART EIGHT

HISTORY, WHENS AND WHERES . . .

LEGENDS AND TRADITIONS

CITY OF ZOHAK

There are some ruins in the mountain range of Safed Koh, the White Mountain, to the east of Kandahar. The ruins include large wells and walls, fortifications of a most impressive kind, like a fairy castle.

The place is desolate, and no inscription seems to survive anywhere in the area. Traditions say that the ruins are of a city. There are two or three old half-demolished brick gates, a castle and a brick pond which it is said was fed by mountain streams, and a hidden channel connected it with the river Indus of India.

Firdausi, the Persian poet, speaks of Zohak as a king who killed Jamshid, the fourth king of the earliest Persian dynasty: who is said to have ruled for seven hundred years, and to have had genies as slaves.

No historical records tell us anything reliable about King Zohak or the ruins of the city in the Safed Koh. There is, however, a local belief that such a king did rule, before the advent of Islam in those regions, and perhaps he extended his military operations as far as Kandahar, and founded this city of Zohak.

Other legends and traditions of the people of the Safed Koh affirm that the city was Zohaka, built by Zohak. About this Persian king a great many stories are told. One of the commonest is that Zohak was cruel and ruled over an empire extending from Basra, on the Persian Gulf, to the Indus. His subjects groaned under his thrall, and invoked the wrath of God to fall upon him.

One night, they say, Zohak arose and found sores or slight wounds on his shoulders. No physician could heal them, and they assumed a more dangerous aspect every day. By and by the heads of two serpents sprouted from Zohak's wounds and grew until they were a yard long.

They bit the King's scalp and ultimately destroyed the bone of his cranium and fed on his brain. He was taken captive by the victorious prince of an invading army named Farindun, and died when the serpents had eaten up all his brain.

Others affirm that he was of Arab parentage and was born with two protruding front teeth. His parents were very proud of him and thought that the child was fortunate as he was born laughing. They named him Zohak. In Arabic, *zahik* means one who laughs much.

The evil qualities which formed Zohak's character, it is believed, had brought a curse upon him, and the two serpents were sent from God to show the people that even a great king like this could be so severely punished in the world.

Zohak has grown proverbial amongst the hill tribes of the Safed Koh and Kandahar, and when they speak of a man whose conduct does not meet with their approval they say that he is a Zohak. A moneylender, the most detested type among the Pashtun people, is sometimes called a son or descendant of Zohak.

BABA FAREED

There is a *mazar*, or grave, of Sheikh Fareed or Baba Fareed in the district of Safed Koh. He was a renowned Sufi. During his younger days as a poor man he roamed about the streets of Kandahar begging bread. None gave him any, and people were all busy with their games and sports. Fareed wanted no alms, for he could at any time produce great quantities of foodstuffs if he desired, but he had heard that people round about were not very charitable and he came to ascertain the truth for himself.

As no-one took any notice of the poor, Faqeer Fareed jumped into the river and caught a fish and held it up to the sun. The sun descended and roasted the fish. The offending people were scorched to death; the water boiled in their vessels and the earth became red hot. Fareed left the town and henceforth the heat of the sun is great over those parts during summer. That legend they say, explains the heatwaves of Kandahar.

One day a man was carrying some things in a covered tray over his head. Baba Fareed asked him what he carried, the man said that it was only bricks. He was carrying loaves but was too stingy to give any away.

'Bricks?' asked the Sufi. 'May they really be bricks then.'

On his arrival at the bazaar the baker found that all his bread had turned into hard bricks. He ran to seek the great Sufi and implored his forgiveness.

'Very well,' said Fareed, 'go. They are bread, and do not tell lies again.' The bricks had once more turned into bread.

One of the disciples of the Sufi had left his land in search of his daughter who had been kidnapped when she was a child. One day, after the evening prayer when everyone had retired, this man felt a pain in his side. Towards midnight his pains grew unbearable and he, in agony, approached his spiritual leader, Baba Fareed, for help.

'Go,' said the Sufi, 'and lie down on the grass of such-and-such a graveyard.' The man could not understand the meaning of this method of treatment, and yet he dared not say anything. It began to rain, and lightning lashed the clouds up above when the sick man went to the graveyard.

He saw that in a *maqbara* – tomb – a dim light was burning, and two men were fighting with swords. He ran to the window and listened, and heard them say to one another: 'The girl is mine'.

He rushed into the building, and the two men took to their heels. 'Rescue me, dear friend,' came a voice from the corner. He saw a veiled woman. She declared that she had been stolen from her parents when she was a little girl by the two villains who had fled. By the description and name the man realised that it was his own daughter for whom he had been searching for fifteen years.

The next day Fareed asked how his disciple's pain was: and revealed that he had told the man to go to the graveyard because of a secret prompting.

THE LAKE WHICH DROWNED A TOWN

In the North-Eastern region of the mountain land of Badakhshan they speak of a certain river as impure and filthy, for it comes from a lake which once drowned a town.

There was a ruler who, though wise and just and a master of a vast and fertile country, had no heir. He prayed to God to give him

281

a son to carry on his line. No answer came, so the King said that he would be content to have a son even if he was as foolish as an ass.

His prayers were heard, and a son was born, but the child, otherwise completely human, had ears like a donkey. The boy was exceptionally intelligent. After his father's death, he managed to govern the country without a regent from the age of ten years.

The long ears were always an awkward problem to him, but he concealed them so well that no one ever saw them.

Only the barbers who shaved his head and trimmed his beard knew the secret, and they were always executed after they had done their work, so the deformity never became known.

However, dissatisfaction amongst the people grew intense, as one barber after another was killed: and they were naturally reluctant to perform that particular service for their King. Whosoever did not present himself when it was his turn was forced to attend, and he was then beheaded lest the secret of the King be disclosed.

One youth volunteered to save his brother's life by going in his stead. He went, and the King, for once, had compassion on him, and taking oaths of secrecy his life was spared, and he was even made the King's Vizier.

They were out together one afternoon for a hunt and the Vizier's horse outstripped that of the King. Rashly, he remarked in glee said that his horse had beaten that of the 'Donkey-eared King'. No sooner had he said this than he realised his mistake and fled, escaping to the nearby mountains where he roamed about for years.

He used to return to the town when it was dark, and his heart one night grew very sad when he saw that they were taking the only son of a poor widow to shave the King's head, and she was in great distress, as the officers of the King beat the poor lad.

The immorality of the town, too, had made a profound impression upon the Vizier, and he prayed that the city be drowned. Water spouted from where he stood, and he ran to the hills; the flood covered even the lofty minarets of the tallest buildings, and a lake was formed in a place where once had stood a mighty city.

THE TOMB OF SHEES

The third son of Adam, whose name was Shees, the Seth of the Bible, is said to be buried in one of the Hazara hills. Shees was of a most extraordinary height, and his appetite was enormous. The deepest ocean would only reach to his knees, and he would catch the bigest whales, lift them up to the sun, and roast them in its tropical rays.

THE MYSTERIOUS KHIZR

In the city of Herat, to the West, near Iran, they speak of the grave of a man who lived for thousands of years. He was a very sacred person, who had met Moses and seen Khwaja Khizr or Khidr.

Khwaja (Master) Khizr is believed to be a most pious old man, commissioned by God to assist all in trouble and show the way to people who may be lost in such places as forests and deserts. Khizr is not ordinarily visible, but he appears in the form of a very old man, with a long white beard, when succour and guidance are desperately needed.

They say that one day the old man, whose grave is at Herat, was picking up dry branches in a wood, when he saw two white-bearded men walking on his right-hand side. They did not talk, but pursued their way in absolute silence. The woodcutter ran up to them, and thinking them robbers or thieves or spies, challenged them to stop and to follow him to the town authorities.

'Do you,' said one, 'not know who we are? We are Khizr and Musa.' The old man fell to his knees and begged their pardon, and asked them what was their mission that day.

'There is a wall,' said Hazrat Khizr, 'in this neighbourhood, where a man has left a chest of gold for his son on his death. The son of that man is yet young and cannot look after himself. The wall where the gold is concealed is in a bad and unstable condition. We are going to put it right and plaster it so that the orphan's treasures shall be secure till he is of an age to dig it up himself.' The two men walked on, and the woodcutter remained astonished.

This woodcutter is made the nucleus of many legends, and as he is believed to have lived for thousands of years, he is reputed to have seen and heard such things as no other human being ever did. Some say that he was a sailor in the service of the Turks, and when a Sultan was much distressed by hordes of robbers who used to steal his gold, he loaded boats with treasure and ordered it to be taken to an island. An unfavourable wind carried it to the coast of Persia, and the Shah, thinking this a gift from God, appropriated the gold and took the crew prisoner. The woodcutter escaped and passed his life in the border hills of Afghanistan.

And yet another version is given of Shahmulla, the sailor or woodcutter – that he was a hard-working farmer in the fertile province of Mashhad in Iran, and had to fly for his life from his native land, for he had elicited the anger of the mighty Emperor Bahram Gur.

THE TREASURE OF SHAHMULLA

Shahmulla, it is related, was once watering his fields, and for two days he was busy with the work. He noticed, however, that one patch of ground was as dry as sand, and all the water there was flowing down a hole. He dug the ground and discovered steps.

Descending them, he saw a large hall, a courtyard and numerous cells. It was dark, and he touched the idols and figures of animals there, which felt like metal. The farmer ran to announce this discovery to the King, and on excavating, the metal animals which he had touched were found to be of pure and solid gold.

The King had them melted down and gave nothing to the poor *dahqan*, or farmer, and when he asked for something the King got so angry that he ordered them to behead Shahmulla. The farmer lived, however, through some miracle, and earned his living by cutting wood and selling it in the bazaars of Herat. There have been so many empires and so many treasures in Afghanistan that this tale perhaps reflects some historical event.

THE FIRST KING OF THE EARTH

In the borderland of Afghanistan and Iran they say that Sabzawar, which is a district in that part of the country, was the seat of the very first King who ruled over the earth. This King was called Kymars. The meaning of the word Kymars is interesting. Kymars was, it is said, originally Gymat, and *gy* or *guo* means in Persian one who speaks or sings in a melodious tone. *Mart* is interchangeable with *mard*, which means man. The combination is 'a man who is a great speaker or singer', and apparently Kymars was possessed of these fine vocal qualities.

Kemakht, they say, reigned over Sabzawar after Kymars, and he was dethroned by rebels and fled to Turkestan, in the North, where he used to dress in the hide of a zebra. *Kemakht* is the word for a silk cloth of many colours made at Sabzawar, and they say that it is that it was during the reign of that king that the cloth was worn by the nobles of his Court to remind him that he was expelled from his country, and in his exile wore nothing but a zebra's uncured hide. His name was Gho, and the cloth was at first named after him as *gho amokht*, *amokht* meaning in Persian 'taught'. The pronounciation has gradually changed, and the cloth is now called *kemakht*.

THE CHESTS OF GOLD

It is said amongst the Kohistanis – the people of the Land of Mountains – that if a boy who is an only child should sleep in the hills he would hear the *ganj-i-Qarun* (*ganj* means, in Persian, treasure; and Qarun is the name of a king) move under the earth. He would hear sounds as if big chests full of gold coins were being moved.

This story they link to the tales of Moses' time, and that of an infidel King, Qarun; the Korah of the Bible. In the Talmud it says, 'Joseph concealed three treasures in Egypt, one of which became known to Korah'. So large was the treasure that 'the keys of Korah's treasure were a burden for three hundred mules'.

This King used to extort money from orphans and the poor, and had amassed a great treasure. Moses prayed to God that the curse of heaven should be imposed upon Qarun. Presently all the chestfuls of gold came running from the *tahkhanas* or treasury cells, and piled themselves up in the shape of a pillar. Qarun fled to the forests but the pillar chased him and stood on his head and thrust him into the depths of the earth. It shall remain so till the Day of Judgment and Qarun's wealth will until then be changing its place constantly under the crust of the earth.

Qarun had many chests full of gold, and each key was about the size of a human finger. Imam Subbee has estimated this treasure to be locked in four hundred and forty thousand chests.

THE CUP OF JAMSHID

Among the Kizilbash clans around Herat they speak of a cave in the Durkat Mountain Range where is buried the *Jam-i-jum* (The cup of Jamshid). Kai Khusro, one of the descendants of Jamshid, had a cup made. In this cup the astronomers had sketched some circles to indicate the motion of the stars. By some hidden means this cypher was read, and future events were disclosed to the King. He could see all that was going on in the world, or if any misfortune were going to befall the ruler or his kingdom. By looking in the cup everything was visible. This cup is also called *Jam-i-jahan-numa* – a cup which reflected whatever happened in this world.

ALEXANDER AND THE MONSTER

They say that Registan (desert) which lies to the south of Kandahar, was once a land where grew immense gardens of pomegranates and figs, and there were many prosperous towns. But during the time of Alexander the Great a beast was born in one of the cities of Registan, and whosoever was caught in its gaze died at once. The beast roamed about devastating the towns and laying waste all that came in its way, and the whole of that part of the country became a desert.

Alexander was very anxious to have the beast killed, but none dared look at the animal.

The King consulted his Ministers, but no-one could suggest a plan nor volunteered to go and face the beast of the desert. Aristotle at last stepped out and said he would undertake to combat the evil-eyed monster.

He caused a mirror of about six feet square to be fastened to a carriage. Sitting in this carriage he propelled it himself, having placed the mirror in front. When the beast smelt the scent of a human being, it advanced towards the carriage, but Aristotle placed the glass in front of the monster, and as soon as it saw its reflection in the mirror it gave a loud growl and died, killed by its own evil eye. The King honoured the Minister and asked him how it was done, and how the monster actually came into being.

'My master,' said the sage, 'the people of that region were very unclean, and this monster was born of filth and a product of uncleanliness, so he purged the earth of such people, and as his sight was death to man, I thought that if he could see himself in a mirror his end would also be complete.'

History, whens and wheres...

TAMERLANE AND THE MYSTERIOUS VOICE

Tamerlane, or Timur the Lame, or as he is called in Persian, Timur Lang (*lang* – lame), was a son of a shepherd in Turkestan, though descended from the great conqueror Changhiz Khan.

His father had died and his mother was old and always ill in bed. Timur used to take his herd early in the morning to the hills and return home at night. Goat's milk and dry bread were their only food and drink, and if the shepherd-boy managed to bring a load of sticks from the hills and sell them in the bazaar, that money added a little to their means of subsistence.

It was a very hot day in summer, and Timur was tired. He made a stone his pillow and lay down on a patch of grass on the bank of a small *chashma* (brook), and the coolness of the shade made him drowsy and he was soon sleeping. Not long had he slept when someone hit him hard with a stick, and his left foot was bruised from the stroke. A voice thundered in his ear from somewhere:

'Rise, Timur, rise! Do not slumber away your life. You are to be a master of nations' destinies and will rule over races and lands never seen by your ancestors. Rise, Timur, rise!' Timur limped home and one day rose to command the nations as was foretold, and was lame in one leg all his life.

Tamerlane the conqueror was an ancestor of Babar, the first of the Mogul emperors, who was born in Kabul, and whose beautiful but simple tomb – at Babar's own request – overlooks his beloved birthplace.

SULTAN MAHMUD AND THE TEMPLE OF SOMNATH

In Ghazni they say that Sultan Mahmud, another Afghan emperor, on his seventeenth invasion of India plundered and ransacked the temple of the rich Somnath. There stood an idol of gigantic height in the centre of the *munder* (temple). This was made of gold and was hollow, and the worshippers used to drop their offerings of jewels into its mouth. Mahmud struck the idol with a hammer, and when his officers beseeched him to spare the idol and accept money from its worshippers, he replied that on the Day of Judgment he would like to be called 'Mahmud the Idol Breaker,' and not 'Mahmud the Idol Seller'. Cartloads of rubies and diamonds, gold and silver, fell out in a torrent from the idol's

287

interior when Mahmud struck it. The wealth was brought to Ghazni, and a portion of it was ordered to be placed at the Juma Mosque, while two other pieces were sent to Mecca and Medina in Arabia, to be used as steps of the mosques. The idolators, it is said, came to Ghazni and sent a petition to Mahmud to say that the jewels of their idol might be retained by the King, but the idol should be exchanged for money.

Mahmud, they say, ordered the idol to be reduced to powder, and that powder, mixed with flour, made the bread for the Hindus at night. The next morning Mahmud said in reply that he had no idol left, for they had eaten up their object of devotion in their bread the preceding night.

For many centuries the matter rankled, and when the British invaded Afghanistan, one of their aims was to recapture the gates of Somnath, which had been carried off, and restore them to their rightful Hindu owners in India. A pair of huge gates were found and brought back with great ceremony. It was soon determined, however, that they were the wrong ones.

A Faqir, a religious mendicant, was asked by Mahmud to tell him the next day at the Durbar where the centre of the earth was. If he failed, he would be put to death.

The Ministers advocated the cause of the poor Faqir saying that he was only a beggar, who knew nothing of geography or of that art in which the Arabs of the desert were so skilled.

But the King of Ghazni would not listen, and said that whoever posed to the people as a saint and possessed superhuman powers would have to prove to the guardians of Ghazni his genuineness.

The unfortunate Faqir was in distress and none of his disciples could save him from his fate, for he knew not where the centre of the earth was. No incantations could he call to his aid, and he sat weeping in his garden, when his daughter saw him and asked the cause of his anxiety.

'I have,' said the Faqir, 'to tell the King the centre of the earth tomorrow. I do not know how to answer, for I am ignorant of the truth.'

His daughter whispered something in his ear and the old man was cheerful.

The day dawned in its usual splendour, and the *Durbaris*, courtiers, all dressed in red sat in grief to see the poor old Faqir's trial, as they were fully aware that he would not be able to answer. He was brought before the King, and after salaams and respects, he said that he could answer the King's question.

It had not, he declared, troubled him at all, for all was known to him; and advancing boldly to the royal throne, he touched one of its legs and said that the centre of the earth was under that leg, for where the King ruled was the centre of the earth.

All were amazed, and Mahmud was much pleased and gave him a robe of honour, a *khilat*: for it is traditional with Eastern kings to reward graceful or ingenious compliments; but yet was sceptical about his honesty, and commanded him further to tell him in open Durbar the next day as to how many leaves there were on all the trees of the King's gardens.

The Faqir's daughter again stood him in good stead, and at the next Durbar he appeared bright and without anxiety, and said that the number of the leaves was one hundred thousand trillion, and if they did not believe him the leaves might be counted. The King was much impressed, and henceforth the Faqir was high in the royal favour.

This tale, with many others of a similar kind, is often recited when people are recounting stories of the great intelligence of women: a favourite Eastern, and Afghan, topic.

THE SULTAN AND THE POET

Mahmud Ghaznavi, they say in Ghazni, was a great admirer of poetry, and not a few poets of all nations were kept at his Court. One day Mahmud was in a great rage and cut the Queen's hair; but when the heat of his temper had subsided he regretted his action, but nothing could re-join the hair. He paced backward and forward in his garden till a favourite poet of his Court, Ansari, approached him and tried to reduce the anxiety of his master.

'Read a poem,' asked the King, 'while I play with small fishes in the pond.'

The poet read, and stopped at the end of each couplet to get the attention of the King, till at last he complained of his Master's inattention.

'The couplet,' replied Mahmud, 'which is really good will compel my attention however much I may try to play with the fishes.'

The poet read another, and it delighted the King so much that he filled his mouth with rubies and diamonds.

Afghan Caravan

MAZAR-I-SHARIF, THE HOLY SHRINE

At Balkh and also at Mazar-i-Sharif to the south they speak of the grave of Shees or Seth, a son of Adam. Both places claim the grave to be in their town; but Mazar-i-Sharif, one thinks, has a better claim to the legend. *Mazar* in Persian means grave or tomb. *Sharif* means respected, holy or pious; and, as the Muslims consider Adam as one of the prophets, it may be that a prophet's son was buried at Mazar-i-Sharif.

It is said that this was a shrine of a holy personage even before it became the burial-place of the Caliph Ali, the Fourth Caliph or successor of the Prophet.

It has also been said that although no-one has seen it, they have a piece of Noah's Ark at Samarkand in Turkestan. The tradition says that the land which appeared first after the Great Deluge of Noah was the Hindu Kush range and the country near Balkh, 'Mother of Cities'.

THE MYSTERIOUS CAVE OF KORGHAN

The inhabitants of the valley of Bamian, more specifically the people of the country near the village of Korghan, in the Central Highlands, speak of a cave in the hills from which cold blasts of air issue during the day. At night a phosphoric light emerges from it and blazes with wild, bright flames. No one dares go near the cave: either in daylight or at night.

The cave is a dark recess of considerable size and not quite natural, for some human hand must have been instrumental in cutting its mouth to such a regular oval shape.

But there is strong evidence to support the possibility that the Greeks or the Buddhists are mainly responsible for the construction of these caves all round the area of Bamian: the world centre of Buddhism for well over a thousand years – longer than the religion has flourished anywhere else in the world.

Some explorations were once made: as the Ameer had been informed by ancestral traditions that in the hills of Bamian there were great deposits of either gold or precious stones. These exertions ended only in discovering prehistoric remains. It is important to observe here that the above legend was so firmly established amongst the *dehqans* (land cultivators) that no-one would accompany the party of engineers when they neared the cave where they claimed were both cold winds and flames.

THE MOVING SANDS

There is a small hill in Kohistan where a white line of sand is visible in the middle of the green herbage. The sand, curiously enough, is in motion, and they say that at the foot of the hill there is a cave where all the *reg-i-rawan* ('running or moving sand') goes down, and weird sounds are heard on dark nights, especially on Thursdays.

The legend goes on to say that there was an old man who took up his abode near the cave of *reg-i-rawan* and proclaimed himself to be Imam Mahdi, the Messiah who is to come at the end of the world. He soon collected followers, dressed them as birds and beasts, and advanced towards Kabul.

The Amir's troops dispersed his followers and the pretender escaped to the hills of Kohistan. But he did not rest, and men from all parts of the country flocked to his banner, and once again they marched on the capital.

The Mullas and Sufis denounced him as a curse to the peace of the Faithful, and prayed to God that the disturber of tranquillity might be severely punished. Supported by the pious men's spiritual zeal, the Afghan soldiers defeated the hordes of the professed Mahdi and killed him near the cave wherefrom he rose.

It is said that his corpse descended into the cave, and from that time the white streak of sand flows from the top of the hill and goes down the pretender's cave to stuff his mouth for speaking blasphemy. The voices heard are his groans as he begs for mercy.

THE SILKWORMS

On the border towns between Afghanistan and Turkestan many families are engaged in the trades of silkworm culture and silk-winding. If one asks them as to how their trade originated, they relate passages from *Qassus-al-Anbia*: Tales of the Prophets; and there still exists a book of that name written in Persian.

Of silkworms, the book says, 'Every prophet has left witnesses to his people, and our brother Job left the worm. All this good came from the patience and mildness of the Prophet Job.'

291

Traditions say that Satan complained to God that he could not combat the Prophet Job as he was rich. God took away all Job's wealth and yet Job was still devoted in prayers to God and preached the truth to people. Again Satan spoke of Job's superiority, inasmuch as Job's body was sound and healthy.

God, to test Job further, brought out wounds on Job's body and created worms in the sores; but the Prophet was patient and humble and offered his prayers as before.

Job's acquittal from his severe test pleased God, and Gabriel was sent to strike the earth, bring out a stream and throw the Prophet in the water. The action of the water healed Job's wounds and the worms scattered in three directions. Some fell in the stream and became leeches, others flew into the air and were made bees, yet others crawled up the trees and were fashioned into silkworms.

Imam Jafar Sadiq, he of great wisdom, the saint who was our own ancestor, who was supposed to be the first silk-winder, is said to have held that a saint, Daud, could not understand the nature of the cocoons. He prayed to God to enlighten him upon their use.

He had not finished praying when a form appeared, and announcing himself to be a Treasurer of God, told Daud to put the cocoons in water and then see the explanation in it. He threw the cocoons into the water, and, taking a crooked stick, he struck the cocoons, saying: 'In the name of God, the Merciful, the Compassionate'.

A thread appeared on the stick, and they called it silk or *resham* or *abresham*. This means 'that which flows in water'.

The trade of silk-winding is considered one of the most honourable ones, and certain rules in connection with different times in the operation of the winding are to be strictly observed.

All engaged in the trade must wash before going into their workroom, and offer prayers on entering it. They should abstain from any intoxicating drugs and speak ill of no man, nor charge excessive prices for their silk.

Due regard and respect must on all occasions be paid to the head of the Guild of the Trade, and beginners in the art should have their gaze directed on the ground and should not stare at their teachers or seniors.

There are certain other preliminary steps which are required of apprentices. They must recite: 'In the name of God the Merciful, the Compassionate. Give us Thy forgiveness, O God; we are sinners', when going to the workshops in the morning.

When the cocoons are thrown into the hot water and a man takes a crooked stick to stir the liquid, they say: 'O Lord, Your happiness has come upon us'. When they take out the silk from the cauldrons they ought to say: 'By Thy wisdom, O God, clean us from sin and keep us apart from guilt'. They should recite: 'Our thanks are due to the Master of Paradise', when putting the thread to the reels, and when winding, a verse should be recited: 'Direct us, O Lord, to the path of righteousness'.

At closing time they must not turn their backs towards the place where the silk may be lying, but retrace their steps facing the loom.

RUSTAM'S WELL

There is an old well some miles from Kabul called Chah-i-Rustam (*chah*, well) of about the radius of ten yards, and a network of iron is placed just under the water. The construction is of red stones, such as cannot be seen in the neighbouring hills.

Rustam is the Iranian equivalent of Hercules, the great champion of the Persians, the prince of the land of Seistan. He fought the White Dragon and struggled for two whole days with Prince Isfandiar, in the Iranic epics.

Seistan is in Western Afghanistan, named formerly Sakastan: Land of the Saka people, the Sakasun, whom some see as the ancestors of the Saxons.

Water is never drawn from the well, which is of a deep grey colour. The well has no date on it, and on the walls big iron chains hang down to the surface.

The legend goes on to say that Rustam, the great wrestler of Persia, after being killed was thrown into this well, and a friend of his fixed these chains, so that Rustam's spirit might climb up and escape; but the enemies of the wrestler placed a net below the level of the water, and thus the dead hero of Firdausi's classic, *The Book of Kings* is forever trapped in that well.

The truth goes against it, for it is to be understood that the water of the well is very unwholesome; and, as it is of very large dimensions, the constructors must have placed the iron network to catch anyone who might fall in by accident, and the chains were to hang onto until help came. Such wells of huge diameter are also seen round about Ghazni.

Condensed from *Afghanistan of the Afghans* by Sirdar Ikbal Ali Shah.

INDO-SCYTHIANS AND HINDUS

Nobody knows who the original Afghans were. Prehistoric remains show a very early human presence. The Vedic literature, scriptures of the Hindus, speaks of Yama, the first king of the Aryans, who lived here five and a half thousand years ago.

The two most ancient religious dispensations of what is now Afghanistan – represented now by Hinduism and Zoroastrianism - have had an influence hardly to be expected from such a small community. Hinduism and its main offshoot, Buddhism, all but conquered the Far East; while the faith of Zarathustra with its preoccupation with morality, has been seen as shaping the thinking of Christianity.

THE BANI-ISRAIL

The supposedly 'very Semitic' appearance of the Pashtun people of Afghanistan (the largest of several ethnic groups) caused some foreign observers to accept their claim to originate with the Hebrews.

The legendary account given by these Afghans regarding their grandsires, although unsupported by history, is interesting. The traditions trace them to a single ancestor with the patronymic of Afghana. The story begins, however, with one ibn Yamin, Bin Yaqub - Benjamin son of Jacob – commonly known as Qais.

Qais and his only son Sarral were, it is said, shepherds on the banks of the river Nile in Egypt. Sarral was a big, stalwart man, nicknamed Tawil, which means 'tall'.

The story continues that one day two sheep of Tawil's herd went astray. While he was searching for them in the desert, he came upon a man called Ismail from the tribe of Lawi.

Ismail, a priest or magician with strange powers, was so impressed by Tawil that he asked him to become the King of the Bani-Israil. The man of the Lawi tribe used supernatural skills to support Tawil's candidature: when he poured some oil over the head of Tawil the shepherd's hair curled up in the shape of a crown fit for kings – and Tawil duly became monarch of the Bani-Israil.

Tawil married into the tribe of Lawi and had a daughter, Iramiah, whom he married to David: it is their son who was Afghana, progenitor of the Afghans of the Pashtun strain.

It is believed that Afghana helped his father David in the building of the Temple at Jerusalem. When misadventure befell the children of Israil, Afghana trekked to the hills of Ghor with his forty sons, and thus the tribe was established in Afghanistan.

This narrative, contained in the ancient books of the Pashtuns and repeated endlessly in story, has caused some to believe that the Afghans are in some way connected with the Lost Tribes of Israel; though this is sharply contested by others. There is no authentic record either to substantiate or to refute the theory.

Several British and other historians have clashed on the matter, which generates much heat among them: though to question its veracity is a killing matter among the Pashtuns, who take such an attitude as questioning their legitimacy. Most, if not all, tribes among the twelve million Pashtuns have detailed family trees tracing this descent.

On the other hand, certain Moslem historians have mentioned that the headman of the Afghans of this descent was summoned from Kohistan by the Prophet Mohammed; but his name is given as Qais and not Afghana.

This Qais is said to have embraced Islam and was given the name of Abdur-Rashid. Later, when Qais distinguished himself in battle, he was nicknamed Pashtun – a rudder – 'he who would steer the boat of Islam in Asia through the troubled waters of infidelity'.

The matter has not been resolved: and readers should beware lest, through cursory reading of one or other of the didactic 'proofs' published in the West, they assume otherwise.

Now, in addition to the Pashtuns, there dwell in Afghanistan people of Mongol, Persian and other stocks. Some, the fair-skinned and often blue-eyed mountain people in Nuristan (formerly Kafiristan) and elsewhere claim to be kin of the Northern Europeans. The people who called themselves Aryans - including the progenitors of the Hindus and the Sakas – either lived for centuries, or originated, in Afghanistan.

The present-day patchwork of different strains is traceable to successive waves of conquests in what the Persians first called the Roof of the World.

Afghanistan has been noted for three important things over the centuries. As a trade route, the Silk Road and other caravan links were the contact between China, the Middle East and the West, effectively ending at Rome. As a highway to conquest, it served the Hindus in their descent upon India, their new home; the Mongols, Huns and others, and finally the Muslim Arabs. Even the Romans (who failed to conquer it) invaded the country, in 305–255 B.C.

The consequence of the trade and military activities was that Afghanistan became famous for one mighty empire, one great religious centre, after another. As early as 549 B.C., the Persian emperor Cyrus had occupied the country: and two centuries later came the expedition of Alexander the Great.

THE GREEKS AND GRAECO-BUDDHISTS

The antiquities of Afghanistan have been much neglected by historians and archaeologists, chiefly because of the political upheavals which have disturbed that country, rendering it impossible to undertake very extensive local researches.

Kabul, the capital, has some of the oldest and most interesting relics of Greek art and civilisation in Asia. Fully two thousand years before Julius Caesar brought his legions to Albion, Kabul had already figured in history. Ptolemy and other ancient geographers applied the term 'Aryana' to a country lying between the Suleiman mountains in the east and the great salt desert of Northern Iran in the west. It was bounded by Baluchistan in the south, and by the Hindu Kush range with the Karabel plateau in the north. From these boundaries one may identify the country with modern Afghanistan: with the addition of Khorasan, 'Land of the Rising Sun', which now forms a province of Iran.

Aryana – ancient Afghanistan – was divided into three provinces: Drangiana (the whole of Northern Afghanistan); Arachosia, the North-Eastern portion; and Paropamisus, the valley of the Kabul river.

The city of Kabul was called Ortospanum, Jalalabad was Plegerium Nagara, Kandahar, Gandhara, and Farah, Phra. The ancient and modern names of the last two have hardly changed. Indeed some people, to this day, call a Kandahari – one belonging to Kandahar – a Gandahari; and Ph is the Greek F.

The early history of Afghanistan is indissolubly bound up with the conquest of Alexander. To several cities in Central Asia and Afghanistan the great Hellenic conqueror is said to have given his name. Herat, for instance, was called after him: Alexandria-Arya; and Kandahar was renamed Alexandria-Arachosia.

The ruins of Opiane in the Kabul river valley can still be identified; near Khojand, on the Jaxartes, are still situated the ruins of Alexander's Cyropolis, the most remote of Alexander's conquests in Central Asia.

Alexander entered Afghanistan from the north-west. Occupying Herat, now in the Iran-Afghan frontier region, he marched on the south-western regions of Afghanistan, capturing Farah, and taking Kandahar and Ghazni.

Having thus almost encircled Kabul, he reduced it. Strategists consider that whosoever possesses the Ghorband and Panjshir valleys, in the neighbourhood of Kabul, holds the keys of Central Asia in his hands. Alexander made these valleys his bases, whence he could proceed to the conquest of Bactria, northwards, and India, to the south.

Another locality which enshrines the memory of Alexander is the Kalif ferry over the Oxus in the north: on the USSR-Afghan frontier.

This place is still regarded as of great strategic importance, and in its immediate vicinity Russians and Afghans have often clashed. The Afghan tendency towards hero-worship has not failed to impart to the Kalif ford – Alexander's crossing point – a considerable degree of reverence. Indeed the local guide insists upon our believing that certain marks in a rock beside the river are the footprints of Alexander, who stood there watching his army crossing the river.

On the death of Alexander, the Greek Empire in the East soon broke up. His generals divided it among themselves. Bactria was under Satrap Philip; Afghanistan under Strasanor and Sibertius; and India under Oxyartes, father-in-law of the dead leader. Discontent about apportioning the empire arose among these Greek generals.

After seven years' fighting, Seleucus emerged as ruler from 'the Euphrates to the Oxus and Indus'. But Seleucus did not have the wisdom of Alexander regarding the natural strength of the Kabul valleys, and failed to retain them as military strongholds. The base was abandoned, and India was bartered to Chandra Gupta for five hundred elephants.

The history of those Greek kings who guided the destinies of early Afghanistan is a stormy one. In 280 B.C. Seleucus was murdered, and was succeeded by Antiochus Soter, who was followed by Antiochus Theos; the latter was undecided as to which of his two wives, Leodike or Berenike, he favoured more, and Leodike, to put an end to his doubts, poisoned him. Seleucus II succeeded him in 246 B.C. and the Bactrian Greeks, in revolt during his reign, occupied Kabul, which henceforth became a Bactrian province.

Diodotus, who had headed the Bactrian revolt, was succeeded, as King of Kabul, by his son Demetrius, merely to be replaced by Eucratides, who in turn was murdered by his own son, whose name remains unknown. From this point history is silent about the doings of the Seleucidas, although the names of two Greek kings are mentioned – those of Menander and Apollodotus. Records cease to be helpful here, and we must be assisted by the no less valuable evidence of monumental structures, coins, and other relics from all over the Middle East, especially in the ruins of Begram.

The plain of Begram, thirty miles north of Kabul, is littered with ruins of the greatest importance to the history of Greek supremacy in Afghanistan. Coins are found in this plain, as the upper soil is washed away by rains or turned by the plough of husbandmen. As many as 30,000 coins are discovered each year. But Begram is not the only locality where archaeological relics are to be encountered. There are many topes scattered over the Kabul valley even farther east than Jalalabad. The topes are immense solid domes raised on round towers, and decorated by green glazed paint. These are the pyramids of Afghanistan.

299

No effort has been made to force an entry into these structures, but one which had been struck by lightning revealed many interesting relics – vessels, coins, rings, signets and seals, some of which bore Greek lettering on one side.

The coins found in Afghanistan have inscriptions both in Greek and the old Kabuli languages, just as the modern Indian rupee bears both English and Urdu characters. The Kabuli inscription is usually a Sanskrit translation of the Greek version.

The cities of the valley of Kabul, like their ancient Greek prototype, possessed mints, and each mint had its own monogram. No less than 150 monograms are known, and from these one can ascertain what part of the country a king had ruled over in Aryana; from the style we can also judge the approximate dates.

When India became severed from Greece, and communications ceased from the mother country, an artistic deterioration set in. The coins of Diodotus, the first Bactrian king, are excellent specimens of true Grecian art. So are those of Antiochus. But the coins of Hermaeus, the last of the Bactrian monarchs, are very rude; even the spelling of the Greek on them is incorrect, and the letters have degenerated to mere barbarous symbols. The coins of the first two kings are of gold, while their successors contented themselves with silver and copper. This may strengthen the assumption that the Greek Conquest had stripped India of such gold as was easily procurable by ancient methods.

The portraits on some of the coins are magnificent, and the four-drachma pieces of Eucratides are very fine indeed. They have the portrait of the king on one side; the reverse contains two horsemen; on the margin are the name and the titles of the Greek king: 'Eucratides, the king, the Saviour'. Apollodotus has, in addition to his title, a novel prefix – 'The lover of his father'. Many coins are square in shape. The Greek gods are frequently depicted on these ancient coins, Hercules with his club, and Apollo with his bow being constantly found. One coin has a fish on it; the owl, as the Athenean bird of wisdom, is represented, while elephants and bullocks also figure.

The coins of twenty-nine kings and three queens, who were entirely unknown to history until the discoveries, have come to light.

The Hellenic kings seem to have reigned for only about 140 years – from 260 to 120 B.C. During the reign of Hermaeus, the country of Afghanistan was overrun by the Scythians, as is shown by the appearance on a Greek coin of the name of a Scythian king Kajula Kadopes.

The rapid succession of these Greek kings in that part of the East gave some of them just time enough to strike coins. Nadir Shah, when he invaded India, set his mint to work during his brief stay of fifty-seven days. Similarly, Sikandar Shah, who reigned for fifty-four days, circulated his own coinage. The exercise of the privilege of coining is the monopoly of royalty in the East. But, apart from this consideration, we have evidence of several Greek kings reigning in Kabul and Bactria at one and the same time.

The coinage enables us to judge local conditions in Afghanistan. King was fighting against king, the father sometimes against his son.

The title of Apollodotus, 'the lover of his father', has a sinister echo, for he was guilty of his parent's assassination. Internecine wars have been never-ending.

The Greek kings of Kabul were idolaters, and their intimate association with the East did not alter their religion. A hundred years after they had ceased to rule Kabul, coins were struck featuring not only Greek letters but the figures of their gods. Some of these on the Indo-Scythian coins are decidedly Indian in aspect, but their Sanskrit names are Hellenised, and are given in Greek characters.

It must be remembered, when thinking about Afghan history, that it was the rule rather than the exception for more than one dynasty to rule at the same time. Frequently the country was divided into smaller states. Each sometimes had its own culture, at times of a very high degree of refinement.

THE TURKI KINGS

During the first Christian century the Yueh-Chi, a Central Asian horde, crushed the last remnants of Greek rule, and also expelled the Parthians. Kanishka was one of the greatest of the Yueh-Chi rulers. When his empire fell to pieces, the Turki kings of his race reigned for several centuries in the Kabul valley, and in the seventh century A.D. the Chinese pilgrim Huien Tsiang, found them still professing Buddhism. Afghanistan was the centre of the great

Graeco-Buddhist civilisation. And, concurrently, the Sakas were ruling in Seistan, to the west.

These Turks were followed by the Ephalites, a division of the Scythians; they by the Tokios, a Mongol group; and then came the Ratbil Shahs. At one and the same period, after 500 A.D., the Sasanians were in control in the west, the Mongols north of the Hindu Kush Mountains, and the Ephalites held the kingdom of Kabulistan.

The Ratbil Shah, as he is called by Arab historians such as the great Tabari and Istakhari, was the ruler of the theocratic Kingdom of Bamian, the world centre of Buddhist teaching, visited by, among others, Chinese pilgrims who have left accounts of the immense monasteries and their warrior-mystic-king.

HINDUS, ARABS AND GHAZNAVID TURKS

About the end of the ninth century the Turki Shahis gave place to Hindu rulers, who finally disappeared before the onslaught of the Ghaznavids. In 642 the Arabs had occupied western Afghanistan, and Herat became one of the principal cities of the Islamic world. The Arabs failed to conquer Kabul, and this war went on for a century. The Arab-Afghan struggle continued for another hundred years.

The Afghans were converted to Islam, and the Arab invaders became Afghanised. Over twelve hundred years later, there are still Arab pockets in the country.

There were two rival Caliphates, headships of the Land of Islam which now stretched from the borders of China to Africa and Spain. An Afghan patriot, Abu Muslim, arose and liberated large parts of the country from the Omayyad Caliphate, ruling from Sind, now in Pakistan, to the Oxus river in the north.

Baghdad, now in Iraq, was the capital of the Islamic State, whose chief advisers were the powerful Barmaki family, former high priests of the pre-Islamic religious centres of Balkh, in Afghanistan. The Caliph Haroun Al Rashid, familiar to the West as the wise ruler in the *Arabian Nights*, was prevailed upon, through treachery, cruelly to destroy the Barmakis. The supporters of the Afghans at Court were wiped out.

Now came the Tahir Dynasty, which declared independence but

became unpopular because they were not independent enough of Baghdad. They were overthrown by the Saffaris, who emphasised freedom from the Caliphs. During their time, in the ninth century, the Arabic language was displaced in favour of Dari, Afghan Persian.

On the break-up of the Caliphate, the Islamic empire in the west, the Safavids ruled for a short time in Herat and Balkh, defeating the armies of what was then the Arabian superpower, only to be beaten in their turn, when King Ahmad was captured and sent a prisoner to Baghdad, where he died.

The Safavids were succeeded by the more powerful Samanids, and they in turn by the Turkish house of Ghazni.

The greatest of the Ghaznavids was Mahmud, who reigned from 988 to 1030. He ruled over Afghanistan, Trans-Oxiana, Western Iran and the Punjab, and founded a university at Ghazni. It was Mahmud who commissioned Firdausi to write the *Book of Kings*, regarded as the major document of Iranian history from the earliest times. Ghazni became the centre of a great culture.

After Mahmud's death his outlying possessions in the north and west fell to the Seljuk Turks; and the Afghan house of Ghor finally dispossessed his descendants of their remaining Afghan and Indian dominions. The greatest of the Ghorids was Shahab-ud-din Mohammed (1173–1206), who conquered the whole of north India.

THE MONGOLS

Afghanistan was next overrun by the Mongol hordes of Genghis Khan. His descendants ruled here until Tamerlane (Timur-i-Lang) subdued the country, sacking Delhi in 1398. When Timur died in 1405 and his empire dissolved, his descendants continued to rule in Herat, Balkh, Ghazni, Kabul and Kandahar.

One of them, Babar, the King of Badakhshan, Kabul and Kandahar, descended upon India in 1525 at the head of a Turki-Afghan army, and at Panipat (1526) overthrew Sultan Ibrahim Lodi of Delhi, who was also of Afghan descent.

Babar became the first Mogul emperor. Now the Afghan possessions become of secondary importance to the Moguls: Badakhshan was occupied by Uzbeks; Herat and Kandahar fell to the Iranian house of the Safavids. All that was left in Mogul hands was

Ghazni and the province of Kabul. In 1708 the Ghilzais of Kandahar threw off the Iranian yoke while the Abdalis (Durranis) - another Afghan family – took Herat and overran Khorasan. In 1738 Nadir Shah of Iran conquered Afghanistan.

THE DURRANIS OF AFGHANISTAN

In 1739 Nadir Shah invaded India and sacked Delhi. When he was returning home he was assassinated and the loot of vast treasures and wealth fell to the Afghans in his army. Among his soldiers was an Afghan general of cavalry, Ahmad Shah, of the Saddozai section of the Abdali clan – a Durrani. The treasure of Delhi falling into his hands, he laid the foundation of the Durrani Empire.

So in the year 1747, the date of the assassination of Nadir Shah, Afghanistan became for a time a national monarchy. This Durrani Empire was never stable: it lasted only fifty years. Under Ahmad Shah a series of well-organised expeditions into India took place, resulting in the famous victory over the Maratha hosts at Panipat, in 1761.

The Durrani Empire included all of modern Afghanistan, Baluchistan, parts of Iran, Sind, the Derajat, the Punjab to Lahore, Kashmir, and the Yusafzai country to the north of Peshawar. Badakhshan paid tribute to Kabul.

NAPOLEON AND BRITISH FEARS OF RUSSIA

Ahmad Shah died in 1773 and was succeeded by his son Timur. Under the son the empire began to decline. Sind in the south fell to the Talpur Amirs; and Balkh in the north became virtually independent. In 1793, Timur was succeeded by his son Zaman, during whose reign the Punjab was overrun by Sikhs. From then onward, until 1818, Afghanistan was the scene of family conflicts between the many sons of Timur. At one time great fears were entertained in India that Zaman would invade it, but he remained too occupied with Iranian troubles and family quarrels. In 1799 Mahmud, another son of Timur, seized the throne.

At the beginning of the nineteenth century (1803), as a result of a conspiracy, the throne passed to Shuja-ul-Mulk. At this time, or rather in 1809, Lord Minto was the British Governor-General of India, and fear of Napoleon caused him to despatch Mountstuart Elphinstone to conclude an alliance with the Amir of Kabul.

While King Shuja's army was crushing a revolt in Kashmir shortly after the mission, he was deposed, and once more Mahmud reigned in his stead. Shuja became an exile at Ludhiana in India. Mahmud was deposed in 1818, which marks the end of the Sadozai dynasty in Afghanistan.

For years following the displacement of the Sadozais, there was considerable internecine fighting, but in 1826 Dost Mohammed Khan, of the Barakzai clan, made himself Lord of Kabul and Ghazni. It was not, however, till 1835 that he assumed the title of Amir.

Amir, an Arab title, originally signifies little more than 'a commander', and was the style used by the governors or viceroys of the central Caliphate, the headship of Islam. Even today, the matter is a sensitive one: rulers using the 'Commander' title rather than 'King', for Islam is opposed to kingship according to high religious authority's opinion.

THE FIRST ANGLO-AFGHAN WAR (1839–1842)

Lord Auckland, the Governor-General of India, now attempted to restore the Sadozai, in the shape of Shah Shuja, because he thought that Shuja, being friendly, would be a desirable ruler of a neighbouring state. It was presumed, too, that Dost Mohammed Khan inclined towards Russia. The whole attempt was a sad mistake. Shah Shuja was installed for a time but the Afghans hated a puppet Amir who was kept on his throne by British bayonets.

The Afghan conqueror Sultan Mahmud of Ghazna, the Idol-Breaker, had carried away the gates of the great Hindu temple of Somnath, eight centuries before. The British proclamation to the Indians after the short-lived victory and capture of Kabul by what is termed the Ever-Victorious Army, was called, by Wellington, a 'Song of Triumph':

Our Victorious Army bears the gates of the Temple of Somnath in triumph from Afghanistan, and the despoiled tomb of Sultan Mahmud looks upon the ruins of Ghazni. The insult of eight hundred years is at last avenged. The gates of the Temple of Somnath, so long the memorial of your humiliation, are become the proudest record of your national glory, the proof of your superiority in arms over the nations beyond the Indus.

Then came the rising against the British occupation, and the loss of the British army. Eventually it was discovered that the 'Gates of Somnath' were the wrong ones. Made of Afghan wood, they were carved with an inscription which had nothing to do with Somnath or its idol . . . The Afghans were free again: or lapsed into barbarism, according to which authority you consult.

According to many of those who lived through that period, Shah Shuja was no malleable puppet; and even the British documentation of the time does not represent him as such. Afghans say that the refusal of many feudal chiefs to support Shuja when he was reinstalled in Kabul meant that he had few supporters (since others wanted the throne) and the opposition, by refusing him support, 'proved' their case that Shuja was helped only by the British.

Shah Shuja was eventually murdered, the British forces were annihilated and Dost Mohammed became Amir and reigned till 1863.

After the second Sikh war in 1849, India and Afghanistan became neighbours and now the frontier troubles began, because up to 1893 no proper boundary line existed between the two countries. The frontier is still disputed. In 1850 Dost Mohammed reconquered Balkh and in 1855 a treaty was signed between India and the Amir. During the same year the Amir captured Kandahar.

It was lucky for the British that Dost Mohammed was friendly in the Indian rising (at that time called 'The Mutiny') of 1857. In the year of his death he captured Herat, and was succeeded by Sher Ali Khan, after much fratricidal conflict.

Proper Anglo-Afghan relations begin from 1869 when Sher Ali Khan met Lord Mayo at Amballa. He wanted a new treaty: a fixed annual subsidy, assistance in arms and men whenever he needed it, a full recognition of his dynasty at Kabul and the acknowledgment of his favourite son, Abdulla Jan, as heir. Mayo could not agree to all the demands, but promised support: of which the British were to be the sole judges in respect of time and measure.

Difficulties once again began to arise on account of Czarist intrigues and General Kaufmann, Governor of Russian Turkestan, corresponded freely with the Amir of Kabul. When Lord Mayo was assassinated, Anglo-Afghan estrangement had reached its climax, to which were added the Perso-Afghan differences over Seistan. When this dispute was handed over to British arbitration, the result went in favour of Iran and animosity towards England grew strong in Afghanistan.

In 1873 Russia annexed Khiva in Central Asia and distinctly menaced the independence of the Khanates of Turkestan. The Amir of Afghanistan was thoroughly alarmed by the wave of Russian territorial expansion beyond his northern border and Sher Ali Khan addressed the British Government for a closer friendship.

Lord Northbrook took a different view. At Simla, he told Sayed Mohammed, the King's representative, that the Afghans should spend less on arms and reduce or abandon conscription to the forces, because Russia had come to an understanding with Britain and was therefore little danger to the Afghans.

In the following year Lord Beaconsfield became Prime Minister, and Lord Salisbury was appointed Secretary of State for India. His Department was delegated to watch Afghan events. Great Britain made a strong demand to have her interests guarded by an Englishman at Kabul rather than by an Indian at the Court of the Amir. The King of Kabul would not agree to the demand, arguing, as he rightly did, that the temper of his people would make him unable to protect an Englishman in Afghanistan.

Lord Salisbury ordered Lord Northbrook to act with a view to establishing a British Resident in Kabul, to 'advise' King Sher Ali on both internal and foreign affairs; rather on the lines of a Resident at the Court of a Maharaja in India. Northbrook resigned in protest. Salisbury hinted that some people were scared of the Afghans because of the disasters of the First Afghan War. He appointed Lord Lytton. One at least of Lytton's military advisers believed that the new technology in weapons now available to the British Army would make the conquest of Afghanistan a simple matter. The Second Afghan War was in gestation.

THE SECOND ANGLO-AFGHAN WAR (1878–1880)

The Second Afghan War arose out of the mere shadow of an excuse. Lord Lytton pressed for a British representative at Kabul despite Amir Sher Ali Khan's repeated explanation that this was not possible. Lytton took it into his head that the Amir's excuse was inspired by Russian intrigue against England. When British troops occupied Quetta, south of Afghanistan, in 1876, the Afghans began to have serious misgivings about the intentions of the Indian Government.

British troops entered Afghanistan, and, the Amir having been defeated, he took refuge in Mazar-i-Sharif where he died. The first phase of this war ended with the treaty of Gundamak in 1879, and Amir Yakub Khan ascended the throne. Sir Louis Cavagnari, British envoy in Afghanistan, was murdered by patriots, which led to British reprisals, and the new Amir had to abdicate, eventually giving place to Amir Abdur Rahman Khan, the nephew of Amir Sher Ali Khan, in 1880. The most important event in Afghan history at this time is that Lord Ripon recognised Amir Abdur Rahman Khan as the ruler in Afghanistan, but he was not permitted to have direct dealings with any foreign powers; all such arrangements were to be carried through the British. This form of dependency did not suit the Afghan temperament.

This was the state of affairs up to and including the First World War, when Afghanistan honoured her undertaking to remain neutral.

AFGHANS AND BRITISH IN THE GREAT GAME: THE THIRD ANGLO-AFGHAN WAR (1919)

For centuries the Afghans had descended upon India, and had ruled it through several dynasties. Their precursors, the Hindus, had originated beyond the Hindu Kush. In the early part of the nineteenth century the British became convinced that the French and Russians were in league to invade India – and that would involve Afghanistan.

In 1839 and again in 1878 the First and Second Anglo-Afghan wars were in large part a result of British and Russian rivalry. Like two clumsy fighters, circling around one another in the dark, both

empires convinced themselves that they were engaged in a vital
struggle to protect their own interests. Reading the records of
those times, one sees that each party, though feverishly engaged in
espionage and political manoeuvring, really had very little information about the intentions or ideas of the other. It is one of the
strangest episodes in history, with paranoia, fear and bombast all
elements in a potent brew.

The British called this preoccupation The Great Game. The
Russian Foreign Minister termed it The Tournament of Shadows.
The tales of intrepid exploits of the rival agents, the sabre-rattling
and the propaganda, have their echoes in the East-West confron-
tations of more recent times.

Once the heart of great empires, still seen in the Eastern and
Islamic worlds as a great nation of soldiers, thinkers and scientists,
Afghanistan after the First World war was sadly small and
weakened.

The British expansion out of India, and The Great Game, had
shrunk the country to an area the size of France, where twelve
million people lived between the Oxus river in the north and the
Khyber in the south. As the price of non-interference, the British
refused to allow Afghanistan the right of an independent State: to
have its own diplomatic representation abroad, and paid the King
a subsidy, as well as providing him with his only source of arms,
imported through India.

Then, on 28 February, 1919, Amanullah Khan crowned himself
King at Kabul. His first proclamation said:

O High Minded Nation!
O Courageous Army!
The Government of Afghanistan shall be internally and ex-
ternally independent and free; that is to say, all rights which are
possessed by other independent Powers of the world shall be
possessed in their entirety by Afghanistan ... from God I seek
guidance and the completion of my wishes.

Politically Afghanistan came under the Viceroy of India, and the
King therefore sent him a letter, three days after his accession,
which contained the words:

Let it not remain unknown to you that our independent and free

Government of Afghanistan considers itself ready to conclude such agreements as may be useful to our Government and yours.

In an infraction of customary courtesy the Viceroy sent no reply, no acknowledgment, within a reasonable period. Sayed Ikbal Ali Shah records that he discussed this omission with Edwin Montague, Secretary of State for India and the Foreign Secretary at Simla, Sir Hamilton Grant. Both agreed that this had been a blunder. Grant, for his part, tried to advise friendly relations with Amanullah, saying, 'There is only one policy, and that is the just and right policy.' For this stand he was later humiliated. The upstart Afghan King could not be allowed to 'chuck his weight about'.

Nearly two months elapsed before an evasive reply was sent by the British Viceroy. It did not acknowledge the freedom of Afghanistan. In Afghanistan, general mobilisation was ordered.

On 6th May, 1919, the Afghans started the military phase of their independence struggle, operating on three fronts, challenging the power of the victors of the recent European War. The Royal Air Force carried out aerial attacks on Jalalabad and on the undefended Royal Palace in Kabul; the world's first bombing of a civilian target. The British and Afghan armies clashed in bitter fighting, while 'money without stint' was poured into the coffers of the tribal chiefs of the Pashtuns in the independent buffer zones.

On one front, the Afghans suffered reverses. On the other two, the commanders Nadir and Abdul Qudus were continuing their advance: following the path of traditional Afghan conquests of India. The third was to be the trump card. The veteran General Nadir Khan marched, on 23rd May, on India, forcing the British frontier garrisons to retreat. Crossing the border into British-administered territory, Nadir Khan took his men and guns by forced marches across terrain considered impassable for troops and suddenly appeared before the British army near the village of Thal: the site of his 'feat of arms'.

Afghan artillery, both accurate and destructive, was admitted by the defenders to be superior to that of the British. The Raj commanders called up air support which (according to British records) was 'effective for the time being, but the relief was temporary'. Yet the Afghans and the British were still negotiating: as Sayed Ikbal writes:

The British Agent was still at Kabul; the Afghan Envoy, one Abdur-Rahman Khan, together with the Afghan Postmaster, was still allowed to go in and out of the country into India; the tribal chiefs and priests were thoroughly on the warpath; the King carried on long communications with the Viceroy (of India), and the war was on all the time.

On 3rd June, the Viceroy sent a letter to the Afghan King, demanding the withdrawal of Afghan troops, British troops to remain on Afghan territory, the Royal Air Force to have freedom of the Afghan skies, and the Pashtun tribes to be dissuaded from making war on the British.

Amanullah replied within a week. He objected to the 'eulogy of the unlimited resources of the British Government', and reminded the Viceroy of 'the internal power of the Sublime Government of Afghanistan, which, notwithstanding its defects of organisation, has repeatedly been the cause of destruction and ruin to foreign powers on its sacred soil'.

He continued that the nation, 'really looks upon fighting with non-Moslem nations as a cause of the revival of its existence and as a means of its awakening; notwithstanding the terrible damage and the probability of extensive losses and injuries'. He underlined the point with, 'it is in the Moslem nature of the Afghans to prefer visible death to subordination to a foreign power...'.

He could not allow aircraft to fly over Afghanistan: it was a violation of sovereignty; and, besides, people could easily shoot them down, which he would not be able to prevent. As to withdrawing troops, this was impossible, since the Afghans made no distinction between warriors and the rest of the people of the country. 'The military and civilians are identical,' he observes, 'and your overlooking such manifest and apparent points is a matter for surprise.'

But the two sides agreed to meet and the Afghan Peace Delegation arrived in India on 25th July and were segregated from the populace, in spite of their protests. It was pointed out that they were technically enemies; and would not be permitted to import any of the ideas of their ruler into India. The Indian nationalists were already agitating on behalf of the Afghans.

The Afghans were inefficient if not irresolute, with all kinds of Court intrigues affecting their conduct of the war. Their forces

311

were in general less well-equipped and their munitions low. The British, for their part, were nervous to hear that there had been an exchange of messages between the Russian Bolsheviks and Kabul. Their equanimity was not increased by the fact that the Afghan Postmaster had a very effective spy network in operation in British India, that (according to Afghan sources at least) the officer corps of the Raj's fighting units contained many poor leaders and some of the British troops were suffering from cholera due to inefficient sanitation. Bad organisation of their supplies had meant that for three weeks some troops lived on bully beef, biscuits, tea and sugar, transport was a shambles and the temperature was at times in excess of 110 degrees Fahrenheit.

The morale of the troops was not good, water was short and hospital accommodation inadequate. They also wanted to go home to Britain.

Peace was signed on 8th August. It abolished the privilege of importing arms and ammunition to Afghanistan via India. Since Afghanistan was now accepted as independent, she was, however, now free to get her arms from anywhere else.

The British subsidy was withdrawn (as a 'mark of displeasure'). This Article restored the freedom of the Afghan sovereign, who no longer had to 'accept the advice' of Britain.

The Afghans agreed to accept the previous frontier.

Afghanistan was free. Both countries claim that they won the war: which is perhaps the best way to end any hostilities.

As a consequence of the two Treaties which followed, the country regained its complete and unqualified independence under Amanullah Khan.

Vast areas of territory formerly under Afghan rule or populated by non-Indians of Afghan tradition, however, remained under British control, administered either as Pashtun tribal territories or as parts of India.

Amanullah Khan instituted a parliament and other social reforms, which enraged ultra-conservatives, who feared creeping Westernisation. A brigand chief, Bacha-i-Saqao, ('Son of the Water-Carrier') seized power and deposed the King in 1929. Anarchy ensued.

A hero of the Third Afghan War, Marshal Nadir Khan, returned to his homeland from his sick bed in France, rallied a volunteer army, notably from among the frontier tribes, and, in October

1929, entered Kabul, which had been conquered by his brother, Marshal Shah-Wali Khan.

Nadir Khan-i-Shahid, himself of noble descent, was acclaimed King of Afghanistan. He ruled until 1933, when he was succeeded by his son, Zahir Khan, who took the title of Zahir Shah.

THE REPUBLIC

King Zahir reigned until a left-wing military coup, organised by a tiny group, together with officers who had trained in the USSR, in July 1973. In 1977 the country was proclaimed a republic, with Daud Khan, the King's uncle, as President. The following year the left-wingers were displaced by a tiny far-left minority group in another coup, and the country was renamed 'the Democratic Republic of Afghanistan'.

The Communist Party (calling itself 'The People's Democratic Party') was the only political organisation permitted. Government was by the Revolutionary Council, and maintained by force, though large parts of Afghanistan refused to submit to this regime.

THE RUSSIAN INVASION

In March 1979, the Communist leader N.M. Taraki was killed and replaced by another Communist, H. Amin. Massive resistance against the minority regime by the people, especially in the numerous mountain areas, ensued. The Communists, about to lose control, appealed for help to the USSR, and in December 1979 large contingents of Soviet troops (known as 'The Fraternal Temporary Socialist Contingent') intervened in order to 'do their international duty' as the Russians called it.

Amin was killed or – according to the rulers in Kabul – 'died of galloping diabetes' during the intervention. The Soviet armies brought with them Babrak Karmal, who had been in Czechoslovakia, and he was made President.

Soviet and Afghan Communist forces continued to fight resisters in all 29 provinces of Afghanistan, year after year. By 1986, eight and a half million Afghans were either dead, crippled or refugees in Iran, Pakistan and elsewhere – or 'internal refugees', having lost their homes and lands in the war.

They had fought the Soviet superpower with few weapons for longer than the entire duration of the Second World War. Afghan casualties were greater than the total number of dead in the combined British and U.S. forces in World War II. General Najib of the Secret Political Police (the KHAD – trained by the KGB) replaced Karmal after the Great Leader returned to Kabul from a protracted stay in Moscow, where the Soviet leader Gorbachev described the Afghan campaign as a bleeding wound. The United Nations, year after year, condemned the Soviet Army's presence in Afghanistan; while the Russians constantly claimed that they wanted to leave, while proposing impossible conditions.

THE RESISTANCE OF THE MUJAHIDIN

Fighting continued, with ever-increasing intensity, with the Russians and their relatively few Afghan supporters controlling only about 15% of the country and living an embattled existence, harried by the patriots, the Mujahidin.

At first, foreign 'experts' insisted that the Afghan resistance would not last more than a few months. As the years went by, commentators constantly expressed amazement that the Mujahidin ('Holy Warriors') could still resist. Those who knew the Afghans, or had read their history, were less surprised.

Those newspaper readers in the free world who were accustomed to sifting fact from fiction, noted the success of Soviet propaganda in infiltrating 'disinformation' into general circulation. Many otherwise irreprochable writers have been induced to believe all kinds of things.

Since journalists often use press clippings for information when writing their own stories, the Soviet-planted 'facts' surface again and again. At times an accumulation of them will produce a grotesquely false article.

The Russians also worked hard on visiting journalists in Afghanistan, showing them 'undamaged' towns and villages, which they represented to be the ones which accurate reports testify they had destroyed.

PART NINE

THE RED BEAR FROM THE NORTH

VISION OF A RECLUSE

Sirdar Ikbal Ali Shah is on record as saying
that this experience, published in 1937 (in *The
Book of Oriental Literature*) referred to the
Barbarians of the North descending on his
country:

Earthly pleasures I had had all, but none opened up my heart.

Wine, gold, and kingdom are chimerical, and nothing more than
illusions, devoid of reality.

Here, look my heart! you have it all for nothing. The lordly
deodars your roof, the velvet grass your carpet, the majestic river
to play music, and the gorgeous lamps of nature as your light. What
more do you desire?

Though once a ruler of men, yet now I have a domain in the
guileless jungle, and reign in the happiness of solitude. Here I stay,
and perchance my blackened disc of mind may yet get bright in
contemplation.

The world's memories are repugnant to my soul, and here I need
recall nothing of life's bitterness. Peace and joy will now abide with
me, and I shall be alone, yet never lonely.

Days go, and shadows of night fall; I listen to the sweet music of
the waters, and roam unhurt amongst my friends of the wild.

No human voice penetrated the wall of mighty hills, no man
floated his barge on the river, and I gloried in my solitary
splendour.

One divine summer evening the perfumes of wild flowers filled
the air, all was calm, all was right and gently peaceful, and I was
kneeling at my prayer. Soon a stupor came upon me, and I knew
not where I was.

For lo! the scene had changed. It was cold; the river, the jungle,

317

and the hills were all gone, the very shape of my hermitage was altered, and I was in a strange land. The stream was small and leaped furiously from stone to stone, the forest was thick, and black clouds threatened storms.

I wondered, however, not long on my surroundings, for I now heard a sound as if lightning had struck a great building and shaken the very foundations of the earth. It was not, as I thought, thunder, but some phenomenon which I had never before seen or heard. A huge tree fell with a crash, and pieces of metal, after striking the rock, rebounded and whizzed past my face.

'What force and power!' said I, 'that can rend asunder such huge trees, and can throw metal in this fashion. What can it be? Where am I? . . .'

Not long had I waited when I heard war-horses at full gallop, and in the distance thunder booming. O Lord and Master! which planet is this? I muttered my prayers. Am I thrown into the pit of demons? Is that not the destination of all sinners after death? A shriek from a thousand voices interrupted my prayer, and horsemen swept down the valley like a hurricane.

'Oh, cruel monster! spare our lives. . . .' A deep moan and a deathlike silence once again. The noise startled me, and presently an old man stumbled over stones to my side.

'Protect me! hide me!' uttered the old man in terror. 'They are killing us. Here is my gold: take it and hide me.'

'Come, father!' said I. 'I seek neither gold nor silver, but am on the quest for the peace of the soul. Your age demands respect; come and hide here; none will disturb the tranquillity of your pious years.' He hid himself under my straw bed, miserable that it was, visible to any who might look.

He could not speak, his arms were bleeding, and he bore a wound on his face, but after a while he said, 'Good hermit, fly for your life; they have drained the wells of brutality to the last drop, and the nails of their heels have torn fountains of blood from the panting necks of the defeated.'

My blood boiled with rage. 'Where are they?' I asked. 'What are they?'

'They are a race of men called the Dragons of War, and come from the North.'

'A race of men? Surely, reverend friend, not men!'

'Yes, men,' replied he, 'in shape and form – and heaven help us if we are discovered.'

'Ay, ay,' said I. 'I understand you now, and all is clear to me. This place – I wondered if it were an abode of demons; it is not, it is Earth, and I have heard of these hordes of whom you speak. Wait here, father, and rest your limbs. To kill may be theirs, yet wrong must be avenged and. . . .'

I had not finished talking, when lo, two men clad in a peculiar garb approached us, and asked me whether I had hidden an old man. 'Concealed!' said I, 'no! Besides what brings evil messengers to the resting-place of a poor hermit?'

'A priest! Ha, ha!' laughed one. 'A priest? A coward – to dress in the guise of a hermit to escape punishment. Feel the edge, now, of this weapon.'

'My order,' said I, 'prohibits shedding human blood, and I am no coward, but have fought and won before, and do not hide behind a priestly cloak. The old man whom you seek is here, but you will have to cross my corpse to pollute his worthy person. I have said that we refrain from killing human beings: but you are no humans; so villains, come and let us fight. My fingers have not yet lost their swordsman's touch.'

They spoke no more, and hurriedly retraced their steps. The old man sat in tears, and at last fell dead from his wounds, and I knelt over him.

Then I awoke.

The waters of the river were like a sheet of melted gold, its flow serene. The evening breeze, loaded with fragrance, produced a music as it glided through the deodar leaves, and the sun was vanishing behind the mountain ranges. The sky was painted red, as I sat by the stream meditating my vision. Was the colour in the sky not from the particles of innocent blood collecting up above: to supplicate and to invoke the wrath of heaven upon the miscreants in the land of my vision?

But visions are visions; there are no such people on God's earth, I thought: and soon I was again at my prayers, in my hermitage.

TALES FROM THE WAR IN AFGHANISTAN

A FORTUNE

Two Afghan guerrillas were discussing the latest news.

'Hey, Abdul, Commander Ahmad Shah has offered a reward of $100 for every Russian killed.'

'That's not bad at all. How many of them are there in the country?'

'They say there's 150,000.'

Abdul embraced his friend. 'Fifteen million dollars – I'm rich! But don't worry, I promise to share it with you.'

RESERVE

An Afghan military engineer had joined a guerrilla band. He became rather nervous on a mission to blow up a bridge when he noticed that one Mujahid was carrying some ancient and unstable gelignite.

'Amin Khan,' he said, 'what will happen if that explosive goes off by itself?'

'That's all right, soldier boy,' said the warrior, 'I've got a spare one in my knapsack.'

THE ANSWERS

Mulla Nasrudin presented himself to the Information Office of the People's Democratic Party of Afghanistan in Kabul.

'May I have some information about our great Red heroes, Comrade?' he asked the man behind the counter.

'Certainly, Comrade; what do you want to know?'

'Comrade, what happened to Comrade Tariki, our former Great Leader?'

'He is dead, Comrade.'

'And where is Comrade General Herati?'

'He's dead, too, Comrade, killed by the counter-revolutionaries.'

'And Comrade President Hafizulla Amin, Comrade, how is he?'

'He's dead, too. But why are you asking me all these questions?'

'Because, Comrade,' said the Mulla, 'I do so love to hear the answers.'

ME, TOO

Three men were talking in a tiny cell in Deh Mazang Prison in Kabul.

They had only a tiny scrap of bread between them, and decided that as it was too small to share, it should go to the man who was the worst villain of all.

'I'm doing thirty years hard labour for supporting the Khalq Faction of the Communist Party,' said the first man to the second one. 'How about you?'

'I'm doing thirty years hard for opposing the Khalq.'

The third man said, 'I *started* the Khalq faction' – and, taking up the piece of bread, put it in his mouth.

HIS VALUE

The Russians arrived in Kabul at the invitation of a handful of desperadoes who had temporarily seized power and could not hold onto it without outside help.

The people of the city knew little of communism, and were at first stunned, not knowing how to react. For their part, the Red Army men were under orders to be as polite as possible to the citizens of the new Socialist Ally.

An old woman with a lot of baggage saw a Russian major standing near a bus and told him to carry her things aboard.

Grinning, the officer saluted and did as she asked, to be rewarded with a five-afghani coin.

'That's too much, Citizeness,' he said, with a laugh, 'one afghani would have been ample.'

'Comrade Russian,' she said, 'five is the right amount: it's Soviet lieutenants that are worth only one afghani.'

THE MESSAGE

This tale was brought from Moscow.

The Russian scientists had discovered a way of reviving a human being, cloning him by using a single cell from his corpse.

Naturally, they obtained a cell from the body of Karl Marx, as a priority – and succeeded in reproducing the great man, perfect in every detail.

Marx insisted on addressing the Soviet people on television.

'Of course, Comrade Marx. You will want to speak for at least ten hours: after all, Comrade Gorbachov spoke for six hours the other day . . .'

'No, I only need thirty seconds.'

'But Comrade Marx . . .'

'Do as I say!'

The date and time were fixed, and, when every single Soviet citizen was glued to his or her TV, the noble head of the great Marx appeared on their screens.

'Comrades, toilers of the Union of Soviet Socialist Republics,' said the Great Teacher, *'I am sorry.'*

QUESTIONS

In an attempt to make things look more democratic, the Red Afghans started mass meetings of the Socialist Toilers for 'questions and consultations' with Party chiefs.

Mulla Nasrudin and a friend hurried to the first meeting.

After the usual hours of haranguing about the New Day, Question Time was announced. Nasrudin's friend put up his hand.

'Yes, Comrade?' said the Chairman.

'Why is there such a shortage of food?'

'The query will be dealt with in a moment. Meanwhile, let us have another question.'

The Mulla raised his arm.

'Yes, Comrade Nasrudin?'

'When are we going to have free elections? And why are those men with guns taking my friend away?'

TOO LATE

The Communists of Afghanistan, notionally united in the People's Democratic Party, early on split into two viciously opposed factions – the Khalq and Parcham elements – and soon became noted for their tendency to gun one another down in the street when tempers flared. The People's Militia, Defenders of the Fatherland Front, police the curfew, which is rigidly enforced. The theory, seldom borne out in practice, is that if the people are kept off the streets from dusk until dawn, the freedom fighters will be dissuaded from attacking the Fraternal Forces of the Brotherly Soviet Union discharging their International Duty.

Early one evening a Parchamite on patrol saw a man he didn't like walking along the main thoroughfare of Kabul, Maiwand Avenue. He took aim with his Kalashnikov, and killed him with a single shot.

A Khalqite rushed up to him. 'It isn't curfew yet! I'll report you to the secret police for committing an anti-revolutionary murder!'

'That's all right, Rafiq – Comrade. You see, I know where that man lives. He hadn't a chance of getting home before curfew time. Trust a Khalqi to lack a sense of dialectical historical materialistic justice-timing.'

OPINION FROM CENTRAL ASIA

Among the Fraternal Limited Contingent of Soviet troops doing their international duty in Afghanistan was a sergeant from Uzbekistan. 'Comrade,' he said to an Afghan in Kabul, 'when you have socialism here, you know what will happen?'

'No, what?'

'One of the first things will be that there'll be a shortage of mountains – you'll have to queue for them . . .'

THE REFUGEE WOMEN

Of nearly six million Afghans who have fled the fighting in Afghanistan since 1979, the majority are women and children. The struggle has already lasted longer than the Second World War, and more Afghans have died than the combined deaths of the United States and British forces in that war.

Members of my institution, the United States International University, were interested in this problem. Being of Afghan descent and working on International Relations at the USIU, I visited the refugee camps in Pakistan, in connection with the United Nations Decade for Women.

Reports and studies of people from traditional cultures are, in the nature of things, generally carried out and consumed by people in the developed world who usually lack the psychological and social background. To appreciate the conditions, realities and problems, some context is first necessary.

The Afghans, living in the mountains and valleys of one of the world's starkest and at times most beautiful and fertile lands, come from a variety of ethnic groups. They comprise Pashtuns (the 'Pathans' of the British), the Persian-speaking Tajiks, the Turkic tribes, Mongols, people of Arabian origin, and the fair-haired folk of Nuristan. These, in turn, have various systems of social organisation. The Pushtuns, the majority, are tribal, and renowned warriors; the Tajiks live mostly in villages; many others have a semi-feudal way of life. The 'westernised' or middle-class, people are generally to be found in the towns. Then there are the Kochis, the nomads, perhaps numbered in millions.

Although there are few social tensions in ordinary times, the lumping together of millions of these people in refugee camps has

324

produced friction which it takes a great deal of their own patience
to defuse.

The Pakistanis, hosts to three and a half of the six million, have
welcomed the Afghans on the basis of a shared belief in Islam. The
Government, aided by national and international aid agencies, has
provided a remarkable structure of administration and support.
Very large numbers of individuals have also taken Afghans into
their homes; some are even sharing two-roomed houses with a
whole Afghan family.

There are over three hundred refugee camps in the north of
Pakistan. One which I visited, Nasir Bagh, houses thirty thousand
people.

One result of the war has been a resurgence of enthusiastic Islam
as a binding force and motor for the resistance.

The problems of the women are especially acute. They have no
homes to call their own, no 'territory' other than a few square feet
in a tent or earthen hut. Most lack the means to carry on their
traditional tasks: weaving, cooking, carpet-making. Few have a
change of clothing. Accustomed to a man as a protector and
provider, they often find themselves alone with their children,
their husbands dead or at the war-front.

Most of the women have given all their jewellery – and any other
possession – to sell for arms and ammunition. Hygiene and washing conditions are below what they are used to. They even help
with the building of rough houses; though the laws of veiling and
modesty restrict their contribution.

Afghan men usually have only one wife, though the law permits
them four ('if they can do equal justice to all'). Many men have
married widows, including the elderly and infirm, to give them the
protection which tradition extends.

The children often refuse to play with toys: dolls and models
containing explosives were dropped from aircraft upon them:
some children are blinded, as are some of their mothers and
fathers, by enemy action.

Just the same, the women are thankful that they have got their
children out of Afghanistan. Tens of thousands, some as young as
five years, have been taken to the USSR, to be educated as 'good
Afghan Communists'. If and when they return, their future will be
most uncertain.

There is one unusual camp called Kerala. It was set up by the survivors from a village in Afghanistan with the same name. Almost the whole male population were killed, leaving some five thousand women. They now all live in Kerala, in mourning.

Most camps have clinics and medical dispensaries; but most of the physicians are men. A significant proportion of the women refugees cannot bring themselves to be touched by a man to whom they are not related.

There are many cases of psychological disorders. I visited one camp and was about to take a photograph of a women, when she had a hysterical fit. She explained that the camera reminded her of the gun which had been fired point-blank at her by a Russian.

Considering their condition and their experiences, some of the latter almost beyond belief, the women have extraordinarily high morale. They are deeply devout and patriotic. As one said to me, 'The Russians will be able to take Afghanistan only when there is not a single Afghan left.' With an estimated one and a half million deaths from a population of just a few million, one's mind is haunted by the possibility . . .

Among the refugees are women who had taken up arms against the invader, and are now wounded, battle-shocked or blinded. Others, fighting in all-women groups, are still resisting in the mountains. They do more effective things than Kipling gave them credit for, after the Second Anglo-Afghan War:

When you're wounded and lying on Afghanistan's plains
An' the women come out to cut up your remains:
Jest roll on your rifle an blow out your brains
An go to your Gawd like a soldier.

One such woman, whose leg had been blown off, has started a school. Others are running small co-operatives, making embroidery and other items for sale. Most of them want education for their children: but there is very little hope of that for a long time to come.

I have not had time to deal with the internal refugees: those who have fled their bombed villages and napalmed fields, and who eke out a miserable existence within Afghanistan – who knows how?

For the refugee women of Afghanistan, whether inside or outside the country, their children are the haunting worry. Inside, when they will be taken away for indoctrination; outside, when they will come and say, 'I am old enough, now, to join the battle for our freedom.'

Tahir Shah

A SHOT AT DAYBREAK

Captain Yusuf Azambai of the Red Army was a member of the Fraternal Limited Contingent of the armed forces of the USSR which descended upon independent Afghanistan at Christmas, 1979.

As the months and years passed, Azambai found the role more and more onerous. The war went on; the Afghans, far from seeing the Russians as liberators, fought them like demons, dying in their thousands. It reminded the Captain, increasingly, of the stories which the old men had told of the Soviet invasion of his own country, Turkestan, just north of the Amu Darya, the River Oxus. And of the forced collectivisation of the lands of his own people, with all its misery, hunger and oppression, just before World War II.

Yusuf Azambai, considered by the Russians to be an officer with a bright future, blew up his army car to cover his desertion and became a hunted man, a ragged guerrilla in the band of warriors who followed the patriot called *The Eagle*.

The band of fighters marched southwards, covering their movements by travelling with a tribe of migrating Kochis, nomads, taking their herds and carpets across the mountains towards Kandahar.

A single shot rang out at daybreak, the sound echoing from the hills which ringed the valley in the high plateau. Birds, just starting their morning song, flew wildly from the trees and hedges, in every direction, away from danger, The *Kochi* nomad, caravan, some thirty families with their animals, resting here on the early Autumn migration to the south, stirred, then the site erupted with noise, as the men leapt to the watchmen's call: '*Khatarde*! *Bedar*! Awake for danger!'

The women stayed inside their black felt tents, the men settled against the tethered and sitting beasts, shotguns ready, watching for the source of the attack. It was a full half hour before they realised that there would be no more shots, and the chief, Malik Aziz, gave them the order to stand down. He had peered out of his tent and seen the waiting figure. Understanding the meaning of the scene, he now had something important to consider.

Traditionally, the Kochis form a very cohesive group. Some are quite wealthy, monopolising the caravan trade through the mountain passes, plying between Afghanistan and Pakistan, dealing in rugs and specialities of all kinds, buying and selling horses, camels, mules. Kochi families very often know one another, and most weddings are arranged by the parents of the bride and groom.

Ordinarily, when a young man is eighteen, his father looks for a bride for him. A suitable girl, about a year younger than the youth, is found and, if she is willing, the engagement is announced. Until the wedding the couple are not allowed to see each other, except perhaps indirectly: in a mirror held by the bride's menfolk, and even then on one occasion only. No conversation can take place.

But there is another way in which an engagement may be made, though it is rare and some do not like the custom. For many women, however, it seems to have a romantic appeal, since they constantly tell tales of how girls have been won by suitors by this method, though mostly, it turns out, somewhere else or in the days of long ago.

If a young man, tradition says, is deeply in love with a girl and fears that her parents will not agree to their being wed, or even if she does not know that he wants to marry her, he can still make his approach.

He positions himself, in his best clothes, or the ceremonial regalia of his clan, in front of the girl's parents' tent, at dawn, and fires a gun into the air. Then, kneeling in homage, head bowed, before her father as he comes out, he awaits the elders' verdict on his suitability.

Today was such a day, and the shot the Kochis heard was such a shot; the father was none other than their own chief, whose daughter, Fawzia, was just sixteen. Every youth in the whole tribe not closely related to her was hoping to be chosen as her mate. Their mothers, cousins and aunts, grandmothers even, had all been working on the question since before the last nomad north-south

329

migration. Fawzia was extremely beautiful, with auburn hair and grey eyes, and the catch of her Kochi generation. Several other tribal chiefs had sent go-betweens to sound out Malik Aziz.

This method of declaring one's devotion was known as the Pledge of the Servant. It dated from the times when youths en-rolled as disciples and apprentice warriors, under a Kochi chief, first placing their service and arms at his disposal, then asking for his daughter's hand.

The old chief wondered which of the hot-bloods of the tribe had had the insolence to anticipate the answer to the question with which the whole community was buzzing. He was still weighing the dynastic consequences of accepting this young man or that; and, of course, her mother would have to have the last say. He didn't like this Pledge business, anyway. It brought the elders too much into the matter. With applications of this kind, if the girl agreed or not, a council of elders would have to sit, to decide whether the ap-proach was to be encouraged or turned down. In Fawzia's case, there were several conflicting groups, each with a candidate. Favouring one over another could cause rifts and enmity which might take years to heal.

But there it was. The chief reached for his ceremonial robe, tied his turban over the embroidered skull-cap, and left his tent with the necessary dignity. He had allowed a suitable interval, nearly half an hour, to elapse. In consequence, the elders and the ladies were already assembled. Only those assigned to the day's duties of watch, work or weaving were, by custom, excluded from the *jirga*. Again by custom, they pretended that they had not noticed; but they were seething, nonetheless, with curiosity. Fawzia was kept in, secure in the women's quarters, by her mother.

The bent figure of the supplicant sat, straight; rifle upright, almost as if presenting arms, still facing the seigneurial tent. Malik Aziz, for all his own curiosity, did not look at him. He walked, slowly and with head held high, towards the centre of the crescent which the people formed, and took his seat on the brightly-coloured camel-saddle which had been placed ready for him.

Now, of course, the younger man had his back to him. In the customary words, the Malik cried, 'Turn around and face us, to explain your behaviour, man!'

The grey-clad figure turned, and stood erect, then bowed in the direction of the silent audience. There was a gasp from the entire

330

assembly as they realised, all at the same moment, that the applicant for the hand of the daughter of the chief, Malik Aziz, son of a chief and son of a son of a chief, was wearing the uniform of a Russian officer, a member of the Red Army of the USSR!

Two thoughts at once flashed through the Malik's head. If this was indeed a Russian, they could kill him at once, and wipe out this insult, this abomination. Or, if it were one of the youths of the community, his garb was a disgrace, and he could be barred from pursuing his intention on those grounds alone. One does not make a buffoon of oneself, and mock the elders, the traditions too, in such a very serious matter as this.

This man did not look like a Slav. Then who was it? Which of their young men? There was a further sound, a low murmur of amazement, when all present, again in unison, realised that they did not know the man at all. A total stranger wanted to marry the daughter of their Chief.

And then the newcomer began to speak. He had a loud, clear confident voice, and he spoke the Dari language perfectly, with no trace of a foreign accent. Was he a man or an evil spirit?

They began to listen to what the apparition was saying: '... aware of the customs of the great Kochi people and the high traditions which must always be preserved, I present myself to you for judgment of my case. This judgment is my right and your duty!'

He was saying the right things, and so poetically. It was like someone on the radio, or like the way the Mulla talked. What could it all mean? There was nothing, surely, even in the legends to compare with this...

The Soviet officer had paused. Now he spoke again.

'I am from beyond the Oxus River, and my name is Yusuf Azambai, son of a chief, and the son of sons of chiefs. I am in love with the lady of the house of your Chief, and I offer myself as her husband. Now you may take your decision!' It was a voice accustomed to command.

As he stopped talking, the elders fingered their rosaries and stroked their beards. He had said all the right things, but there could be no question, of course, of accepting his proposal. The Russian army was trying to take the country – not that they had much chance of doing that – but as to marrying their daughters...

As the Kochi saying had it, 'Whatever word is stronger than "impossible", that is the one I want'.

Nor did the Malik feel otherwise. Still, the proprieties might as well be observed, and this madman humoured before they shot, or, at the least bastinadoed him.

The answer was already specified by tribal law.

'The elders will consider it,' he shouted, and called for his water-pipe.

Exercising his prerogative of interrogation, the oldest greybeard then held up his hand.

'Why are you in the infidel army, and why are you wearing his uniform? This is most unseemly, and for that alone you should be punished!'

Azambai was ready. 'Respected whitebeard! I was born in the Soviet Union and, in spite of being oppressed by the Russians in my own land, I was able, by my own merits, to rise in *their* army to a rank that millions of their own troops can never reach. This uniform is therefore one of high degree. I wear it only to show you the status which I have attained, acknowledged even by our enemies!'

The Kochis stirred, uneasily. Then one shouted, 'Why don't you take the uniform off, and join the fighters for freedom?'

'I *have* been fighting for some months now, and I come to you as the right hand of the man whom we all admire, the Eagle! I'm one of the guerilla band that has been travelling with your caravan these past few weeks.'

After that, the Turkestani got his permission to court the lady; a restricted one, it is true, and the pair had to be seen keeping, modestly, much apart until they were married. Neither of them, of course, dared to confide in the Kochis that they had known each other for weeks. It was Fawzia who had briefed her fiancé in the best way to win her hand, as the Kochis and guerrillas had marched southwards, and camped side by side.

Azambai was now regarded as a member of the tribe, an honorary Kochi, and even as a useful acquisition. He deferred to the elders and sat for long hours hearing their songs and legends. The women started to plan the wedding preparations, and the tribal bard began to compose a suitable ballad.

This, the people told one another, would indeed be a tale to pass on to future generations. Why the elders dropped their objections, even though this meant the failure of their many schemes, is still unknown: unless it be because a romantic event can have a decisive effect on human minds.

And the untold part of the tale, how Azambai, all alone, stalked and killed a Russian officer, to gain the garb 'of achievement' – having left his own behind when he deserted – remained for long tight-locked in his heart. Nobody had missed him from the caravan on that night, as the guerrillas had lain low near a Soviet camp in the high mountains. In spite of the dramatic words he had used to win his bride, Yusuf Azambai was not a boaster.

Idries Shah

FROM A LETTER OF A
FRIEND IN AFGHANISTAN

I saw the clouds of helicopters and the long lines of tanks, the marching men, the power and the hard steel of the latest Empire which had come to take Afghanistan.

And I looked again, and here and there among the mountains I saw the poor, small bands of fighters as they threw themselves against this massive force.

Hunger, fatigue, wounds, sacking tied around their feet... Hand-filled cartridges with homemade gunpowder... Bandaged wounds, shining eyes...

Was it a century, a thousand years ago, that I had sat in my own garden, eating peaches, drinking pure water, heard the voices of my children as they played, of my wife, of the neighbours, asking us to share their plentiful fare?

I sat down by a small waterfall and looked into the pool of water below. Taking off my shoes, I cooled my feet; one foot struck something hard, and I reached down and picked it up.

It was a flat, quite heavy stone, of some very dense rock. It must have been lying there for centuries: through the middle was a hole, clean, large, as if punched by a fist.

Then I thought I heard a voice saying, 'Look at the hole, and think of what weak water can do against the hardness of a stone. Drops of water, no more than that, were the instrument. Are the people of Afghanistan any less?'

That night, we 'bandits and counter-revolutionaries, hirelings of the Americans' destroyed three armoured personnel-carriers. For that we paid with thirty lives.

I wear the stone, held to my stomach by a cummerbund. It reduces the pain of hunger on the long marches.

THE SIGH OF THE OPPRESSED

Quatrains by Ustad Khalilullah Khalili,
Poet Laureate of Afghanistan

They killed humanity and called it Politics
They laid the world waste and said that it was wise
In the guise of goodness towards men
They destroyed – this is real cleverness!

My heart, in every state, is my support
In this world of being it is my king
When, from the deceit of reason I am weary
I call God to witness – I am grateful to my heart!

The greatest joy is the company of the Friends
To be parted from them is the misery of death
Since they, in time, are gathered in the dust
So life and death, to us, are one and the same

Alas! Life is but a breath and pain
A heart, a torture, an eye filled with tears
Either enduring, day by day, oppression
Or oneself stamping the jackboot upon the rest

For the desperate, what happiness or sadness can there be?
The dead taste neither the bitter nor the sweet
With our freedom's riding-camel sunk in a morass
What matter if our goal be near or far?

When just one drop of blood falls on the earth
The ring of heaven's lost a precious jewel
Tyranny, beware! For an oppressed orphan's sigh
Will yet again destroy your mighty throne.